Dreaming No Small Dreams

Dreaming No Small Dreams

William R. Harvey's Visionary Leadership

by

Lois Benjamin

Tapestry Press
Irving, Texas

Tapestry Press
3649 Conflans Road
Suite 103
Irving, TX 75061

Library of Congress Cataloging-in-Publication Data
Benjamin, Lois, 1944-
    Dreaming no small dreams : William R. Harvey's visionary leadership /
by Lois Benjamin.
        p. cm.
    Includes bibliographical references (p.) and index.
    ISBN 1-930819-31-5 (hard cover : alk. paper)
    1. Harvey, William R., 1941- 2. Hampton University
(Va.)--Presidents--Biography. 3. College presidents--United
States--Biography. I. Title.
    LC2851.H317 .B46 2003
    370'.92--dc21
                                        2003010218

Cover and book design and layout by
D. & F. Scott Publishing, Inc.
N. Richland Hills, Texas

*This book is dedicated to Mrs. Norma Baker Harvey,
the wife of Dr. William R. Harvey,
who has supported and sustained the visionary and his visions.*

Dreams
Hold fast to dreams
For if dreams die
Life is a broken-winged bird
That cannot fly

Hold fast to dreams
For when dreams go
Life is a barren field
Frozen with snow

—Langston Hughes

Contents

Acknowledgments

First and foremost, I would like to thank President William R. Harvey for entrusting me to tell his story. Indeed, I consider the opportunity a privilege and a sacred trust.

Second, I would also like to thank members of the Harvey family, friends of the Harvey family, members of the Hampton University family (past and present)—including the Board of Trustees, administrators, faculty, staff, students, and alumni who so willingly cooperated in providing interviews for this project.

Third, I am appreciative of the support of Cassandra Herring, Carolyn Acklin, and Margaret Dismond Martin, who took time out from their busy schedules to provide editorial assistance. I am also indebted to Frances H. Hawkins for her editorial and typing services.

Finally, I would like to thank Carl Jeffrey Wright for his help in bringing this project to fruition in a timely manner.

Introduction
What Manner of Man is This!

William R. Harvey's years at Hampton University may be
"liken[ed] to bread that is cast upon the waters."[1]

Surrounding President William R. Harvey is an aura of a dreamer with a destiny, a dreamer who aims and grasps for visions of excellence, like the tentacles of a giant octopus. His emanation reaches into every crevice and corner of Hampton University's historic, picturesque and pristine 254-acre, waterfront campus and beyond. When he physically enters any space there, to engage in hyperbole, it is like Moses parting the Red Sea. His commanding presence signals that it is time for business, time to make those dreams a reality and, now, "Let's get on with it."

The last opening plenary session of the twentieth century—the 1999–2000 academic year—was no exception. As the President entered McGrew Towers for the Fifty-Fourth Annual Educational Staff Institute, he greeted a scattering of administrators, faculty, and staff with an affable smile and a warm handshake that welcomed them back for the new academic year. Then the chatter ceased and a hush fell over the room as his handsome, indomitable six-foot-three, 200-pound frame, towering like the giant Emancipation Oak tree, and nattily attired in a three-piece, navy blue pin-striped suit, accented by a red tie and handkerchief, strolled toward the dais.

What manner of man is this whose presence can command such stillness? Is it his persona? He is charming, congenial, and effervescent. His dignified and regal bearing is the quintessence of an indisputably ardent, charismatic leader. It shows in his long and lofty strides, where each step is firmly and sure-footedly planted on steady ground. According to the tales of Langston Hughes' Simple, "Feet Live Their Own Life." "If you want to know about my life," said Simple, ". . . don't look at my face, don't look at my hands. Look at my feet and see if you can tell how long I been standing on them."[2] If there is a grain of truth in the lore of Simple's tale, Harvey's feet have the purposeful strides of a master dreamer, like Joseph, and he has been dreaming no small dreams and holding fast to them for many seasons.

Even though Simple counseled, "If you want to know about my life, don't look at my face," proceed anyway and take a closer gaze at Harvey's. Notice that in the furrows of his brow are the sagacious visions of Isaiah and the wisdom of Solomon. Search the windows to his soul, his piercing owl-like eyes, and find the courage and compassion of David; the zeal of Jehu; the spiritual fortitude of Daniel; the power of Elijah; the fearlessness of Shadrach, Meshach, and Abednego; the daring of Gideon; the perseverance of Hannah; the faith of Job; and the temperament of Paul.

And whereas Simple said, "If you want to know about my life, don't look at my hands," go ahead and examine Harvey's. His palms foretell a financial wizardry with the golden touch of King Midas, and his hands augur a seasoned master builder with the leadership of a Moses. So it appears from Harvey's persona, the sagacious Simple is surely vindicated. Not only do "feet live their own life," but maybe the face and hands as well.

But is it solely Harvey's persona that defines him? Does it answer the question, "What manner of man is this whose presence can command such stillness?" Is it his ethical and spiritual philosophy of life? Harvey is quick to say, "When the taproot of life is out, the plant withers and dies." So always, at official gatherings of University constituents, the program begins with a prayer by the University chaplain. Sometimes it is a silent meditation. But often, as that day in the Faculty Institute, it is a verbal supplication given by Timothy Tee Boddie, the University chaplain, who beseeched:

> Eternal Creator, gracious Redeemer, merciful Sustainer of all life, we come this morning, not out of mere routine, ritual, or ceremony, but we come recognizing that if it had not been for the Lord who was on our side, we know not where we would be. We thank thee, O God, for a president and CEO who dares to "dream no small dreams"; for an administration who has the audacity to nurture those dreams; for a faculty and staff who demonstrate the "moxie" to attend to the every detail of those dreams; and most especially, for a student body that is not only the beneficiary of those dreams, but that is also the reason for them.

If it is not solely Harvey's spiritual grounding producing such stillness, perhaps Harvey's introduction at the opening plenary session of the final academic semester of the second millennium can offer some clues. With Hampton in the hands of this master dreamer and master builder, he has accomplished some extraordinary achievements in his twenty-five-year tenure. To digress momentarily from his apprentice's discourse about his deeds and deftness, let us step back in time to the pre-Harvey era, and listen to Wendell P. Holmes. Upon retiring as chair of the Hampton University Board of Trustees in April 28, 2000, Holmes reflected on the status of the University when Harvey arrived in 1978.

> In 1978, our institution, then called Hampton Institute, was experiencing one of the most difficult periods in its history. Some real concerns that the Board of Trustees and others had included the following: (1) Years of deferred maintenance had caused the physical plant to deteriorate badly— buildings were not painted, windows were broken, and there was general decay; (2) Because of the lack of adequate fund-raising and deficit spending, the institution had tapped into its endowment; (3) The endowment had eroded from a high of approximately $36 million to $29 million in 1978; (4) There were instances when faculty and staff raises were deferred or delayed in order to ascertain if enrollment goals would be met; (5) Faculty and staff morale was low.

The precariousness of the University, Holmes noted, induced "one of our former Board members who was the grandson of Hampton's founder [to recommend] that we cease operation as an institution of higher education and become a college preparatory school."

Harvey's apprentice's introduction, more than two decades later, presented a striking portrait in contrast. Here, Martha Jallim-Hall, then assistant to the provost, noted how he has artfully blended a benchmark of edifices and academic excellence with sound fiscal management that has sealed his success on the celebrated and scenic campus that he calls one of "God's Little Acres." Moreover, since 1978, the twelfth president of Hampton University has been dreaming up blueprints, successfully framing his dreams, and, like Moses, delivering on his promises.

Under Harvey's ingenious leadership, a legion of accomplishments, as reflected in the growth and quality of the University's financial base, physical facilities, academic programs, and student population, was cited. First and foremost, in the master builder's framing plans, he has dug a solid financial footing, producing consecutive fiscal growth and stability for Hampton University during his tenure as President. When Harvey arrived on campus in July 1978, the University's budget had a deficit of nearly $500,000, and for the preceding five consecutive years, the budget was drowning in a sea of red ink. He resuscitated the University's budget by blotting away the red ink and achieving a surplus during each year of his tenure. Moreover, when Harvey took the reins, he securely framed the financial walls of the University. The endowment, which stood at $29 million, now exceeds $180 million. The University's first capital fund-raising campaign in 1979 had a goal of $30 million. That campaign raised $46.4 million. When his five-year capital campaign project, with a goal of $200 million, was officially launched on October 22, 1998, some $110 million had already been raised. Two years later, the University surpassed the initial $200 million goal by $16 million, so Harvey increased this campaign to $250 million. Second, when the master builder arrived, he found, as Wendell Holmes previously noted, run-down buildings with cracks and peeling paint that were rapidly falling into a state of disrepair. So Harvey rolled up his sleeves for a long day's work. He designed a master plan for the University's physical facilities, bringing it out of dark crawl spaces into sunlit rooms. He strongly believes a "physical environment is conducive to learning and living." Accordingly, Harvey erected between 1978–1999 fourteen new buildings at a cost of over $65 million; between 2000–2002, he built four new structures at a cost of $37.8 million. And between 1978–1999, he spent almost $30 million on the renovation of existing facilities and infrastructures. Moreover, employing his financial ingenuity, he hammered out a plan for a university-owned commercial development consisting of a shopping center and 246 two-bedroom apartments. The after-tax profits from the Hampton Harbor Project are used primarily for student scholarships. Additionally, the Hampton Harbor Project created jobs, provided services, increased the number of African American entrepreneurs, and expanded the tax base for the City of Hampton.

Third, in his framing plans, he moved Hampton to university status in 1984. Faculty members increased from approximately 190 to 350. According to data from the president's office, Harvey initiated 64 new degree programs between 1978–2002, which included undergraduate programs in physical therapy, marine science, music engineering technology, sports management, criminal justice, chemical and electrical engineering, airway science, journalism and communications, emergency medical systems management; graduate programs in business administration, museum studies, applied mathematics, chemistry, and medical science; and Ph.D. programs in physics, pharmacy, physical therapy, and nursing. The University also offers a value-added course in equestrianism. These additional programs have positioned Hampton at the cutting edge of the competitive landscape of higher education.

Fourth, the builder raised the roof of student enrollment and academic excellence at Hampton University. The student body increased from approximately 2,700 students to nearly 6,000. The SAT scores of entering freshmen spiraled approximately 300 points. "Without a doubt, the catalyst and leader of this overwhelmingly positive growth and development has been our President, Dr. William R. Harvey," said Wendell Holmes. "When many speak of a successful college and university presidency, they use Dr. Harvey as a role model."

Fifth, the master builder and the architect of the Harvey Model of Administrative Leadership developed, in a decade, eight college and university chief executive officers, one bank CEO, and an athletic commissioner.

In the framing plan of "God's Little Acres," Harvey, the role model, has also built on a solid foundation, like the joists that carry the house load. So he has incorporated a truss of "movers and shakers" and people of "influence and affluence" on the local, national, and international scenes in his vision of building a world class institution. Being connected to such a network of girders has resulted in his appointments to national boards by four United States presidents. He has served on the President's National Advisory Council on Elementary and Secondary Education, the Defense Advisory Committee on Women in the Service, the Fund for the Improvement of Post-secondary Education, the Commission on Presidential Scholars, the President's Advisory Board on Historically Black Colleges, and the United States Department of Commerce Minority Economic Development Advisory Board, the First Union National Bank (Mid-Atlantic Division—South Carolina, North Carolina, Tennessee, Virginia, Washington, D. C. and Maryland)—Newport News Shipbuilding, Inc., Trigon Blue Cross Blue Shield of Virginia, and Fannie Mae.

Locally and regionally, Harvey, like the block and tackle, has pulled together individuals and organizations for uplift of the community. As the visionary framing planner of several community and educational initiatives, he chaired, in 1994, the Virginia Peninsula United Way Campaign. He was the first African American to head the organization's annual drive and raised a record setting $6.6 million. Harvey has also chaired the annual fund-raising dinner for the National Conference of Christians and Jews, and hosted the first celebrity luncheon for the Hampton Roads Chapter of the American Red Cross.

For drawing up successful framing plans and developing them, he has been recognized in *Personalities of the South, Who's Who in the South and Southwest, Who's Who in Black America, Who's Who in American Education, International Who's Who of Intellectuals, Two Thousand Noble Americans, and Who's Who in America.*

Harvey, also known for his entrepreneurship and business ventures, is listed in *Who's Who in Business and Finance*. As the sole owner of the Pepsi-Cola Bottling Company of Houghton, Michigan, he received the Donald M. Kendall Pepsi Bottler of the Year award in 1997. In addition, Harvey, along with a group of North Carolina businessmen, received approval from the Arena Football League to launch a team in Raleigh-Durham, North Carolina.

So on this day, August 23, 1999, during his remarkable introduction, the "Moses of Hampton University," with eyes peering over his glasses, thumbed through the program of the Educational Staff Institute, "Institutional Change: Preparing for the Future Through Teaching Standards, Tenure Options, and Technology-Based Instruction." When the acclamations ceased, he rose briskly and gracefully to speak of ways to lead his people out of the educational wilderness by building an academic tower that will prepare them to meet the educational and technological challenges of the twenty-first century. In a forceful voice, he conversed extemporaneously, saying, "This academic year, colleagues, as we turn the page of the twenty-first century, it promises a number of changes and challenges that will enhance the process of your work and at the same time will require your energy, enthusiasm, and expertise." He brought attention to the "newly wired [for internet services] campus that includes every dormitory and every building on campus," which has given the University the distinction, according to Yahoo, of being among the 100 most wired campuses in the country. So Harvey could justly and proudly proclaim that day, "We are one of the most wired campuses anywhere," as he discussed the implications of the new technology for living and learning. "It translates to one of the most immediate and direct accesses to the world's resources for students and faculty by the way of the World Wide Web. It means communication between students and faculty by the way of the University Intranet and HUNet, which will allow increased interaction with students beyond the perimeters of the traditional classroom environment and office hour settings. While faculty can e-mail students and direct their research through the Internet, students can also contact instructors about the course materials and ask questions. Both are sure to benefit the teaching/learning process." He also stressed that "faculty have an obligation to teach. It is the highest priority, unless otherwise, we have failed." And that "students must be prepared for the skills and competency required of a twenty-first century workforce." Indeed, he also asserted that

> faculty must be full participants in the area of their discipline, and thereby current on trends. They must contribute to the canons of knowledge through presenting papers, articles, books, and maintain an active record of grantsmanship. Furthermore, in asking the legislature to work with us in getting some of the things we want, it is incumbent upon faculty to present the vision or the strategy to get to the vision. Next, we have an obligation to participate in the HU community and to offer students an "Education for Life." Education for living reinforces the values of integrity, honesty, respect for themselves and others, hard work, and responsible behavior. The experience should be inside and outside the classroom, should bolster their minds and spirit for their life's journey. These are the experiences that characterize the unique Hampton experience. These types of value-added experiences are why people come to Hampton. It is our individual and collective responsibility to ensure that they have them. It better serves our student body, heightens our quality of work

and satisfaction, and ultimately improves the whole of Hampton University. . . .

Harvey sat down and listened to the introduction of new faculty. Then he slipped silently out of the room, stepping in respect to Hampton's past legacy as he continues to build for the present, and to plan for the future, while "dreaming no small dreams." Like Langston Hughes, he, too, believes:

> *First in the heart is a dream*
> *Then the mind starts seeking a way. . .*
> *Then the hands seek others to help*
> *A community of hands to help*
> *Thus the dream becomes not one man's dream alone*
> *But our dream*
> *Belonging to all the hands who build.*

"This is my dream, this is my prayer," he said at his Inauguration in 1979. It is also his legacy from ancestral leaders. He acknowledged that,

> The African American leaders of the past surely were unswayed by those who tried to convince them of the impossibility of their dreams. Because they dared to try and better the condition of African Americans and humanity, they were called radicals. Yet they persevered and worked tirelessly to persuade both the believers and disbelievers to assist them in the transformation of their impossible dreams. Not every radical is dangerous and not every dreamer dreams idle dreams. That was their legacy to us then. Can those of us who are African American leaders do any less today?[3]

Leadership Blueprints of the Master Dreamer and Master Builder

"Men can shape their institutions to suit their purposes . . . provided they are not too gravely afflicted with the diseases of which institutions die—among them, complacency, myopia and unwillingness to choose."

—John Gardner

Though Harvey's accomplishments are many and his persona is imperial, such qualities do not sufficiently answer the question: What manner of man is this whose presence can command such stillness? Could it be his effectual transformational leadership? But what is effective leadership? When he humbly accepted the 100 Black Men of Virginia Peninsula's award for role model of the year in 1999, he stated that "able leadership is, in its purest form, a contribution to our community and to our society-at-large. It is that peculiar human trait, that as evidenced through the course of history, possesses the potential to right wrongs, ease human suffering, provide guidance and direction, uplift the downtrodden, and—ultimately—change the course of the universe."[1]

For Harvey, leadership, "in all of its perspectives and dimensions," is a subject of intense interest. Speaking at an African American History Month Observance on February 4, 1999,[2] Harvey philosophized about leadership and its building blocks. "I believe in leadership because it is one of the keys to success of any cause, or effort. Show me a corporation, city, ball club, university, hospital, organization or any other entity that is successful and I will first show you effective leadership," he contended.

But what are the building blocks of a good leader? What are the ingredients of mixed mortar necessary for bonding strong, secure leaders? The preeminent characteristics are decency, self-respect and self-responsibility. Quoting William Penn's 1669 *No Cross, No Crown*, Harvey argued that, "No man is fit to command another that cannot command himself." Thus, for Harvey, "Command of self—or responsibility, decency, and self-respect—is a characteristic common among every great and successful leader and is, in fact, the very foundation upon which leadership is built." He argued forcefully, "Show me a man or woman who holds others responsible for everything that befalls him or her, who succumbs to anything and everything because he or she holds no standards for living or for right and wrong, or who carries him/herself in such a way that is crude, loud, or offensive, and I will show you a person incapable of leadership. Perhaps by deceit or manipulation, such individuals may gain a foothold at the helm of a movement or a cause, but the intrinsic demands of true leadership will render his tenure temporary and her efforts in vain."

Although cognizant of the foibles of leaders and the challenging demands imposed upon effective leadership, Harvey reiterated that, "True leaders—successful leaders—possess and exhibit the capability to handle themselves in such a way that they can live with their own conscience and that they gain the trust, respect, and even admiration of others."

"Upon the foundation comprised of responsibility, decency, and self-respect is the vitally important characteristic of respect for others," noted Harvey. This portentous base eludes many who "might aspire or be called to leadership." Therefore, "respect for one's fellow human being has less to do with likes and dislikes or the desire to win friends, as much as it has to do with listening to and understanding human desires, needs, value, and rights." In essence, "one cannot be a leader if one is not first a follower—a follower to the extent that he is keenly aware of his surroundings, the trends of his community, and the voices of his peers and constituents. A leader, by mere definition of the word, has a following. No one, however, has ever followed a person who is deaf to his cries or aloof to his condition," asserted Harvey.

Another foundational element of an effective leader is the "possession of sound judgment." On life's path, he posited that we each encounter adversities, which are "par for the course of human existence and are, in many respects, the building blocks of character." But those "experiences that are based in nature and that serve to diminish the value and dignity of life are their antithesis; one's ability to discern the often-fine difference between these two extremes is a prominent feature of leadership." Harvey reminds us that "strong leaders, past and present, have possessed the ability to analyze the individual and minute particulars of an occurrence or situation in order to effectively critique the sum of its impact. They had the skill to objectively evaluate a matter, all the while avoiding hypersensitive and knee-jerk solutions to complex or complicated issues." Such attribute—like the building blocks of responsibility, decency and self-respect—"is not easily acquired, for it demands of humans the nonhuman tendency to evaluate a situation from a broad and other-centered perspective—as opposed to a narrow and self-centered perspective," he boldly claimed.

For Harvey, courage is still another definitive ingredient of "capable and right leadership," which ranks in importance with the primary building blocks of "responsibility, decency, and self-respect." In theorizing about the significance of courage, Harvey reasoned that, "no matter the purity of a man's character, the clarity of his insight, the reason of his ration, or righteousness of his cause, if he lacks the courage to stand up, come forward, and lead, his attributes are rendered silent and in many respects—in large scale—useless."

Harvey deemed that the most noble quality of a leader is the yearning to serve others. "If you can help somebody—do it! If you can alleviate someone's pain—do it! If you can brighten some-one's day with a kind word—do it! If you can be less bureau-cratic—do it! If you can reach out and positively touch just one somebody—do it! If you can alleviate just one somebody's mis-ery—do it!" In a forceful conclusion, he reiterated: "If anyone really wants to be a leader, if anyone really wants to be great, if anyone really wants to be a person of honor, they must do as Jesus says; they must serve others."

Though geographically separated by age, time, and space, a resounding chorus of University constituents—administrators, alumni, faculty, students, trustees, family, friends and even foes—spoke with one voice when asked, what descriptive words come to mind when they think of Harvey's leadership. Among the collective definitive phrases, *effective* and *visionary leadership* spewed forth. The late Margaret Simmons, an English professor at Hampton Uni-versity who had known Harvey since 1978, believed, along with others, that he is not only an effective leader, "he can, like the eye of the eagle, see beyond reality. It is almost uncanny the way he can do that. And once he makes a decision, he follows that. You know, if it's an unpopular one, he doesn't care if he thinks he's right. He says, 'Be sure you're right and then go ahead.' And that's the main thing you have to admire about him. And so many times when I'm sure I, as well as others, wondered why are we doing this, and then you come to see that he is the man with the vision." He is not only the "man with the vision," but the man with a plan, who, instead of watching things happen, makes things happen. No doubt Harvey would fully concur with Woodrow Wilson, who pro-claimed, "No man that does not see visions will ever realize any high hope or undertake any high enterprise."[3] So, for Harvey, being a planner and a doer encircle his visions, which have a mis-sion with lucid goals, objectives, and strategies that are results-ori-ented. But more importantly, he is able to translate his visions to others around him. Take, for example, the gala where Wendell P. Holmes, an alumnus of Hampton University for over fifty years, past-president of its National Alumni Association, and former chair of its Board of Trustees, paid tribute to Harvey at the "Kickoff of Hampton University's $200 Million Capital Campaign and Tribute to the President on his 20th Anniversary," on October 22, 1998, in Hampton, Virginia. It was evident, from Holmes' passionate delivery, that this one man's vision was now a shared one for the participants—trustees, alumni, administrators, faculty, students, staff, corporate donors, family, and friends of the University.

> We who are here come for the laudable purpose of inaugurating to initiate and generate resources for Hampton University and at the same time pay homage to President William R. Harvey. . . an intellectual giant of a man who has devoted his life toward the cause of creating and optimizing an educational environment for young men and women, which will serve as a model for institutions of higher learning across this country. For twenty years, Harvey has served well and with distinction. He has exemplified the type of visionary leadership, guidance, commitment that is needed to propel all of us into a challenging twenty-first century. . . . Dr. Harvey is determined, as are the trustees, and as you believe as evidenced by your presence tonight, that we will achieve the goals we set for ourselves. . . .

So what are some distinguishing composite characteristics of his leadership style that sway others to follow the dreamer and his dreams? Some descriptive phrases, in addition to visionary and effective leadership, of University constituents, as well as family, friends, and foes, were accountable, aggressive, bold, challenging, committed to excellence, competent, competitive, creative, decisive, dedicated, demanding, democratic, determined, dictatorial, dynamic, efficient, effective communicator, entrepreneurial, fiscally conservative, hard-working, hard-nosed, brilliant money manager, no-nonsense, perfectionist, perspicacious planner, policy-oriented, results-oriented, self-assured, skilled tactician, of sound judgment, team builder, and time manager. These characteristics are blended with personality traits, described by the aforementioned constituents of the University, such as astute, affable, approachable, charming, compassionate, extroverted, highly confident, gregarious, personable, precocious, self-assured, short- tempered, unpredictable, and the need always to be right, to be in charge, and to make the final crucial decisions. The respective comments further illuminate his leadership style. Ben Head, a twenty-year member of the Board of Trustees and a banker, stated that Harvey has a "dynamic leadership style."

> He makes an excellent presence. He's a tall man, distinguished-looking, he speaks well, and he's prepared when he makes a talk. It's obvious that he has researched the project when he discusses one, when he makes a statement about what has happened within the school year, or certain periods of time. His leadership style is that he wants to get a general feeling of opinions on matters and he is very quick to say that the Board of Trustees makes the final decisions and he carries them out. But I think it's best to say that he also sets out an agenda and a schedule for things that he feels should be done for a given period. He enunciates clearly what his plans are, and then he asks the Board for its approval or suggested changes. I would say that when changes are necessitated, he will argue his point hard.

Rosemary Brinkley, a former member of the Board of Trustees and an alumna of Hampton, agreed that:

> Harvey is democratic in his leadership style. However, I feel that even though a person uses the democratic side of leadership, that person comes to the situation with a predetermined goal in mind. Dr. Harvey is working with so many people that he has to be as democratic as possible in order to make people feel that they are part of the decision-making process. I think he's a person that delegates responsibility, and I think this is important because no one person can do it all or has the knowledge to do so. So I think you surround yourself with people who are competent, who can carry out the assignments that they are given. And I think that's another characteristic of his—he's able to find competent people. And those persons help to make him the great president that he is.

Lucius Wyatt, an alumnus and a retired vice president for fiscal affairs and treasurer, who was on Harvey's first administrative team and who has known him for over twenty-five years, assured us that: "Dr. Harvey always has good ideas, and he is quite a visionary in terms of the program and educational needs of society. . . . He is a good planner, and very aggressive in carrying out those plans. It's the kind of style that gets things done. His management style and leadership style are just about one and the same. And he feels that the leader or manager has possibly the responsibility for making the final decision."

Similarly, Martha Jallim-Hall, who has known the president since 1982 in her status as student and in her professional capacity at the University, enthusiastically endorsed Wyatt's assertion that his leadership style parallels his managerial style. "Oh, he's a great manager. And he does not want you to waste time. You have to do a job efficiently and effectively. It really doesn't make sense if you spend a lot of time and not be effective. There are times when he would say, 'Well, if you would get here on time, then you can do everything you need to do before five o'clock.' If you budget your time, work smarter, and do your research first, then you don't have to waste a lot of time in trying to find answers in all the wrong places."

JoAnn W. Haysbert, provost, stated that: "As a manager, he is a policy person. He wants those of us in his administration to follow the policy. His administrative council enacts policies governing the day-to-day operation of the University. Which means, as a manager, it is a team effort and a participatory process, because we can make the policies, with the understanding that policies are subject to review and change when needed and appropriate. But once the policies are made, then the managerial side of the President is to follow the policy. And to recognize that each administrator should operate where the buck stops here."

The University's constituents have spoken. So what does Harvey have to say about his own leadership style? In a *Daily Press* profile of the President by Kirk Saville, Harvey likens his role to that of a basketball player. "I don't shrink from leadership, from adversity," he said, "When the game is on the line, I want the ball.

I want to take the shot. Some people call that arrogance. I'm not arrogant. I am confident."

His wife, Norma, agreed. "He doesn't like to sit back and see things happen," she said. "He's a doer."[4] For Harvey, the power of wisdom, boldness, and vision has been the hallmark of his administrative leadership and his catalyst for change. In these qualities "lie the difference between pedestrian performance and extraordinary achievement." To effect visionary changes in a race-, gender-, and class-conscious society, an aggressive and competitive, demanding leadership style that is business-oriented fuels Harvey's engine. Charles M. Schwab argued that for "a man to carry on a successful business, [he] must have imagination. He must see things as in a vision, a dream of the whole thing."[5] Accordingly, Harvey, the entrepreneur and educator, expresses his stock idiom, "I run Hampton like a business for educational objectives." This style of leadership incorporates Harvey's "notion that the rights, interests, and privileges of Hampton [University] take precedence over the rights, interests, and privileges of individual faculty, staff, students, administrators, trustees and alumni. Hampton is greater and better than all of us, because it is all of us—not just one of us."[6] Adhering to this environmental assumption for twenty-five years, Harvey has effectively employed a leadership and managerial mode at Hampton University to achieve his educational goals. In doing so, he identified three principal ingredients on which the axis of success turns for his administrative leadership: obtaining and retaining competent people; developing sound programs that maintain the reputation of the University; and following the Harvey Leadership Model for Academic administrative Success.

Harvey's successful blueprint, which has ten steps, involves vision, a good work ethic, academic excellence, team building, innovation, courage, good management, fairness, fiscal conservatism, and results.[7] "First, there is vision," Harvey affirmed. "Visionaries can see the big picture. They look beyond the horizon as they plan, and, yes, as they dream. Visionaries are creators. Visionaries are undeterred by challenges. Visionaries see stumbling blocks and turn them into stepping stones. Visionaries can persuade others, even critics, cynics, and enemies to follow their lead. Visionaries can get others to take ownership in their vision." If that be true of visionaries, JoAnn W. Haysbert, who has served under Harvey's leadership for over twenty years not only as provost, but also as faculty, assistant provost, and interim provost, no doubt would see his administrative success as a "vision in motion." "I call it a vision in motion—because of the movement from when he initially conceptualized it to the actual fruition of the product," she avowed. She cited examples to support her contention. "When we became a university in [1984] that was one of the things that Dr. Harvey talked about when he initially came here. If you were to look at his Inaugural Address, you will find that everything he said that he wanted to do, he has done that. On one occasion, he was [the Opening Convocation] speaker, he talked about ethics, character, and conduct. As a derivative of that we now have the Hampton University Code of Conduct. If you think about the physical facilities, he talked about that long before we got them. In terms of programs, long before we initiated a school of pharmacy, a Ph.D. in physics and physical therapy, he talked about the direction we were to go in the sciences." Much of "this talking" was in conversations, in administrative council, and in addresses to faculty. She trumpeted his vision, "If you were to go back and look at those papers, you will find that he has always forecast where we ought to go long before we got there."

Harvey's Vision

As Haysbert hinted, let's go to Harvey's Inaugural Address of March 24, 1979 and rewind his "vision in motion." When the 38-year-old Harvey stood center stage to deliver his vision for the Hampton University family, he was surrounded by his lifelong supporters from across the United States. From the deep South, a multitude of family and friends from Brewton, Alabama and surrounding counties came to acclaim an old home boy who had done well—his beloved and doting mother, Claudis P. Harvey, his Southern Normal High School mentors, Kenneth Burwell Young and Mai Graham Young, and his classmates from Southern Normal. His sister, Anne Harvey Allison and her family, came from Atlanta, Georgia, and other relatives, friends, and classmates came from Mobile, Birmingham, Pensacola and Washington, D. C. Others traveled from as far North as New Jersey and as far West as San Diego, California. His lovely young wife, Norma, sartorially correct in a two-piece, ecru silk suit, beamed with excitement and pride. Beside her were their two well-mannered children, eight-year-old Kelly and six-year-old Christopher. Leslie was not yet born. The family, with Norma and her pulchritude, grace, charm, and intelligence, along with the rising star of her handsome husband and their attractive children, was perhaps, in the minds of many, Hampton's own version of Camelot.

As this youthful president, full of vim, prepared to share his vision that day in Odgen Hall, he was aware of strong supporters, like Lucius Wyatt, who had served on the presidential search committee that selected the 37-year-old President, as well as detractors. It was Wyatt's recollection that:

> At the time that we were winding down the selection of a president in 1978, I had an opportunity to participate in a presentation by two candidates who were the finalists for this selection committee. One of them was Dr. Harvey, and the other was Dr. Prezell Robinson, who, at that time, was the president of Saint Augustine's College. The President was graceful and had a good self-presentation and a good appearance. The women on the committee were taken aback by his pleasing personality and handsome appearance. After the two candidates had made their presentations, I was asked which man would I recommend as president of Hampton Institute. My response was, if the college was looking for a person with experience as a college president who could step in and continue to head the college, or lead the college as it had been in the past, or as it was being lead at this time, then you would select the experienced president. However, if you are looking for a younger man who would lead this college

> into the next century, with new ideas and really improve the
> University, then I would select Harvey. And that was the way
> it was.

But it was not that way with the doomsayers and doubters that also
encircled him, like the heavy, overcast clouds during the ceremony.
Martha Dawson, former vice-president of academic affairs and a member of his first administrative team, probably said it best when she
introduced Harvey at a speaking engagement on October 1, 1982: "So
many said that it could not and would not be done. He was too young,
too self-assured and too much of a dreamer. Particularly not for
Hampton Institute, the venerable, historically evolved barometer for
black higher education. Hampton, the self-proclaimed 'consultants'
would argue, needs a man of experience ('which can only come with
age') and one who can maintain the status quo. Certainly not some
37-year-old hayseed country boy (Brewton, Alabama) with no 'real
name.'" Perhaps his critics, too, believed the biblical admonition, in
Joel 2:28, that "Your old men will dream dreams and your young men
will see visions." What they saw was a visionary in the fullness of his
youth and heard the dreamer with the wisdom of the old.

That day of his inauguration, Harvey was also cognizant that
a major factor that would enlarge the success of Hampton University would be "its ability to wed successfully the dictates of historical tradition with the demands of a changing environment."
As Winston Churchill once noted, "The farther back you can look,
the farther forward you are likely to see."[8] So the young president
would begin his address by looking back at Hampton's founder,
Brigadier General Samuel Chapman Armstrong, and the Hampton
legacy. Armstrong, born in Hawaii to white missionary parents,
had fought on the Union side in the Civil War and commanded
black troops. After the war, he worked as an agent with the
Freedmen's Bureau, and he genuinely desired to help blacks. It
was Armstrong's belief that "education would uplift the black
man while helping him to appear less of an 'uncivilized threat' to
white society."[9] Though a complex man, Armstrong was, on the
one hand, paternalistic and condescendingly racist in his assump-

tions about the capabilities of blacks for a more classical education. On the other hand, he had a noble vision, though myopic,
about the need to educate the newly emancipated African captives as manual laborers and as teachers for an agricultural and
industrial economy in the post-war South. Armstrong's vision
was clear: "To train selected Negro youths who should go out and
teach and lead their people, first by example, by getting land and
homes; to give them not a dollar that they could earn for themselves; to teach respect for labor, to replace stupid drudgery with
skilled hands, and in this way to build up an industrial system for
the sake, not only of self-support and intelligent labor, but also
for the sake of character."[10] At age 29, Armstrong's vision became
a reality when he opened the doors of Hampton Normal and Agricultural Institute on April 1, 1868.

At age 37, when Harvey took over the reins of Hampton University in 1978, he was the youngest president since its founder.
Like Armstrong, he had a vision. But Harvey's was more farsighted
and progressive for blacks at the last quarter of the twentieth century than Armstrong's near the latter quarter of the nineteenth
century. When Harvey took control of the leadership at Hampton,
as in the times of its founder, the country was in a crisis. Though it
was not wracked by war, it was undergoing an economic and social
imbroglio. The economy was in deep recession with high inflation
and an oil crisis. The trauma after the Watergate scandal resulted
in a lack of confidence in government, a general credibility gap in
leadership, and a sense of moral and spiritual decline. Changes
were also occurring in the field of higher education and its very *raison d'etre* was being questioned; times were particularly trying, in
1978, for HBCUs. Endowments had decreased, enrollments had
dipped, and some institutional staff had to cut back due to bal-
looning budget deficits. Along with the rising cost of education in
a declining economy, black schools were experiencing a brain
drain of quality black students and faculty who were exiting to traditionally white universities. Many schools had cut their class

offerings, as well as student aid. Dire predictions abounded about the demise of black institutions.

This bright-eyed President could have accepted a position at a white university. But, instead, he chose a predominantly black educational institution because he wanted to be a role model and put his energies and talents in a black setting. He saw a linkage between the past status of blacks and the milieu of the late seventies, and, like a prophet, he gave warnings and offered his dreams to help shape the future.

So, in the President's Inaugural Address, there was no dialectical tension between the past, present or the future path of Hampton; between materialism and spiritualism; between the academic enterprise and the moral enterprise or the business enterprise; between collective responsibility and individual responsibility; between service to others and self-help; between being tender and being tough; between science and art; between seeing points and understanding patterns; between theory and praxis; between the universal and the particular. Rather his vision, as a transformational leader, accented a positive synthesis of Hampton's rich tradition and his desire to build upon it and link it to a new era. Though no spellbinding orator, Harvey, a man of prodigious intellectual and moral profundity who speaks with clarity, dignity, passion and purpose, said on that day, March 24, 1979:

> From the beginning, Hampton stressed General Armstrong's concept of "education for life," and "learning by doing." Students learned their lessons about the dignity of labor, the value of self-sufficiency and self-reliance, the appreciation of the value of time by experiencing the act and sensing the satisfaction of achievement. They learned to build character through building buildings on campus and in the community. They learned bookkeeping by keeping their personal ledgers balanced and ready for inspection at all times. They learned to write by writing not only their lessons, but letters of appreciation to friends and donors of the institution. These values... are as much a part of the Hampton Experience today as they were then.

And these values would continue under his administration. "We shall continue to strive for truth and beauty and excellence in all of the things that we do. We shall emphasize dignity and decency. In curricular and extracurricular activities, we shall promote the ideals of self-reliance, learning by doing, and the dignity of labor. We shall demand of ourselves and all who are associated with the College high standards and exemplary performance." The dreamer reminded his audience of the timelessness of excellence and its embedded tradition at the venerable institution. "Emphasizing excellence and high standards is not to be nostalgic about a bygone era, for I myself believe in those things and establish them as hallmarks for a continued prosperity. Furthermore, this is the Hampton way. Hampton Institute is more than an educational institution of excellence. It is an institution that has a soul, a tradition of hard work, loyalty, high academic pertinence, warmth, character building, spiritual vigor, and yes, sacrifice. This institutional soul guides us, sustains us and pushes us as we move forward on a daily basis."

Harvey spoke of the embodiment of these ideas, which was manifested during the preceding week of Inaugural activities. Reiterating the challenge given to the college community by Father Nathan Baxter, an Episcopalian rector, who spoke at the Sunday morning Inaugural services, Harvey echoed his call for excellence: "Students should be faithful to their capacity to achieve and the sense of purpose related to that achievement. Administrators, he said, must be concerned with more than survival. They must be committed to excellence. Faculty must ignite the classroom with a power, a presence and a purpose. They must challenge and inspire students with their own excellence of skill. This was an inspired message challenging us all to the pursuit of excellence."

Still another event that week, the initiation of the First National Conference on the Black Family, sponsored by the Alumni Association and Hampton Institute, provided Harvey an opportunity to state that this was "Hampton Institute's way of challenging society—both black and white America—to return to the basics of moral and social decency and to recommit itself both spiritually and financially to restoring the family, which is the microcosm of a nation, to its rightful place as the benchmark of the social order." He cited a litany of social problems and social neglect: unemployment and underemployment; a failed welfare system and economic dependency; high incarceration of youth and the failure of the penal system to rehabilitate offenders; the poor status of the health care system; the drug crisis; and the wretched quality of the educational system. Because he does not see the University as an ivory tower, separate from the larger community, he reminded the gathering that, "as an academic institution that has historical commitment to turning out good doctors, lawyers, craftsmen, engineers and teachers, we took the opportunity of the Black Family Conference to issue a loud clarion call to Black America."

For Harvey, that call is to begin to "do more for ourselves and the first step is with the family. It is my firm belief that a strong family unit is the greatest source of strength that this nation, or indeed, the world has to offer. The need for this uniqueness and reliance on self-sufficiency and other proven strengths is just as great today, not only for Hampton Institute, but for our nation and world. The need is so great because the problems are so many."

Speaking at that moment in history, the visionary saw a connection between the age-old crisis of leadership, the societal problems, and a nation afflicted by a profound spiritual vacuity. "It is no accident that in these grave days the thoughts of men should turn to religion and to God. We are living through one of the recurrent crises in history that offer a special challenge to the very spirit of man."

Continuing, he asserted:

We who have rested our security and our mighty weapons; we who have been free from the stark hunger that crushes the spirits of millions of other people; we who have trusted to our ingenious use of nature to continue an incredible prosperity and high standard of living, now feel ourselves threatened and in a danger that has never before been as close, as real or so uncompromising. We know now that although we might fight, we cannot in the horrible end conquer either what we seek or need. Our weapons are futile against intangible ideas; our statesmen may debate political realities but without conclusion; we talk only of war . . . as if thereby we might still the deep and sickening uneasiness of fear. It is no wonder that man's thoughts turn to religion and to God. It is either this or empty futility.

And for Harvey, the Bible provides a frame of reference for the social crisis of that season, noting, "Students of the Old Testament remind us that there have been other such periods when men were stirred by social unrest and strife of classes, by a decline of national morale, by the weary threat of war, military service, the miserable lot of displaced persons in unfriendly countries, and the desperate appeal to God: 'Oh that thou wouldst rend the heavens and come down.'

"We know, too, that the trouble then and now was moral and spiritual decay, and that in the end the decisions to be made are those made in the minds and hearts of the millions of men and women like ourselves," he speculated.

Clearly, Harvey understood that no matter our social standing, we are connected globally by our common humanity. "Whether we like it or not, we are all bound together on this one earth—the rich and the poor, the famous and infamous, the king and the common man, the black and the white—we are inextricably bound. We need God and we need each other."

Hence, he reminded his audience, "We are better off here in America when there are no wars in the Middle East. We are the healthiest when all disease has been eradicated. No man should consider himself literate until all men can read and write. None of us are free until all of us are free. Eugene Debs perhaps said it best: 'As long as there is a lower class, I am in it.

As long as there is a criminal element, I am of it. As long as there is a man in jail, I am not free."

And he asked and answered the meaning of all his prophecy for Hampton, which is revealed in a plan. "What does this mean to those of us here at Hampton Institute? It means that in our efforts to remain responsive to the special concerns and challenges that each age has presented, we shall emphasize self-reliance, hard work, the dignity of labor, and learning by doing to provide an education for life. To meet this challenge, Hampton will continue to base its forward-looking and innovative posture on its own creative quality and genius of history, tradition and culture." While looking backward, the master builder was moving forward with a proposed plan to restructure the academic program, which would stress character building and emphasize a scientific and professional curriculum, with a strong liberal arts undergirding.

In engaging others to share his visions and dreams, he reaffirmed the importance of collective effort. "We can continue to move ahead. We can only do so if we work together, however. With my Hampton Institute colleagues and me working together, and the help and prayers of others, what can be accomplished is limitless." As he ended his Inaugural Address with Langston Hughes's poem, he also avowed to "accept the challenge, responsibility and privilege of leading this magnificent place we call 'Our Home by the Sea,'" and added, "I pray for the wisdom and courage to provide stable leadership while dreaming bold new dreams."

"Dreaming bold dreams" seems effortless for Harvey. Robert Binswanger, Board of Trustees member, remarked that Harvey's "interesting characteristic is that he is a Vesuvius of ideas. They keep popping out. And they pop out so frequently, if all of them aren't picked up, if all of them aren't implemented, that doesn't seem to stop him in terms of ideas and initiatives. He just keeps getting more."

Margaret Dismond, the president's executive assistant, agreed, and is quite amazed at his creative power. "He'll come up with an idea, and on the one hand, I will say it's brilliant. And on the other hand, I will say, but it is so simple and straightforward and anyone looking would easily see that it is just the move that the University needs to make next, but no one else has come up with the idea. Without a doubt, I believe he is a visionary. He sees into the future and comes up with ideas." Citing an example, she noted: "A lot of colleges and universities are moving toward distance learning, and this has been something that he's talked about—that we need to move in that direction so that we can remain competitive in that area. He asked people for ideas about where we might be able to set up a distance learning program—not just a few courses—but a degree-granting program. And he came up with this idea in conjunction with the ministers' conference that's been taking place here a long time. There are a lot of ministers who participate in the conference and who are pastoring very large churches but are not credentialed ministers in that they don't have degrees. So, since we have this group of people who come here every year, and they support the University in that way, it makes sense that if we offer a distance learning program in religious studies or philosophy, we have a target group right there. And it is so apparent that anyone on this campus should have been able to put those two together. But he did—he's the one that did."

Martha Dawson, Harvey's former vice president of academic affairs, recalled that while in Harvey's presence during informal gatherings, she might have been "having fun or joking" with the President, and suddenly an idea would come to him. "And I have seen him take a napkin off the table and jot notes down," she said.

One wonders how many ideas have been conceived on a table, at his friend, Arthur Greene's kitchen table, or during a midnight reading of a mystery novel. Perhaps his serendipitous moment for the Leadership Institute happened in such a spot. His visions, like the Leadership Institute that has been transformed into reality, are not fleeting thoughts that are tossed, like idle doodles, into the dustbin; he nurtures them to fruition. Harvey's

"Can Do" philosophy, along with his faith and purpose, propels him to say: "I truly believe that we are limited only by the boundaries of our imaginations. Whatever we envision, we can accomplish; whatever we dream, we can become." He spoke those words at the Hampton University 125th Anniversary Gala Celebration on April 1, 1993. It was fourteen years after his Inaugural Address and he had already transformed those dreams and visions into actuality. For Harvey, whose administrative leadership philosophy parallels Langston Hughes, "The dream does not belong to the dreamer alone, but all the hands that helped." For those hands that offered no help, some of these doubters and doomsayers were made believers in the dream; some gazed upon the shining star and followed. Some receded into the sunset, while others fell down in the sea of despair and drowned in their own envy and resentment. But Harvey kept on dreaming. He "hit the ground running" when he arrived on campus in 1978, and only looked back annually in his yearly reports to see how far he had come. His "vision in motion" was always expanding.

Continuing to build on Samuel Chapman Armstrong and the Hampton legacy of training leaders, in his 125th Anniversary Gala Celebration speech, "A Vision for Our Time," Harvey dreamed of building an academy for leadership to train leaders to serve, as did Armstrong, and to correct the ills of society. After Harvey sketched the historical foundation of Hampton's proclaimed ethos of "Education for Life," highlighting the tenets of learning by doing, strong moral character, leadership development, and community service, he reaffirmed Armstrong's resolve that Hampton should prepare students who were technically trained and morally inclined to "lead and serve." Moreover, he praised Armstrong's willingness to adhere to the courage of his conviction against all odds, noting, "Now, as then, our nation cries out for men and women 'who will not be bought or sold . . . who in their innermost souls are true and honest . . . men and women who are not afraid to call sin by its right name . . . men and women who are as true to duty as is the needle to the pole . . . men and women who will stand for the right though their heavens fall.' In short, like Armstrong's world, our world today cries out for men and women who are willing to exercise the courage of their own convictions, and promote what is right and what is fair, without regard for popular acclaim."

Offering weighty commentary on the changing state of African American communities and the changing value system, he defined the problem and sounded an alarm:

> It is not enough for educational institutions to produce successful physicians, accountants, or systems analysts if they are unwilling or unable to transfer those experiences and sound values to those who walk beside them and to those who will succeed them. For all the progress of the 1950s and 1960s, too many of us became too prematurely self-satisfied with short-term "illusions of success."
>
> We relaxed our resolve and tabled those experiences which gave us that "grit in our craw." For example, we stopped those precious annual oratorical contests in our schools and churches, and now too many of our young people are unable to manage basic oral and written communications skills. We stopped our open discussions of values, ethics, and character and their development in the classrooms, and began to insert sensational, empty and directionless "rap sessions." We became so caught up in blaming others, that we surrendered the responsibility for our own lives, our own cultural preservation and community sustenance. We bargained away those sacrifices made by our forebears. The result is our continuing suffering and languishing with social, political and economic inertia—the willingness to hoard and the unwillingness to share those accumulated blessings with those truly in need. That, my friends, is a crime . . . and we will and are paying dearly for that crime.

Next, Harvey proposed a solution of collective and personal empowerment and responsibility to the problem, saying, "It is time for us to take back our neighborhoods, our responsibilities, our todays, our tomorrows, our legacy. We must save our children. Somebody said that 'children are the message that we send into the future.' We must reclaim, rekindle, reignite and reinvigorate the hopes and aspirations of our children—the greenest, richest and most precious Plants in their Garden called Life. In this society, many of us have made children and their hopes and dreams an afterthought and such callousness must cease."

He reassured the audience that we must "return to being unashamed and unapologetic in openly discussing with young people values, character development, and ethics clarifications. We must stand for what is right and not tiptoe around what is wrong. Let us call it what it is: we need to propagandize—yes, evangelize with a holy fire—make clear-cut distinctions between right and wrong. We must outline our lofty expectations and be clear about what is non-negotiable. We must become the embodiment of men and women striving to do what's right against hapless but popular alternatives. Our young people are hungering for leadership. Someone to stand up, straighten and stiffen their backs, take a stand for justice and truth and acknowledge the responsibility for our destiny. . . . We are the problem: Therefore, we must become the solution."

Then Harvey began his enlarged vision for our time on how to solve the ills of society and empower community and self by training the ethically grounded, best and brightest students to lead and serve.

> In my vision of the future, Hampton University will attack these national problems by becoming once again not only an academy for learning, but also an academy for leadership and service. In my vision, you would see the hundreds and thousands of young people who leave their Home by the Sea in Hampton, Virginia, and go out into the world with a lifetime dedication to correcting the ills in our society.
>
> You would see hundreds of the best and brightest young people in this country—young people totally committed to leadership and community service—young people recruited and trained for just this purpose. You would see a curriculum focused on critical and analytical thinking skills, problem solving, the issues of race, economics, crime, morality, and a required community service component at some point during the student's four years.

In this vision, you would see talented young people fully
indoctrinated with the ideals of self-sufficiency, ownership
and community as the foundation for true liberation. You
would see thousands of young, well-trained people of impec-
cable character, leaders committed to becoming great teachers, and artists, and scientists, but also committed to ridding
our communities of crime and illiteracy, to improving the
environment, to moving our race from a position of consumership to ownership, to creating a world where man's
inhumanity to man is the rare exception rather than the pre-
vailing rule.

Like Armstrong, these servant leaders would "gather to scatter." He
remarked, "If I could render up for you a portrait of the kinds of
young leaders this academy would produce, you would see a proces-
sion of Sojourner Truths, Samuel Chapman Armstrongs, Booker T.
Washingtons, W. E. B. DuBoises, Thurgood Marshalls, Marva Col-
linses and Martin Luther Kings."

"In order to translate this vision into reality," Harvey said, "it
would mean building a leadership program into the entire University structure."

In concluding his address, he entreated the congregants,
saying, "Call me a radical, a visionary, a dreamer. I welcome the
designation. General Samuel Chapman Armstrong was a radical, a
dreamer. And because he dreamed we find ourselves this evening
in this time, in this place, revering his dream. Armstrong had a
vision for his time. And I have a vision for our time."

"Therefore, call me a dreamer, but better yet, join me in the
fulfillment of this dream. For as Langston Hughes so eloquently
put it, 'The dream belongs not to the dreamer alone, but to all
who helped to build.' Whether you know it or not those of you in
this room tonight, those of you who have given so generously to
the University's scholarship fund already share the dream. Moreover, you too are inspired by what Hampton University was and
motivated by what you know she can become."

When the dreamer sets forth his multitudinous visions, and
signs off his talk with "Let's get on with it," the web of the Harvey

Leadership Model for Academic Administrative Success is being woven. Beside vision, it incorporates the following interconnection of elements: a good work ethic, academic excellence, team building, innovation, courage, good management, fairness, fiscal conservatism, and results. Although, each component of Harvey's model is discussed separately here, each overlaps and is integrally intertwined with one another.

Shoring Up the Vision
Weaving the Web of the Harvey Model

A Good Work Ethic

"Having a good work ethic is essential," said Harvey. "I don't care how smart you are, how much vision you may have, or how assiduously you plan, you cannot get around having a good work ethic." In warning others of its importance, he stated: "An absence of hard work is telling because you cannot fool people for long. They can see it in your results... Hard work cannot be compromised."

For Harvey, hard work is also an integral component of excellence. "Excellence is really a synonym for effort," declared Harvey. Although most people picture themselves as an "extremely hard worker," they are "really operating on less than half power." In terms of effort, "they may never get over 50 percent although they think of themselves as 90 percent producers. Therefore, to get 100 percent, one must aim for 110 percent. In my opinion, the world belongs to those who aim for 110 percent. One hundred percent is not enough."

"Nor should we expect anyone to do more than we do," he asserted. "The real test of every man and every woman is how much they give of themselves. When a person likes his job so much that he enjoys coming to the office every morning, he is fortunate. When a person likes his job so much that work above and beyond job description becomes routine, then he is also fortunate. Sometimes we want something very badly, but when it comes to a little extra work or study we all fail to generate the extra effort."

Academic Excellence

Academic excellence is, as Harvey envisions it, "a *sine qua non* in any higher educational setting." "I personally believe in setting the bar high. There are those who would like to make excuses for their performance because of family background, financial status, peer groupings, or some other crutch. All of us have heard about students in high schools and colleges that have dumbed down because they did not want to be considered geeks by their so-called friends," Harvey stated. He knows, however, that "education is the keystone in the arch of freedom and progress. Nothing has contributed more to the enlargement of this nation's strength and opportunities than our traditional educational system. For the individual, the doors to the schoolhouse, to the library, and to the college lead to the richest treasures of our open society; to the power of knowledge—to the wisdom, the ideas, and the culture which enrich life—and to the creative, self-disciplined understanding of society needed for good citizenship in today's changing and challenging world... Through the pursuit of excellence, we can travel a long way up freedom's road."

Inherent in his vision of building a premier educational institution is the "pursuit of excellence in all of our undertakings." Academic excellence is inseparable from his holistic concept of excellence, as noted in a speech entitled, "Black Americans and the Struggle for Excellence in Education," that he delivered at a Department of Defense Black History Month Program on February 10, 1984. Harvey wistfully professed: "I wish that there were more of us who held excellence and scholarship in such high esteem. I don't mean that everybody ought to try to become intellectual giants. I do believe, however, that every professional person should strive for a style of intellect and sensibility which he has freely chosen in order to express his own needs, thoughts and feelings in an appropriate and spontaneous way. The life of an intellectual is indeed only one among many. But the intellectual tools of truth and excellence should vigorously grip and hold on to every young man and woman."

Harvey views excellence as a "never-ending preparation." "This means preparation for an assignment, a briefing, a meeting or any other endeavor. We do ourselves, as well as the people we interact with, a disservice by being ill-prepared," he contended. And Harvey strongly asserted that, "Excellence is always doing what you believe is right. This may not be popular or expedient, but it allows you to sleep at night."

"Excellence is paying attention to details. A lot of people can conceptualize big ideas and new schemes, but they always fail to see them become a reality because they are unwilling to attend to the necessary details," said Harvey.

In the quest for excellence, Harvey urged us to "never take anything for granted or waste an opportunity. For every day that is wasted is one that can never be made up. Unless progress is made each day, you are going to get behind or someone is going to get ahead of you. There must always be total dedication and concentration."

Team Building

Harvey, the quintessential model of a teamworker and motivator of people, believes that "teamwork is very important and that collective competency is better than individual competency. Teamwork ignites the creative juices for all of us." Like the architect who conceives the plan, Harvey, in signing off with his signature trademark, "Let's get on with it," always turns to his team to help carry out his "vision in motion." As a transformational leader, he attributes team building as one of the principal components of his administrative success. He asserted that, "the teamwork concept undergirds sports and numerous other successful ventures. Teamwork is learned behavior, which means there are rules/understandings as well as penalties. Individuals may want to 'star,' but they soon become aware of the need for team support, exhibiting oneness of purpose, thought, spirit and style, and the subordination of all parts to the general effect. Teamwork fosters unity of purpose and unity in action."[11] Martha Dawson agreed that Harvey believes in teamwork and is a team builder who brings people along with him and raises them to a higher standard. A true visionary leader is not "the person alone." The builder part of Harvey's personality works in collaboration to "get everybody to come along with him" and to help build the dream—alumni, trustees, administration, faculty, and students.

JoAnn Haysbert, calling Harvey a master builder, concurred with Dawson: "I have been in the position to interact and observe [Harvey] over the past nineteen years. I have watched him build not only in the natural things, like physical facilities, but I have watched him build a team of professionals. In fact, I recall his first administrative council in which he gave each of them a portrait—a hand drawing of each of the administrative council members on a white background with a black frame, and he called it his first team." Members of that first team included Vice President for Academic Affairs, Martha Dawson; Vice President for Fiscal Affairs, Lucius Wyatt; Vice President for Development, Leron Clark; Vice President for Administrative Services, Oscar Prater; Director of Student Affairs, Alexander Strawn; Robert Bonner, Dean, Pure and Applied Sciences; Mary Christian, Dean, School of Education; William Kearney, Dean, School of Arts and Letters; Elnora Daniel, Dean, School of Nursing; and Secretary of the College, Mae Barbee Pleasant.

Continuing, Haysbert added: "I have observed him build a team of academic leaders, a team of devoted, committed and loyal faculty, and I can say that because I am among that group. I have watched him and observed him build academic programs, build physical facilities, and environment. He has, in essence, built a mystique at Hampton. He has built the alumni association and the unity; he has taken the cliché 'home' and built it into a reality. I think you will probably find some of the most devoted and committed individuals at Hampton University that you will find at any other University you may go."

"We thrive on what I call the team management approach," explained Harvey. "Although I provide the leadership, my vice presidents and deans are given the responsibility and authority—

with the appropriate controls and lines of communication—to get things done. We all feed off each other's ideas; no one should work in a vacuum."

Twice a week Harvey meets with his administrative council, which serves somewhat as an in-house board of directors. It is comprised of his vice president of academic affairs and provost, vice president of administrative services, vice president for fiscal affairs and treasurer, vice president of student affairs, vice president for research, and his vice president for development. Other principals, like the school deans, are included in his weekly expanded administrative council. In addition to group meetings, he manages to meet with each of his chief officers once a week, if only to brainstorm. Once a week, the provost and vice-president of academic affairs convenes the Academic Leadership Team, which consists of the deans of each school and directors, to discuss academic issues. Once a month the two groups, along with the department chairs, meet to discuss larger, school-wide issues. Deans and chairs also meet regularly with faculty to help carry Harvey's vision forward.

Martha Dawson felt that the administrative set-up allowed for "a great deal of cross-fertilization" and diverse perspectives. As she pointed out, at some schools, academics often run their "little shops in isolation," but at Hampton people can "bounce ideas off each other and understand the ramifications an action" would have on another unit.

Innovation

Essential to Harvey's administrative success and vision is innovation. While team work is crucial, Harvey maintains that, "Every enterprise takes into account the initiative of individuals and of the organization which results in innovation, coordination and flexibility so that new opportunities may be seized and adjustments to change may be continual and orderly." The Strategic Plan of 1992–1993, designed to improve the total University milieu, is an example of such innovation, which resulted in a newly emerging shared culture, emphasizing "academic excellence, character building, and efficiency and

excellence in all things." A clear mission of the University material-
ized from the Strategic Plan, one where the curricular emphasis is
scientific and professional, with a strong liberal arts undergirding.
Unquestionably, Harvey understood that building a distinctive,
diverse academic program was key to remaining competitive in the
vista of higher education. "In order for us to remain on the cutting
edge of the higher educational enterprise, in order for us to compete against the Harvards, Yales and Virginias for the very best and
brightest black kids in this country, in order for us to continue to
attract between 15–20 percent white students, we must continue to
build high quality and diverse curricular offerings," contended
Harvey, when he spoke at the "Kickoff of Hampton University's $200
Million Capital Campaign and Tribute to the President on his 20th
Anniversary" on October 22, 1998. "As this new millennium approaches," he continued, "we cannot rest on our laurels and be successful with the formula that caused us to be successful fifty years
ago. Therefore, only a minor part of this campaign deals with new
buildings. Other institutions seek to build bricks and mortar. We
seek to build a world-class institution!" So in building quality academic programs, Hampton University has established, for example,
a Center for Atmospheric Sciences, which is responsible for studying
the earth's atmosphere and assisting NASA in its quest to understand and explore the heavens.

Courage
Harvey noted that "Just as a leader must think outside of the box, a
leader must also have the courage to stick to his convictions." Discipline and perseverance are elements of courage. "I will tell you that
your thoughts and ideas will be tested—and that is good, you must
have the courage to listen and receive input on any subject. However, in the final analysis, after you have had a great deal of analysis,
input, challenges, you must have the courage of your convictions.
Sometimes you must say, win, lose, or draw; this is what we are
going to do," Harvey contended.

Good Management

As Harvey sees it, "Management is different from leadership." Yet, "both are completely necessary if one is to be effective." For Harvey, "management is the brains of an effective and efficient operation. Management is an enabler. It helps people to better utilize skills and knowledge. It helps them to do a better job. Every organization needs as many good managers as possible," since the human potential is critical to organizational success. Moreover, he feels that any organization, including a university, that lacks effective leadership has "little chance for survival." "It will be reduced to the controls of, at best, efficient clerks and their orbits. Organizations must be led to overcome their trained incapacity, to adapt to changing conditions. Leadership is what gives an organization its ability to translate that vision into reality." In the tradition of transformational leaders, Harvey believes that great leaders inspire their followers to excellence by pointing out how their labor advances worthwhile goals. Furthermore, he added that "leadership cares about the development of their people, predicting how they will behave in response to your leadership attempts, and directing their behavior are all necessary for effective leadership." In essence, he feels a good leader, who must also be a good manager, must devote time to nurturing his/her followers' "leadership potential—motivation, expertise, decision-making and problem-solving skills."[12]

In being a good manager, the leader also understands the importance of effective communication, accountability, and planning in the organization. Harvey recognized early in his administration at Hampton University, when speaking at a Faculty Institute on August 27, 1979, that effective communication is an essential tool of good management. "Part of my job is to interpret and relay appropriate information and news, whether good or bad—to the Board and to the college's various constituent groups. One of the tools used to indicate relationships in the communications process is the organizational chart, which sets up a formal system of responsibility. Often, however, the top executive does not get all of the communication as it flows through formal channels," he said. Unquestionably, he was cognizant that, "Much information provided the chief executive by administrative colleagues is either unintentionally or willfully inaccurate." He enumerated rationales why this occurs. First, he said, "No subordinate wants to have his superiors learn of anything which he interprets to be actually discreditable to him. So he filters out items of information that are potentially threatening in transmitting information upward." Second, he believed, "The subordinate learns what his superiors want to hear and becomes adept not only at avoiding the unpleasant, but also in stressing the positive. Now the individual may consciously be entirely sincere and accountable, but his personal anxieties, hostilities, aspirations and system of beliefs and values will shape or color his interpretation and acceptance of what he has learned and is expected to transmit." Third, Harvey maintained that, "each subordinate often desires to impress the chief executive with the superiority of his contributions to the enterprise." Fourth, "There is finally the inability of many chief executives to comprehend and accept valid information even when it comes to their attention. No wonder subordinates seldom tell the whole truth."

Therefore, Harvey contended, "For communication to be effective, it must be two-way. There has to be feedback to ascertain the extent to which the message has actually been understood and accepted. Otherwise the chief executive may be isolated and not know what is transpiring below him. As a result, he is often forced to make major decisions on the basis of unreliable intra-company intelligence. Further, his orders to those in the lower echelons may be distorted or even blocked at any supervisory level in between. It is therefore important to realize that communication problems exist at all levels, particularly top management."[13] To avert a crisis, the President developed open lines of communication on a regular basis between various constituent groups. He initiated monthly meetings with student leaders, bi-weekly meetings with his administrative council, weekly meetings with the expanded administrative council, monthly meetings with faculty, periodic visits to freshman halls, and an "open door" policy every Thursday from 3:30–5:00 PM.

Accountability is also crucial in the chain of command in higher education, and Harvey sees it as assuming "ever encompassing dimensions." He posits that, "Every person in an organization is responsible in some degree to another person or position for something for the accomplishment of an objective to be achieved with certain constraints." Accountability is inextricably linked to planning, which includes short-term, intermediate, and long-term planning.

Accordingly, Harvey maintained, in his remarks made on January 6, 1981, at Saint Augustine's College, that to "plan successfully for future contingencies, accurate and pertinent information must be available to the planner along with an objective analysis of those data. To promote orderly growth or retrenchment and to prevent future disasters in higher education, much more sophisticated approaches to planning must be implemented than have been used in the past." Here he identified some basic planning process characteristics for which to strive. These "basic planning elements should include and make explicit (1) the statement of mission; (2) the external environment; (3) internal assumptions; (4) program objectives; (5) budgets; and (6) evaluation plans. This approach requires the involvement of third, fourth and perhaps fifth-level administrators in the planning process. A major question as to the validity of this approach is whether or not department chairmen, unit managers and the like have a desire and therefore can be trained to do serious planning and whether the faculty can accept the results."[14]

Fairness

Harvey advocates fairness in his interactions with others. He advocated that, "In all that we do, in every decision that we make, in every interaction that we undertake, we should always keep fairness at the center of our being." For, Harvey noted, "It doesn't make a lot of difference if decisions are not popular. It is important, however, for decisions to be fair. If I cannot be fair, even to enemies, then I have failed."

Fiscal Conservatism

Harvey espouses the notion that Hampton should be run "like a business for educational objectives." Thus, it is imperative for him to look at both sides of the ledger. "If you have a dollar, you cannot spend a dollar and twenty-five cents," is Harvey's fiscal philosophy. So in his hands, he holds the pen to avoid deficits, to demand a balanced budget, to eliminate excessive overtime and waste, to institute presidential line-item budget review, to issue all contracts, and to allocate the budget on a quarterly basis to guard against deficit spending. His bottom line is "Where do we get the money?" When Martha Dawson was the vice-president for academic affairs, she met with him at least once a week and acknowledged how Harvey minded the University ledger with a jeweler's eye: "I would prepare to go in there, because if you went in there and you say, 'Dr. Harvey, I would like to start this program.' He would ask you lots of questions. 'Where's the money coming from, Dr. D?' 'What does that do for Hampton?'" Harvey also has an acute understanding of the activities and needs of each department. Laughing, Dawson recalled that sometimes he knew more about what was going on in your area than you did. She saw his actions as helping them to grow as educators, by teaching them how to plan judiciously and question themselves.

Surely, Harvey knows that to make "dreams realities," one needs "good ideas, sufficient capital, persistence, a little luck, and inspired leadership."[15]

Results Oriented

When the web of the Harvey model of administrative success is woven, the master builder's vision results in a finished product. The product is sometimes in the form of a tangible structure, like the Harvey Library or the Student Center, that catches the eye. It is sometimes in the form of an intangible idea, like the Honors Code, that touches the heart and builds character. It is sometimes in the new academic programs, like the Ph.D. in pharmacy and physical therapy, that stir the mind. It could be changes in the athletic program that condition the body. It could be renovating the art museum as a storehouse for treasures of the soul. His pursuit of excellence is transcendental. For his tenure at Hampton has taught him, as he stated in the *President's Annual Report, 1996–1997*, that "no matter how strong the faculty and staff, how boundless the potential of our able students, how solid the financial base, and how superb the physical plant, to remain great, we must do more. We must and will continue to raise the bar."

Arguably, by all accounts, some readers can apparently see the master dreamer's blueprints and can feel the heart pulse of the master builder hammering away at his plans. They are set to listen and watch how Harvey's "vision in motion" unfolds. But others marvel and still ask: What manner of man is this whose presence can command such stillness? For answers, we look to the cornerstone of his leadership—from the ground up—those who help to lay the foundation of his character, community, and culture—his family and friends, mentors, and those who continue to influence him and are influenced by him—his constituents—in his work at Hampton University.

From the Ground Up

For man, knowledge is important; more important is the ability to use knowledge; but most important of all is what a man believes; what he thinks good or bad; whether he has clear values and good standards and whether he is prepared to live by these standards and values.
—Sir Richard Livingstone

We know what a person thinks not when he tells us what he thinks, but by his actions.
—Issac Bashevis Singer

The Foundational Underpinning of Harvey's Leadership

The roots of Harvey's phenomenally successful leadership reach back to Brewton, a small hamlet in south central Alabama, known as the "richest little town in the South." A forest of yellow, long-leaf pines grow so bountifully along Murder and Burnt Corn Creeks in Brewton that its timber, the wellspring of a natural industry, built lumber mills and created thirteen lumber barons. Here, in the red clay of Alabama, where these pines sprouted so abundantly, he learned to see both the trees and the forest and to dream that he, too, could one day become an educational or "money magnet"[1] baron. From the moment of his birth on January 29, 1941, in this racially segregated town, the timber of Harvey's character was molded at the knee of his devoted and

45

loving parents, claudis P. and Willie D. C. Harvey, and cast by his caring black community.

In their middle-class home, this son of a successful building contractor and a housewife, along with his sister, Anne, learned valuable lessons, such as the importance of family, that set him on the prosperous path he has trodden. These messages, like the brick firing in the kiln, are baked into the very fiber of his being, and are central to his tenets of leadership. First and foremost, as the son of a Baptist deacon, he had a strong spiritual foundation. His parents taught him and his sister that "in time of crisis as well as other times, lean on Jesus. No matter what our professional fields are, we need an ethical philosophy of life. When the tap-root of life is out, the plant withers and dies." Because they understood, as Harvey professed, that:

> *On Christ, the solid rock I stand; all other ground is sinking*
> *sand.*
> *My hope is built on nothing less*
> *Than Jesus' blood of righteousness;*
> *I dare not trust the sweetest frame,*
> *but wholly lean on Jesus' name.*
> *On Christ the solid rock I stand; all other ground is sinking*
> *sand.*
> *All other ground is sinking sand.*[2]

For the perplexing questions about life—good and evil, faith and doubt, joy and suffering—the Bible offered him a framework for understanding and solving the existential mysteries of the human condition. In Sunday school, church worship, and Vacation Bible School, he identified with strong biblical characters of the Old Testament, like David, Jeremiah, and Job, whose faith remained unshakable, even when strenuously tested. Their faith taught him that it is always better to light a candle than curse the darkness. Repeatedly, he heard his parents and the elders of the community counsel that, "There are times when it seems that God withdraws from the world and we cannot make contact with Him. We seek and do not find

Him. We ask and do not receive. We knock and no one answers."[3] Even David spoke of such an encounter in the Thirteenth Psalm: "How long, O Lord, wilt thou forget me forever? How long wilt thou hide Thy face from me? How long must I bear pain in my soul and have sorrow in my heart all the day? How long shall my enemy be exalted over me?"[3]

Harvey discerned from the elders that "David was like every man in that he had his own dark night, but he was unlike some men in that he was not willing to surrender to it. He did not understand it, but neither did he believe it represented the whole truth about God or the will of God. God is a righteous God whose mercy extends to the end of the earth. David knew this and so deeply did he believe that he sought out God and complained about his suffering."[4]

Though David, Harvey theorized, "had no better answer to the mystery of human suffering than any other man," he "never doubted that God held the solution to his problem. God is the answer to crisis. . . God is the one who can enlarge our vision. When your doctor says that he can do no more, turn to the one who can. God is the master doctor; He is the master preacher; He is the master teacher. God can deliver."[5]

Unquestionably, his faith-based religious and spiritual foundation holds sway over his visionary leadership, and his "Can Do" philosophy. Therefore, he firmly believes that "there is no mountain of obstacles so high, there is no valley of despair so low, there is no burden of frustration so heavy that God cannot empower us to deal with them positively. And so, with God's help, we can climb the mountains of obstacles; with God's help we can be victorious over the valleys of despair; with God's help we can, like Jeremiah, bear our burdens in the heat of the day."[6] From his strong spiritual upbringing springs his self-confidence to dream big dreams and to envision how to build on them.

Fortunately, he had a quantity and quality of role models to light the way of his life path, like his father, from whom he gleaned the art of building. Willie D. C. Harvey built houses and buildings over southern Alabama and Pensacola, Florida: William, his son, would learn to build institutions. From his father, an entrepreneur who died in 1975, he also grasped his business acumen. At the same time, he learned his money management and fiscal conservatism from his mother, who would always remind her children, "If you have a dollar, you can't spend a dollar and twenty-five cents." His mother, who died in 1997 and whom he regarded as "near perfect," taught him by words and deeds the valuable lessons of "decency, dignity, fair play." She taught her children to be fair to others and to give people an opportunity to succeed. Although Harvey asserted that she did stress "no one should be given anything, but should work for it." Both parents instilled in him the way you get ahead is through hard work. His parents did not believe in giving their children allowances, so they had to work for it. Work always came before play. As an enterprising youth, he performed sundry odd jobs around Brewton—picking, pulling and hoeing cotton, shaking peanuts, picking strawberries, cutting grass, planting pine trees in the forest, delivering newspapers, and collecting and selling coat hangers to dry cleaners. "I have always worked and I have always had high ideals. I think that came from my father who was a civil rights leader and successful businessman. I don't know how I could have had any other thoughts." He reminisced about one of his jobs selling religious placards.

> I remember seeing an advertisement about selling placards in a book and I asked my daddy if I could write to get the materials to sell. I don't remember what it was now, but if I sold a placard for a dollar, I think that I had to send in maybe seventy-five cents and keep twenty-five cents. I remember my father telling me that I could get the materials to sell, but only if I treated it responsibly. Therefore, he made me practice how I would sell it. I would come by and ring the doorbell and he would answer the door and I would have to say my name, "Hi, my name is William Robert Harvey and I am selling . . ." I rang the doorbell. And Daddy answered the door, and I

was grinning, smiling, and carrying on and he closed the door. Then I wanted to know why he closed the door and he said, "I told you I want you to practice. I want you to practice as if you are going to a house and don't even know the people." So Daddy made me ring the doorbell and I had to go through my spiel and only after he was convinced that I could do a good job did he let me send away to get the things. Then when they came, I was successful. I also used to sell candy; and all kinds of other things because I always believed in working my way.

In an article by Stacy Burling, "Hampton's Best Seller," that appeared in the *Virginia Magazine*, July 10, 1983, she quoted Harvey's mother as saying, "He wasn't a child that would throw away his money. He loved to save." According to the article, Harvey's mother noted not only qualities of thriftiness and sound money management in his early formative years, but qualities of leadership, compassion, and generosity. Clearly, other children followed him. "You know how a hen would have little chicks following her, that's the way the little boys would follow him," his mother was quoted as saying.[7] Although he did not identify himself as having leadership qualities or assuming leadership during childhood, he recalled: "I was always out front in everything as early as I can remember. I don't know that I considered that as assuming leadership; however, I can remember when I went to school in Pensacola, Florida, I was asked to be a patrol leader, which meant that I would be the one to stop the cars to let the kids pass by on a very busy street in front of our elementary school. I credit my parents with whatever leadership acumen that I have because they were such great examples, and I am not sure that was not almost an innate kind of thing by simply looking at them and being counseled by them to serve, to do the kinds of things that helped one's community." As a Boy Scout, he remembered organizing "the fellows to go pick up trash on the streets in our neighborhood. I don't know where I got that from. I don't know if one of my parents suggested it, or I saw it on TV, or heard it on the radio. I don't know where that came from, but I remember doing it. When I was eight or nine years old, I also remember organizing a bunch of guys so that we could go out and cut a field and make a baseball field, so that we would have a place to play. But I am not sure that I considered that leadership at the time. As I look back, I can see that it probably was."

Harvey's family was an affluent black family in the lumber mill town, so he had more toys than the other boys and they looked up to him. Yet, his mother indicated "he was generous with his possessions." "I was the only black kid that had a basketball goal in his yard at that time, and the little boys would always be at my house. On Saturday mornings, for example, I would get up early, as I do now. The doorbell would start ringing, but my mother wouldn't let me go out. She would say, 'Well, he can't come out until ten,' so I would read on the couch in the living room, because they always had books for us. I developed at a very early age, as early as I can remember, the joy of reading, and I still read every night, wherever I am in the world. At ten o'clock I would then go out and we would play ball all day."

Growing up in the brutally racist milieu of southern Alabama, Harvey's parents primed portentous race lessons that serve as a guidepost for his leadership. Although his father, a civil rights leader, sheltered his children from the most virulent racial storms, they, too, were occasionally struck by a lightning bolt of racism. Their house was the meeting place of civil rights leaders. He recounted that his father never allowed his children to drink from a colored water fountain or use the colored restroom. One day while traveling through Alabama, he stopped for gas. When he asked to use the restroom, which had three signs— men, women, and colored, his father announced, "My son and I are men and we want to use the men's bathroom. My daughter and wife are women." When the gas attendant refused their usage of the restroom, his father balked at paying for the gas and asked the attendant to remove it. Unable to do so, the attendant angrily told the Harvey's to "just git on out of here." On that day, a free gasoline fill-up was received as a result of the racist South.

In another account, Harvey and a cousin were spotted playing tennis at an all-white school. Police stopped them on the way home and told them that blacks couldn't play on the tennis court. Harvey's father stormed downtown to the mayor's office at city hall. He informed the mayor that "if the tennis court was not integrated, he would start a sit-in by the weekend." The next day, construction started on a tennis court at a nearby black school.

These racial lessons taught Harvey survival skills, self-respect, and the courage to stand up for what is right. "I have very little fear. My father would say to my sister and me, "If you are right, don't worry about the consequences." It also fueled his spirit of competitiveness. He asserted, "Given the kinds of things my mother and father taught us—give no quarter and accept no quarter—I have never taken a back seat to anyone." His father always pushed Harvey and his sister not to accept "second class citizenship, to accept only the best." His parents emphasized, "Whites can make you inferior only on your own consent." Harvey contended, "I just never thought of myself as anything other than one of the best." While urging their children not to submit to racism, his parents implored them not to use it as an excuse for not being the best or as an excuse to hate whites.

As a corollary to his racial lessons, his father instructed him on the reality of politics, while underscoring the imperativeness of political independence. His father, who headed the local chapter of the National Association for the Advancement of Colored People and other civil rights organizations, always repeated two admonitions, asserted Harvey during an introduction of Virginia's Senator John Warner in 1996 at a political debate. "One was to always be a financial card-carrying member of the NAACP. I heard him say many times that if one got into political difficulty in parts of the racist South, you could always count on an NAACP member for support." "The second thing my father also stressed was that we do not have permanent friends or permanent enemies; rather, we only have permanent interests. . . . I am a political independent in the cherished and true Virginia tradition. As an example, I am an ardent supporter of Senator Warner and Senator Allen, both Republicans, and I also supported Senator Chuck Robb, Governor Doug Wilder, and Congressman Bobby Scott, who are Democrats."[8]

More importantly, Harvey contended that his father taught him that he "could never refuse to use the skills and influence" he has cultivated over the years to work for what he feels is the "public good"—as long as he has an "informed opinion." And being a Boy Scout, he learned always to be prepared to have one. While Harvey's philosophy of leadership, views of service, and compassion for others emanated from both parents, it was especially his father who influenced him.

These multitudinous moral messages and values of his parents undergird the aim-for-excellence outlook imparted to Harvey and his sister. Not only did Claudis and Willie Harvey reinforce their children's moral underpinnings by sending them to Southern Normal, a private school affiliated with the Dutch Reformed Church of America, they also wanted them to get a first-rate education. Their parents bolstered the process in the home by encouraging their children to work hard, study, and read. Through reading, Harvey's world expanded beyond Brewton. "There were always a lot of books in the house and I loved to read, mostly biographies," Harvey said. "We didn't get a television set until I was about 12, so there was plenty of time to read."[9] His late-night passion for reading, especially those spy novels, is a carryover from his early school days. At Southern Normal, which was one of the best schools at that time, blacks from all over the country sent their children, and here Harvey met mentors, like Kenneth B. Young, the director of Southern Normal and, his wife, Mai Graham Young, the guidance counselor. When I interviewed the then 92-years-old Mai Young in 1999 in Tuskegee, Alabama, she explicitly recalled meeting "William Robert," as she often referred to him, in the fall of 1955 as a

tenth grader: He was a "member of an outstanding class of thirteen." Even then, she observed that he was "a very aggressive
youngster and very affable and easy to meet." He demonstrated
leadership qualities, "by involving the class in projects that he
wanted them to accomplish," or by participating in youth forums.
Having followed this rising star since high school, she noted that:

> You could see early in life that Harvey had a vision. He
> always seemed to have wanted to reach up. You could see it
> in him. He always wanted the best and he always wanted to
> associate with the people who could help him climb to that.
> Looks like to me, he just knows how to touch the right peo-
> ple at the right time. You could see it within him that there is
> something that I am aspiring for. And when he came to
> Southern Normal, it looked like it just did something to him.
> He seemed to say, "Well, Lord here are some people I have
> been waiting to emulate and I haven't had that opportunity,
> but they are here now and that's what I want to be."

Young and her husband became mentors for Harvey and close
friends of his parents. At Southern Normal, Harvey said that the
"leaders, directors, and teachers provided a leadership that was
probably unequaled. They believed in the academic side but employed discipline." But the Youngs were also interested in a more
holistic development of their charges, so they gradually included a
social component in their maturation process at this Christian
school. She recalled with amusement how she taught "William Robert" to dance and how she imbued him with other social graces that
helped prepare him for upward mobility. "I think the thing that fasci-
nated me the most is that he [and the other boys in his class] didn't
know how to dance and that was strange to me because I had lived
in an area where dancing was a part of [the social setting]. So when
they came to counseling that day, I took them on the porch to teach
them how to dance. Well, William Robert's feet were so big, I was
afraid he was going to mash mine. I taught them, him and his cousin,
the one-step, and finally they got it. When they came to the banquet,
they could kind of move."

Harvey graduated from high school at sixteen, having started school a year early and skipped grade two. A high SAT score and good grades earned him scholarship offers from almost thirty colleges. But when he was offered an early admissions scholarship to Morehouse College, Mai Young counseled against it and instead encouraged him to attend Talladega College. "I told his mother, 'Listen, if William Robert goes to Atlanta, you will lose him. The women will take him. He's that kind, and those women in Atlanta will eat him up.' He wanted to go to Morehouse, but he listened to his mother." Young noted, "He was a real mama's boy. I used to tell her, Claudis, I wouldn't marry William Robert if I was a gold lady. That's your heart and he could do no wrong in anything." After he listened to the advice of his mother, Mai Young was influential in his matriculation at Talladega College, where he was awarded a scholarship.

There he was involved as a leader in the Civil Rights movement and in sports as an outstanding basketball star and tennis player. The foundation of his athletic talents had begun in Brewton, where so many people coached him during the summer in little league baseball, basketball, football, tennis, and during high school at Southern Normal, where he played split end on the football team and forward on the basketball team. Playing sports aided him in learning teamwork, in increasing his competitive spirit, and in understanding rules and how the game of life is played.

After graduating from Talladega College with a degree in history in 1961, he spent three years in the army as a history writer for the Department of Army in Europe. There he was also a basketball stand-out. The army reinforced the discipline of home and school, "to be all you can be," and it helped him to "grow up." After his tour of duty, he returned South to Pensacola, where he taught high school history for a year in 1965–66.

Staking and Laying His Leadership Foundation

After he left the Army and his brief teaching stint, he headed for Virginia State College (now Virginia State University) in Petersburg, Virginia to begin his graduate work in history. Although he completed his course work at the institution, he never wrote a thesis. There he was deeply influenced by Ed Toppin, a history professor, and the first person he ever met who had written a book. He encountered another person that would also play a significant role in his life. Here, he staked out his soul mate in the school's library on a Sunday afternoon in 1965, the enchanting daughter of a brick mason and school teacher, Norma Baker of Martinsville, Virginia. So enamored was he by her comeliness, he asked a friend about her. Norma Harvey told this story with mirth to me: "I was sitting at one of the tables [in the library] and he came over and sat down beside me and I got up and moved. And he loves to tell how he punished me for two months by not speaking to me. I tell him that I hate to burst his bubble, but I did not know that I was being punished, because I did not even know that he existed. That was our first unofficial meeting. A couple of months later, he introduced himself and we started going out." With his future wife, Norma Baker, Harvey discussed his high aspirations as he mapped out his plans for a career in the field of higher education. Sharing similar values, which stressed the importance of religion, family, education, excellence, self-respect, decency and dignity, she would become the portal to his heart and his mooring for equilibrium. They married in the summer of 1966. From that day forward, commitment, the brick and mortar of their marriage, has held the builder's son and the brick mason's daughter together for over thirty-seven years. "When we went into marriage, we [made] a commitment and it was us. It has to be the melding of we. . . . I am a firm believer, that in order to make things work, you have to do it as partners. And that's the way we have remained together all these years because we do things together; we make decisions together; and I think this is the key to a successful relationship," she counseled. In pledging their allegiance to one another, Harvey never fails to introduce her as the first lady of

Hampton University and to acknowledge publicly that she is the most important person in his life and the best thing that ever happened to him, other than his mother. "I think upon my wife as I did my mother who has passed; and my wife, who is with me now, is a crown of gold. My wife really is the glue in my life. I really feel that without her, I am nothing. And I pray to the Lord that she and I will be able to be together for a long time because she truly is the straw that stirs my drink." When he received the Alumni Council Award at Harvard University on June 8, 1988, he also acknowledged, "My wife. . . has been a solid rock of support and strength for me and our three children. Without her, my life would not have the equilibrium in which to function."

After their marriage, they moved to Alabama, where he worked for a couple of years as a deputy director of the Equal Opportunity Agency in Daphne, Alabama, before he accepted a fellowship to Harvard University in 1968.

The Harvard Experience

In 1968, when the Harveys arrived at Harvard, it was a watershed epoch. It was the height of the Vietnam War, of campus protests, urban rebellions, white flight from major cities, youth rebellions, the counterculture movements, and the Black Nationalist movement. For the first time, white universities were recruiting people of color in larger numbers. Within the context of these historical events, the impact of the Harvard experience on Harvey's leadership development is told through the eyes of Robert Binswanger, one of Harvey's mentors at Harvard. Binswanger, who later became chair of the Hampton University Board of Trustees, has known Harvey for over thirty years. He noted that Harvey entered the School of Education at Harvard during a time when the institution was beginning to acknowledge that the higher educational enterprise, and those controlling it, was reflective of the white male-oriented larger society. In his view, "Harvard came to the conclusion that it had a duty and responsibility to reach out and bring persons of color to the campus and to offer them an education for leadership in [the field of] education. And Bill Harvey was admitted, not because he was black, but admitted with a group of other students of color. In the time period he came, he was an important figure, not because he was Bill Harvey, but he was someone the school was counting on to take a leadership position in American society." The school had established a new program, called the Administrative Careers Program, designed to train individuals for innovative educational leadership on the federal and state levels. Although there was a core curriculum, Harvey knew what he wanted and planned his own. Binswanger remarked: "It's nice to have a graduate student who is bright enough to be accepted through the admissions process who truly knows their direction. He knew why he wanted the degree; he knew what he was going to do with the degree; and he knew that he had to jump over certain obstacles to get the degree. And there was no argument about that. And he went right to work and decided that if I am here and I have all these riches, I am going to find people who are going to make a difference in my education."

So Harvey took courses at Harvard Business School in human resources and in organizational dynamics, and at the law school—not introductory level courses but upper level ones—in the development and enforcement of laws. He wanted to take courses with distinguished professors, like Henry Kissinger, John Kenneth Galbraith, and Nathan Glazer, to broaden his thinking. "Bill was not a quiet student. He had strong opinions and a strong set of values, and he stuck to them. When I said he was opinionated, I should have added that he wasn't afraid to judge things and still isn't," asserted Binswanger. Clearly, Binswanger remembered that "he was focused on having a leadership role in education" and had "entrepreneurial instincts—in the sense of leadership, in the sense of direction, in the sense of taking charge of things, in the sense of planning, in the sense of judgment." When Harvey was a graduate student, he recalled thinking, "Here's a student who does know who they are and what they are, learning it at the graduate level of education. That's very unusual. But I had the feeling that Bill Harvey, because of his values, because of how he looks at the world, and because of his aggressiveness, wanted to build something. And I think that's what he's done at Hampton."

Preparing to Build

After receiving his Doctor of Education in College Administration at Harvard University in 1971 and serving there as assistant for governmental affairs to the dean, Harvey, the planner, knew his career aspiration was to become a college president and to build someday a quality institution. But first, he wanted to acquire the proper tools and training to do a successful job. Although courted by New England institutions, like Harvard, Dartmouth and the University of Connecticut, Harvey wanted to apply his energies and talents to building a quality black institution of higher education, where he felt role models were most needed to help promote upward mobility and, therefore, democracy. As a student of history, it was irrefutable then as it is now for him that "the struggle for equal educational opportunity is still at the heart of our desire for equal opportunity in America, and higher education plays an enormously important role in equalizing human conditions. . . .Vital in this process—though little heralded in the past—will be black colleges. Historically, out of their bosom has come strength for this nation over and beyond the thousands of students directly touched in the classroom and set on the road to solid citizenship—often to local, national, and worldwide distinction. The very concept of this nation and its origins has been magnificently advanced by black colleges," Harvey stated in a speech before the U. S. Department of Transportation on February 4, 1987. The President is an example of someone who came out of the bosom of a black high school, black undergraduate school, a black graduate school. He went to Harvard and competed exceptionally well with people from all walks of life. Though he is enormously proud of his doctoral degree from Harvard, he said, "I am equally proud of my association with

Talladega College and Virginia State University for their careful nurturing of those skills and talents which rendered that achievement possible." Accordingly, Harvey chose the arena of an HBCU, because he wanted to give something back to the community that so enriched his life. He believes that black institutions have been a creditable model: they have provided a positive psychological and psychosocial milieu for students' living and learning; have offered them opportunities for leadership and to learn about their history and heritage; and have "served as a bridge between the haves and have-nots." He wanted to provide the same opportunity for future generations as he had experienced.

In preparing to one day assume the mantle of college president, he and Norma moved to Nashville, Tennessee. There, he spent two years as administrative assistant to the President of Fisk University, before moving to then Tuskegee Institute. He was there six years and served in two administrative posts, the vice president for administrative services and vice president of student affairs. These experiences allowed Harvey to further hone his team-building skills and his business acumen before accepting a college presidency. He told Scott Walsh, a journalist, after he had become President of Hampton, that:

> Brilliant scholars often go on to become college presidents, and fine ones at that, but some may pull their hair out when confronted with a budget sheet. That just happens to be where I have focused my energies, realizing that everything academic emanates from our financial base. My last two jobs exposed me to the entire gamut of administrative, academic, and planning duties. My job at Harvard took me to Washington once a week to work out educational funding opportunities with all sorts of federal agencies. The theoretical side of my education complements all that, so I guess I've developed my own pragmatic approach to the job.[10]

Armed with a vision, along with possessing management and budgetary deftness, Harvey was ready to be called to duty as a college president. According to Mai Graham Young, Harvey and his wife, Norma, were about to travel to Oklahoma to accept a position at a university there. But on that day in 1978, a different fate awaited them. Prior to their scheduled departure, he attended the funeral of Booker T. Washington's daughter. After the service, they had planned to go directly to the airport. But when Norma Harvey sent him by his office for something, he learned Hampton Institute had called to offer him the position as its twelfth president.

Building His Family Life at Hampton

The Harveys and their two children—Kelly Renee and William Christopher [Leslie Denise, their third child, was not born until 1980]— set off to build a new life at Hampton University in their ten-bedroom, three-story nineteenth-century mansion overlooking the Hampton River. It has been home to the school's presidents and their families since 1868. The walls of the family room are lined with portraits of family members, bespeaking the importance of family. While he traveled extensively raising funds and building a quality institution, Norma Harvey, now a consultant for the Hampton University Business Assistance Program, kept the hearth fires burning and took care of their young children. Now that the children are grown, she has no regrets. "I told people when I moved here that was my commitment. My commitment was first to my family, and then second, it was to him. . . . I felt our children needed guidance and I knew my husband would be traveling a lot, so that made me commit to the values and nourishment that children needed at that age. And I have always felt that family came before anything else," she said. Although she was committed to her children, she supported her husband in his pursuit of excellence. "I try to help as much as I can. It goes back to teamwork. One can't do everything alone."

Leslie Denise, the youngest child of the Harveys, agreed. "The role of the first lady is very important. Not only is she the wife of the President but the backbone. My parents work hand-in-hand. The success made by my father is all a result of teamwork. My mother has always been a sweet and sophisticated woman whose personality fits right into the role of first lady. She is filled with compassion and helps people whenever she can. My mother is a people person, which is good because she has to interact with so many people in her role as First Lady." Dubbed the gracious hostess, she unarguably entertains royally at receptions and "last minute luncheons" at the Mansion House. "It's not something I am afraid to do, and I think that's important because the person that he may bring in the last minute could eventually give us millions of dollars," said Norma.

Kelly, their oldest child, presented another side of the teammates. Norma, the calm in the storm, is the emotional center for her husband and the family. "Mommy is gracious, beautiful and together, and oftentimes people think she is submissive and he's dominant and it's not like that at all. At home the [emotional] roles of my parents are reversed. . . . You know he gets kind of disheveled when things aren't going right or something didn't happen like he wanted it to. Daddy is the emotional one and Mommy is levelheaded and keeps everyone calm. And he goes to her for a lot of things in terms of decisions I've heard at Hampton and in their business dealings together. You have to know when to be a lady and when to let your partner take the lead. She knows here at home they are equals, and they both understand their roles in the other's life," remarked Kelly. Her parents have explained there may be times in a relationship where one person may have to take a lead and the other may follow. Even though Harvey spent up to eighty percent of his time away from campus raising funds while his children was growing up, family life is important to him. "I'm always going to be Daddy," Harvey said. "I'm not always going to be president. My family comes first, even before the job." Norma Harvey agreed with her husband, noting that, "Some activities he had to attend as a commitment to his job, but he never left the children unattended. I remember that he was in New York on business on one occasion when Kelly had a dance recital. He left New York early to be back for her. And that's the kind of person he is, he never makes a promise to his children that he does not keep."

His oldest child, Kelly Renee, who claimed that she is a daddy's girl and "his clone," agreed that, while growing up, her father has "always been there for me, my brother, and my sister. I've heard him tell people that he would come back from business trips to make it to my dance recitals. I didn't know he was cutting them short, because he was always there. He'd always be in the audience. He and Mommy both." Speaking for William Christopher, her brother and Leslie, her younger sister, she stated that when "Chris was a football player and a basketball player, they would be at every game." Kelly remembers another occasion when she was elected as "Ms. Homecoming" at her school, Hampton Roads Academy. She was to be crowned on the Saturday which conflicted with Hampton University's homecoming. She asked, "which event do you think my daddy attended?" The answer, of course, was the crowning of Kelly, the first Black Homecoming Queen at Hampton Roads Academy. When Kelly, most recently a television reporter and weekend anchorwoman with a local CBS affiliate, had her sixteenth birthday party, she remembered, "My parents gave me a pearl necklace and pearl earrings. That was my sweet sixteen birthday present. And I still have those. I love them. As a debutante, I also remember how much I enjoyed the daddy dance we had."

When talking about her father, Kelly is so fond of him that a wellspring of emotions rose up. With tender tears cascading down her cherubic cheeks, she declared, "He's just a wonderful person! A lot of people feel intimidated by him and a lot of people ask me questions about him. But you know, to me, he's not the president. To me, he's Daddy. Daddy has always been there. I guess I'm learning more now about his accomplishments. I never thought of him as the president—only as Daddy." Growing up, several events stood out in her mind to illustrate his sense of caring. She cited this example. "I was a junior in high school and I was in a dance class at Hampton, and I was coming downstairs at the studio and I missed a step and turned my ankle. It was so severe, they said it would have healed faster and with less pain if I had broken it. Well, my mom took me to the emergency room and she called Daddy. And he, of course, rushed right over as he always did. I remember being on a stretcher, being in so much pain and crying, my leaning on him, and his hugging me and stroking my hair. He said, 'Darling, I'm so sorry. If I could take the pain for you, I would.'"

Leslie, too, concurred with Kelly. She said that "Dad has always been supportive of me. When I look back on my childhood, I think of the dad who held on to the back of my bicycle and kept holding on because I was scared I was going to fall. The next thing I knew I was riding and he wasn't even holding on. He made me think I wasn't riding by myself but I was, and I wasn't scared anymore. I think of my dad who would throw me a football in the backyard when I was going through my tomboy stage. I think of a dad who would dance with me when the music for Monday night football would come on."

Kelly feels "lucky that the Lord put her with these two people," caring parents, who passed on the important values of family, education, respect for elders, hard work, self-reliance, and the importance of ownership, money management and a service orientation. In her formative years, she contended, "My father ingrained in our heads that family comes first. And the other things he always said to me is that 'No two people in this world will love you more than your mother and I. Not your husband, not your children—your mother and I.' And I have grown up believing that." Leslie absorbed similar values from her parents, noting that her father imparted, "Family members are the only ones who will tell you nothing wrong and never do anything to hurt you."

Margaret Simmons, the late professor of English and a close friend of Harvey who died in 2002, attested to his sincerity about the importance of family. "I was talking to him on the phone one night, and he said, 'I had better call you back, I got to give mother her medicine.' Here is a man who could have people to administer every dose, but he did it himself. He missed convocation and a board meeting for the first time because he went to be [with his mother]. He had people he could depend on, but the first thought was his mother." For Simmons, it was another side of the "big giant of a man, who sometimes seems unrelentless in his insistence and the push and drive; to see his compassion, to see William Harvey, the son, to see him as the person who cares about other human beings and tries to bring out the best in everyone."

Mai Graham Young, his Brewton mentor and close friend, has an inkling of what Kelly and Simmons pointed out. As a family friend, Harvey's sense of caring has been extended to her. When her husband, whom Harvey looked fondly on as a dad, was infirmed, Harvey told her: "Bring him to Hampton! Don't put him in a nursing home! I'll get somebody to take care of him and you won't have to worry." Young responded, "Bill, I couldn't put that on you." "But I want to do it," he said. Young stated that "he never consented for me to put him in a nursing home. And then when I did put him in a nursing home, he said, 'I told you not to do it. I told you to bring him here.'"

Arthur Greene, Harvey's closest friend, who is a successful orthopedic surgeon, also acknowledged that "he is a tremendously caring person. When there is illness or trouble in a friend's life, he does things that he doesn't really want people to know that he's doing for them—whether its giving some assistance, visiting them, or allowing them to know that he's thinking about them. These are things I know everyone does, but you would think the president of a university wouldn't have time to do those things. But we have agreed that we believe that family and friends are the two most enduring assets anyone can have." Hence, Harvey and Greene, with a friendship of more than twenty years, are more like brothers. They can now in their mature years express that sense of caring with "I love you" and not feel their manhood is threatened.

With what Kelly has heard and seen within her family and within the circle of family friends, it should come as little surprise to know that her best friends are her parents. "I go to them with everything—life, love—and when I talk to Daddy or Mommy about love, he'll say, 'Every stone you're traveling, I've overturned at least once.' But they always have good advice. Daddy always has good advice about everything. Daddy knows everything."

Kelly sees her daddy as a "staunch disciplinarian," who taught lessons of respect. "I know that for a fact he did in my home," she said. He taught us to "respect elders and respect your parents. Daddy always says, 'I'm just as much older than you are today as the day you were born.' [Harvey's mother] used to say the same thing. I've heard her say it to him. I said, 'That's where he got it from.' And it was just respect, not merely do as I say. It was more 'I've been here longer, and I've been through things and I have a lot to impart to you. Yes, I'm your father; yes, I'm your grandmother, but I've walked the walk a little longer, so I think I know what I'm talking about.'" As a teenager growing up, she remembered, "I didn't think I should have a curfew an hour earlier than everyone else, so I tried to express myself then. But they just were not having that," said Kelly.

Norma and William Harvey taught their children those values of hard work, time management, money management, and self-reliance as essential qualities for succeeding in life. According to Kelly, her father would say, "His children were not going to sit in the house all summer and do nothing. He did not want to spoil his children." So each of his three children went to work at about ten or eleven years of age. "I worked in his office answering phones, running errands for people, and eventually I was a camp counselor on campus at Hampton University's Kiddie College," said Kelly. Although the President and his family had housekeepers, Kelly remarked that, "We were not waited on hand and foot. We were expected to pull our weight in this house as a family unit.

Oftentimes, successful people do not make their children do that, so they don't learn what it takes to get where they are. They think it's just handed to them. Daddy and Mommy have not forgotten what got them here, and that's basic hard work." When the children were not working, they were busily engrossed in other extracurricular activities like tennis. Kelly reiterated, "We did not have time to sit down and not do anything because his children were not going to be lazy and sit on their butts. We were going to learn the values of discipline and time management." Furthermore, "Daddy is always talking about saving money, even if it's only ten dollars from your check." While she was matriculating at Spelman College in Atlanta in the early 1990s, her allowance was a nonnegotiable $200.00 monthly for four years. Furthermore, she was required to stay on campus for the entire four years of her undergraduate studies. Kelly was allowed to have a car in her sophomore year, but when her grades slipped, her parents took it away.

Along with Kelly, Christopher and Leslie worked during the summer. Their parents told them that they "would not be handed anything if they didn't work for it." Moreover, Kelly remarked that her parents did not take their children along on their trips around the world to China and Japan. "My daddy would say, 'If we take you when you are a child, you will have nothing to look forward to as an adult.'"

Clearly, Kelly absorbed the life lessons of her parents. In a 1983 feature story about President Harvey, entitled "Hampton Best Seller," the writer observed that, "Kelly Harvey was showing off her collection of Coca-Cola bottle caps. She was one word short of completing a sentence with the words printed inside the cap, and of course winning $50,000. What would she do with the money? a family friend asked, Buy a car? Fly to Disneyland? "I'm going to put $20,000 in savings and give the rest to Hampton Institute," the 9-year-old replied. "I just know the money is not being wasted here."[11]

Undoubtedly, she learned her compassion and service orientation from her father. She grew up hearing her "daddy's stories" and other black intellectuals discourse about the Civil Rights movement and the state of black America. It inspired in her a passion to help students in her profession of journalism. She noted that, "He is always helping people who are trying to get into school or get a job." She cited the example of how, with his own money, he set up a college fund for the family of Christopher Harper, the late Chief of Police at Hampton University, who died unexpectedly, leaving his pregnant widow and two children. Kelly assures us that "Daddy isn't one who needs accolades in terms of being able to help people. The gift that he gets in return for doing that is knowing that this woman won't suffer. She just lost her soul mate. But she won't have to worry about sending her kids to college because my daddy put that together for her. But that's enough for Daddy— her coming up and hugging him and saying, 'Thank you.' That's enough for him because he's very humble."

Although Kelly thinks that he is humble, she may have captured the duality of his personality when she contended: "I think we are both highly opinionated and I think we're both very emotional. I think as a woman I am not afraid to wear my emotions on my sleeve. I think men are more guarded of that. Both of us just care a lot about other people. I think I got that from him. Like I say, Mom says we're two peas in a pod. He's opinionated; I'm opinionated. And oftentimes we clash. We clash a lot because we are a lot alike." One disagreement centers around their racial politics. While Kelly, whose parents cautioned her "never to use race as a crutch," is more politically liberal, she thinks he is more politically conservative. On the one hand, she believes racism is ever present, and even though one should not employ it as a crutch, racism should be acknowledged as a barrier to achievement. On the other hand, Kelly maintained that, "Daddy preaches self-reliance. And while I think he realizes that there are variables that sometimes don't let people pull themselves up by their boot-straps, I think it goes back to not using race as a crutch. He knows that there is racism and it's very real for some people. But I think he thinks that if you take out that variable and really work hard, you can achieve."

Harvey's way of viewing racial politics is perhaps linked to his "Can Do" philosophy. "If you imagine it, you can achieve it." But Kelly thinks, "Sometimes Daddy expects people to perform—he has higher standards—at his level. And not everyone is capable of doing that. You know, everyone has strengths and everyone has weaknesses and its a matter of being able to pick up on people's strengths."

Kelly has picked up on her father's many strengths. Yet, she is aware that "Sometimes, because of everything he has been through, because of everything he knows, sometimes he is too narrow-minded to see another's person's perspective. I think this is his weakness," she stated. "I think as I have gotten older, maybe it's just family. He says, 'Everyone listens to me. My children sometimes don't listen to me.' And I say, 'But Daddy, that's because they see everything good you do. We see the good and the bad.' And you know we are like two peas in a pod and we have clashed a lot of times because he has been unwilling to listen to my perspective. He sees me as a child."

Kelly has just begun to take a look at the professional side of her father. As she reflected about growing up with her prominent parents, she said: "I have two wonderful parents. Their life was us. And so it was always about me, Chris, and Leslie and what we were doing—making sure our homework was done and our papers were done."

Kelly, most recently a television reporter and anchorwoman, is married to Sean Jones. William Christopher, who is employed as a real estate development executive, is married to Valerie Magliore, a resident physician, and they have a daughter, Taylor Jean Marie. Leslie Denise, a 2002 graduate, is the first child of a sitting president to graduate from Hampton University and is the first child to be born to a sitting president since Samuel Armstrong, the founder, and his wife had a daughter, Margaret, in 1893.

Building the Hampton Family

Much of what Harvey is, much of what his leadership mandates, and much of what he yearns for Hampton University and its students is rooted in his childhood and is augmented in his own family. What his leadership commands and what he desires for his constituents is to hold fast to core values of academic excellence, leadership, character, community service, respect for oneself, respect for others, decency, and dignity. These values are embedded in his family of orientation and family of procreation. And it is best illustrated in a well-known anecdote about Leslie Harvey. This time the storyteller is Charles Wilson, Board of Trustees member, who praises Harvey as a "rare bird" in the way he has blended his skills as an "administrator and educator to build Hampton University into a first-class university." In his version of the story, when Leslie disclosed to her father that she wanted to attend Hampton University, President Harvey purportedly said, "You wouldn't want to come to Hampton." She responded, "Why, Daddy?" He stated, "Because you would have to get the lumps if the food wasn't good in the cafeteria. They would say, 'Your daddy did it.' If the instructor wasn't there and the building wasn't there, 'Your daddy did it.' Whatever went wrong at Hampton, you would have to take my lumps." "But, Daddy," she said, "you always wanted us to go to the best and I think Hampton is the best."

Prior to selecting Hampton, Leslie Harvey, in her own words, said:

> When it came to choosing the college I wanted to go, it was a very tough decision. My senior year in high school I applied to various colleges including Xavier University, Spelman College, William and Mary, University of Virginia, and last but not least Hampton University. I fooled myself into thinking I wanted to go to Spelman but my heart was really at Hampton University. I had always wanted to attend a historically black university and Hampton was at the top of

my list. My family didn't want me to go because I grew up in Hampton and they thought I should get away. It wasn't just my family who felt this way but so did my friends. Everyone thought I should leave and experience a new city and new people. I figured I could experience all of those things in graduate school. It was my decision to make and I enrolled at Hampton. During my freshmen year at Hampton, I was warned by many people that I would get a lot of criticism for attending the school that I loved so much. ...

My father told me that I would have to prepare for a lot of negativity about my going to Hampton and about him as president. I didn't care because I thought I could handle anything that was to come my way. I was a freshman enjoying the freedom of college. Things were said to me that were negative about attending the college, which hurt my feelings. This was when I discovered I wasn't as tough as I thought I was. I felt like people were judging me before they even got to know me. This brought me to the conclusion that I wanted to transfer the following year. This was a hard decision for me to make but I thought I would be happier at another school. It wasn't until the last semester of school that I became comfortable with myself that I realized that I shouldn't cater to other people. I was at Hampton for Leslie and it shouldn't matter what others felt. I couldn't believe I was so close to giving up my dream of attending Hampton University and leaving all of the friends I had because of the ignorance of others. I came to believe people will talk about you wherever you are, so who cares.

Like her father, Leslie, too, only wanted the best, a virtue reinforced by Harvey's family of orientation. Kelly Harvey Jones reminds us that, "He was raised on higher standards, not that he thinks he's better, he just wants to do better. He says too many people settle for mediocrity. But he doesn't. And that's exemplified in everything that he has accomplished; everything that he has done. Its just a higher standard that he expects people to work towards—to live up to. He wants black people to succeed and he wants the best for Hampton University and its students. And you know you're only as strong as your weakest link, so how is Hampton going to be successful if the people that are running it don't think that way?" Like his own family, Norma

Harvey knows that her husband "loves Hampton," is committed to it, and works zealously to make all the links strong. "The time, and all his energies, that he has put into Hampton shows that," she said.

Agreeing, Robert Binswanger noted: "What he has done is take a warm, dusty institution and made it one of the leading black colleges or universities in the United States. And that's a major accomplishment, particularly in times when there isn't enough money and all kinds of competing interests. He has had a clear vision of where he wanted to go and has given the time— twenty-some years—to move the institution forward." Binswanger felt that Harvey's seasoned leadership is an asset. "The institution would not have made the progress without single leadership." And this "continuity is very unusual in higher education. We're down to presidencies being three and one-half to four and one-half years. And by the time a new president comes in, it takes them a year to understand it—a year to figure out what they want to do. And in a sense, they have left before they have time to see the results of what they have been thinking about. And continuity in higher education is vital, and the changes that he has made are essential ones to take Hampton into the twenty-first century."
Although Binswanger recognized Hampton University's historic strong presidential leaders, he surmised that many people had not "imagined the moves forward that have been made of strengthening [the University] in terms of broadening faculty disciplines, strengthening in terms of the facilities that have been built." He maintained, it was a "major task that I don't really believe either the faculty, staff, or alumni were aware of until the train left the station."

JoAnn Haysbert, his provost, was one person on Harvey's train who understood and supported his administrative model of academic success—vision, good work ethic, academic excellence, team building, innovation, courage, good management, fairness, fiscal conservatism, and results-orientation. She concurred with Binswanger that he has built edifices and excellent programs, but she suggested that he has also constructed an institution with a soul. As noted earlier, she indicated that Harvey has taken the "cliché home and translated it into a reality." Compassion is one of its underpinnings. "Oftentimes one does not associate compassion as one of the virtues of a successful dynamic leader. Typically, you think about people who are separated from the group of folks that they lead. Not physically separated, but keeping themselves at a professional or comfortable distance. I find Dr. Harvey to be a person who is intricately involved with those people around him that he serves and who serve him. I have seen him cry, when others have cried, and then, perhaps, when others have not," remarked Haysbert. She recalled an example from her own experience when she was the assistant vice president of academic affairs in the 1980s. "I had come to a point in my life when I was faced with a life and death illness. But I did not want my illness to jeopardize my job. I had put in too much of me as a personal professional to let my health affect what I was doing." She discussed her situation with Martha Dawson, her immediate supervisor—then vice president of academic affairs—and she suggested that she speak with President Harvey. "And I did. It was a turning point for me. All the things that I thought about Dr. Harvey, based on my interactions, came to full circle when I shared with him the condition of my health. Because he was so emotionally tied to another human being's fate, he shed tears. I remember reaching on his desk and getting a Kleenex from a box of tissue and handing it to him. So his compassion for me caused me to drop tears, and I was giving him a tissue in lieu of his giving me one. I will never forget it as long as I live." As a result of their conversation, Harvey picked up his phone and explained to Carlton Brown, then dean of the School of Education who later became president of Savannah State University, about Haysbert's health status and her desire to return to the classroom. Harvey asked the dean if he could find a position for her. She had previously held a position as an associate professor in the school, and fortunately, a vacancy was available. When Harvey completed his conversation with the dean, he turned his attention to her. "But now you are sick," he continued his conversation with Haysbert, and to ensure her "future health" and for her "to continue to contribute to the University, do whatever is needed, but let me know." He then allowed her to work a half day for the remainder of her contractual period.

Haysbert pointed out another example of Harvey's sense of humanity and family, which is often personalized because of his phenomenal retentive memory. "Dr. Harvey probably knows every groundsman by name, and groundswoman. I have walked with him, or have been behind him, or in front of him when he passed different people that are working on the [grounds] and it is "Hi! Mr. Whatever," or a short chat with the person that's putting out the flowers, the man that's mowing the lawn, the one that's cutting the hedges. And it's a first name in many cases and where it's not a first name, there's a name." Similarly, she related her feelings when Harvey gave his first team, as previously mentioned, the hand painted portrait. "I was not in his administrative cabinet at that level, at that time, so I'm not on it. But I was so struck by his recognizing that this is my first team, not my administrative council, but my first team."

Haysbert saw Harvey's compassion and generosity extend beyond kind words to other acts of good. "I remember one year we had met a balanced budget and there were some dollars remaining. Dr. Harvey gave every single human being that worked full-time for Hampton University a certain amount of money. And I don't mean just professors and administrators, I mean the groundskeepers, everybody. I was so struck by it at the time that I recall writing him a letter to say not only thank you, but in amazement almost, because I had never seen anybody do this before," she said. In doing so, she contended, "You are building a cadre of folk that are dedicated to the institution. Why? Because the person in charge recognizes your service, regardless of what place that service is rendered." Likewise, Ben Head also noted that Harvey "recognizes people who have done something good for the

University, whether he is a professor or employee. I think he recognizes talent and ability, and a job well done, and gives that person proper credit."

Moreover, Harvey never fails to publicly thank his constituents during public ceremonies or in his *President's Annual Report*. His 1981–82 Report is an example.

> Indeed, our greatness must be ultimately attributed to the diverse skills and talents of the many faces of Hampton [University]. Its successes are the result of the collective vision and the concerted effort of members of the Board of Trustees, faculty, support staff, alumni, student body, parents, contributors, friends. Without them, we might have well been caught up in the confusion, uncertainty and despair which have paralyzed other institutions. With them we have risen above the tide and continue to grow. There are those whose efforts have not thrust them into the spotlight, have not brought them headlines, adulation or fame. These are the ones who prepare the food, maintain the beautiful physical plant, drive the vehicles and maintain the equipment. Although their effort may seem to go unnoticed, they continue to affirm their commitment to Hampton [University] through unrelenting service.

His "down home" sense of decency and good manners are codified into the Hampton University Code of Conduct, a shared ideal culture, that he first advocated at the Opening Convocation in 1983, and which came to fruition in the academic year of 1993–94. Harvey strongly subscribes to the notion that the Hampton University experience is best accomplished through the University family spirit that is upheld through the coordinated efforts and dedication of each student, faculty, administrator, and staff member. Therefore, the Code of Conduct is exemplary of this family spirit.

> Joining the Hampton Family is an honor and requires each individual to uphold the policies, regulations, and guidelines established for students, faculty, administration, professional and other employees, and the laws of the Commonwealth of Virginia. Each member is required to adhere to and conform to the instructions and guidance of the leadership of his/her respective area. Therefore, the following are

expected of each member of the Hampton Family: 1. To respect himself or herself; 2. To respect the dignity, feelings, worth, and values of others; 3. To respect the rights and property of others and to discourage vandalism and theft; 4. To prohibit discrimination, while striving to learn from differences in people, ideas, and opinions; 5. To practice personal, professional, and academic integrity, and to discourage all forms of dishonesty, plagiarism, deceit, and disloyalty to the Code of Conduct. 6. To foster a personal professional work ethic within the Hampton University Family; 7. To foster an open, fair, and caring environment; 8. To be fully responsible for upholding the Hampton University Code.

The rewarding of constituents' efforts in upholding the Code of Conduct through recognition, remuneration, respect, decency and dignity has helped Harvey to achieve a shared vision, a shared faith, and a shared commitment among his followers. Using her own commitment as an example, JoAnn Haysbert asserted, "I am not an alumna, but if you were to talk with me, one would assume, as many have, that I am, because of my commitment to the University. And I attribute that to a leader—a leader that I observe that took the time, in my estimation, to know that he was building just what he has, and that is a cadre of committed, loyal and dedicated professionals, programs, student body, and facilities."

"Harvey knows people," said Charles Wilson, Board of Trustees member. And he agreed that the "titular head of the University" has "developed loyalty and respect with people who work with him." And this loyalty, along with Hampton University's national image, "did not get their by prayer. It got there through efforts, sweat, sleepless nights. That's Harvey's contribution, but he had to have a team to do it."

Martha Jallim-Hall also acknowledged that Harvey is "dedicated to making sure that Hampton is really the best school it can be. It has the types of programs that students and faculty would like to brag about or to say I am a Hamptonian, or I work at the University." When "people see his dedication, and if they are not as dedicated, they become dedicated themselves." Harvey is not only "committed to the goals of the University and what he believes in," but also "the goals and objectives of individuals of the University and what others believe in, whether they are students, faculty or staff."

Martha Dawson can attest to Jallim-Hall's observations that he supports others' vision by giving them an opportunity to grow, which is also the mark of an effective leader. "In my experience of working with Dr. Harvey, I grew, because he allows you to grow. If you had an idea and it was a good one, he would be very supportive. He didn't give you a blueprint. You brought him the blueprint and he added to it and then helped you to carry it out. But you didn't go in there with a half-cocked idea," she remarked. She cited an example where one of her many ideas was supported. When the University revamped its academic structure from directors to deans, Harvey and Dawson wanted the revisions to represent more than a title change. They wanted the academic chairs and deans to have the necessary leadership development credentials to carry out the President's vision. "Dr. Harvey was supportive of a program that I started with training the leaders. We called it SALT—Special Administrative Leadership Training," said Dawson. Since her idea was a good one, she remarked that," Throughout my tenure, he allowed me to have money to have a series of these workshops. The first couple of years we had them practically every six weeks. Then, we would go on administrative retreats with the team. He never questioned if you said you were bringing in somebody on time management. We brought in outstanding people from all over this country until we developed a cadre of people who could really implement the vision he had. And that was the glory that I got out of working with it. In fact, when I would go in for budgeting, he would say, 'Well, we'll keep that in,' because he saw the results." She is resolved that "it's no accident that all of these people who worked for Dr. Harvey have moved on to [a presidency] position." Since 1990, eight administrators from Hampton University have assumed the position of CEO at an academic institution; one administrator has become president of a bank; and another one has been appointed as an athletic commissioner.

Clearly, from the aforementioned comments of university constituents, Harvey has built a shared culture of excellence and commitment, and a team spirit within the Hampton family to bring his vision into fruition. Dawson, who retired from Hampton University in 1991, captured her relationship with Harvey this way. "If I could put in one capsule my relationship with Dr. Harvey is like a person in the family who really cares. You're working together to build this family. And that's the thing about the Hampton family, sometimes you'll agree, and sometimes you disagree. But everything was for the good of the whole."

To make everything work for the good of the whole, Harvey, the concert master, has sought a "community of hands to help"— his wife, Norma Harvey and their children; his Board of Trustees; government, foundations, and corporate donors; his friends; and alumni—to work in unison and to buy into his vision of excellence. To bolster the community of helping hands, he looks backwards to the past and blends the philosophy of Samuel Chapman Armstrong, Hampton's founder, and Booker T. Washington, Hampton's most illustrious graduate, with the ancestral legacy and spirit of W. E. B. Du Bois. In making everything work for the "good of the whole," Harvey has fit Hampton like a finely mitered corner. In the relatively short season of today's college presidents, he has a lengthy tenure of twenty-five years. He said on his twentieth anniversary, in his *President's Report, 1997–1998:* "I have been both fortunate and proud to lead this great institution to the position of excellence and world-renowned reputation it enjoys today. I have aimed high; I have faced challenges, and my rewards have been many. It is no secret that my work is my passion, and given the opportunity to serve my twenty-year presidency again, I would gladly accept it. And I would change nothing—not a plan, a decision, an accomplishment. Every aspect, every nuance of my life at Hampton has been that precious to me. I love Hampton University—my Home by the Sea." That bespeaks of a man for all seasons, with no season to rest.

What manner of man is this, who remains fresh like dew in the spring or in the fall? To JoAnn Haysbert, Harvey is a "twenty-first century role model," who is "traveling a hero's journey in the academy." To Tony Brown, the television personality, he is "the second Booker T. Washington." To Joffre T. Whisenton, the former president of Southern University, he is the "President of presidents." To Martha Dawson, he is a "Renaissance man—a master builder, an entrepreneur, a human engineer, a national mover and shaker, a creative genius. He is a living sermon!" But Harvey sees himself as a man who espouses "simple values of God, family, equality, country, and work."

The man with simple family values still shows up at the home of his high school mentor, Mai Graham Young, without calling. He will drive from Atlanta or nearby Montgomery or wherever he is in the vicinity to check on Young. "He is the only person that comes to my house and never tells me that he is coming. My own two children do not do that. He will ring the door bell and I will look up and see him. Then he will tell me what he wants to eat. I say, 'Boy, you're the only person who comes to my house and doesn't tell me.'" He will look in her refrigerator hoping to find some Southern prepared collard greens. She looks at her "adopted son" and bursts with pride at seeing the seasoned leader, who has taken photos with presidents and worked with diplomats, great scholars, corporate CEOs and other national and international movers and shakers and who even has the Hampton University library named after him and his wife, do so well. When she tells him how proud she is of him and how far he has come, to all this, Harvey responds, "I am just an old country boy from Brewton."

To paraphrase Isaac Bashevis Singer, we know what the "old country boy from Brewton" thinks not when he tells us what he thinks, but by his action. After laying the foundation of his

Hampton family, the master building has insulated its financial walls; has developed a facilities master plan; has restructured the academic programs; has anchored art and athletics; has opened a philanthropic window of opportunity; has installed a service door; has created a student stairwell of living, learning, leadership, and service; has braced for storms and weatherstripped for critics; has developed broad beams of leadership for women; has made college presidents; and, in the process, has become a living legend.

Insulating Financial Walls

"I believe that the wise use of finances is the cornerstone of any successful operational entity. . ."
—William R. Harvey

When President William R. Harvey assumed the mantle of leadership, in July 1978, at Hampton University, the school had an endowment of $29 million and actual revenue of more than $15.6 million, coupled with a deficit of nearly a half million. Under his presidency, which emphasized sound, conservative, fiscal management, the endowment ballooned by the end of the century to $169 million and the actual revenue to nearly $110 million. (See Figures 1 and 2.) Furthermore, in each year of his presidency, the University has operated with a balanced budget and a small surplus. As Joseph French Johnson once said, "The man who works for the gold in the job rather than for the money in the pay envelope, is the fellow who gets on."[1] Indeed, Harvey works for the gold in the job and gets on with the business of developing relations and making connections, building the University's war chest, and managing its finances.

Building Relations and Making Connections

When Harvey is in his office, he works the telephone like a switchboard operator, to connect with presidents of Fortune 500 companies, Wall Street lawyers, U. S. presidential aides, or celebrities. No shortage of constantly ringing telephones exists in his ornately

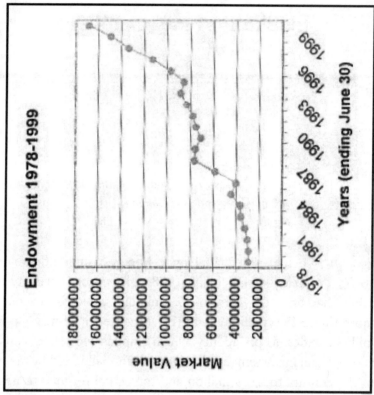

Figure 1

Year Ending June 30	Market Value
1978	29334000
1979	29364000
1980	30320000
1981	32356000
1982	36031000
1983	36656000
1984	44476000
1985	40129000
1986	58785000
1987	76572000
1988	75860000
1989	71201000
1990	75359000
1991	78221000
1992	83628000
1993	88922000
1994	86199000
1995	97441000
1996	113046000
1997	133906000
1998	149375000
1999	169026000

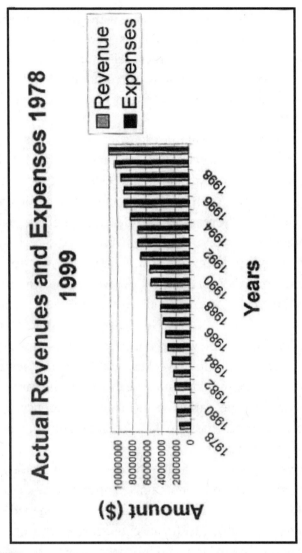

Figure 2

	Revenue ($)	Expenses ($)
1978	15635524	16118040
1979	18980539	18936026
1980	22221904	21947371
1981	21967976	21898173
1982	23909704	23841413
1983	25845183	25762218
1984	31072436	30991544
1985	34192941	34115228
1986	37569455	37480993
1987	40991720	40924380
1988	47062846	46998333
1989	54311762	54212233
1990	55791277	55692264
1991	67651106	67552312
1992	71564759	71466165
1993	70943509	70824091
1994	81395231	81277866
1995	89902653	89781768
1996	90007525	89881763
1997	94155450	94027961
1998	1017119379	101590883
1999	109614387	109496163

adorned office, where the foyer is lined with art masterpieces and photographs of himself with presidents, governors, and senators. He is seldom an arm's reach from these telephones. They are his life-line to individuals and institutions, to corporate boardrooms, to foundations, and to government agencies—the movers and shakers of this country.

When he is not on campus, he spends fifty percent of his time "covering the country like the dew," meeting chief executive officers in their own boardrooms, and inviting future donors to visit the campus and to join him for a round of golf or for a ride on his yacht. In his early years as President, he spent as much as eighty percent of his time traveling. On a good day, he would cover four or five corporations or foundations, flying, for example, to New York City for one day of "well-orchestrated meet-ings." Mindful of his use of fund-raising time and money, he would also plan a week's stay in New York. "We would maximize our time. One flight to New York, or headquarters of major cor-porations in other cities for a week, would eliminate the need to go back two and three times and save money at the same time," noted Harvey.[2] In the earlier years of his presidency, he was known to sometimes pass up fancy restaurants for fast-food chains to save on expenses.

In "covering the country like the dew," there are few areas where he and his development team, led primarily for many years by Leron Clark, have not blanketed. Harvey has even made some inroads internationally, in African countries, in the Caribbean Islands, in Spain, in England, and in Japan. In 1991, for example, he, along with Norma, his wife, at the invitation of the Japanese Foundation, visited Japan and met with people such as the chair-men of Sony and Canon, and the American ambassador. He addressed the Tokyo Chamber of Commerce and also met with the president of Tsuda College, which was one of the most exclu-sive girls' schools in Tokyo.

"Fund-raising is not difficult," Harvey is fond of saying. "You have to work at it." But working at it requires building relationships with individuals, alumni, corporations, foundations, and the government before passing the hat. "Today it is very important to develop relationships—partnering, if you will—particularly with corporations," he said. "Try to make sure that they can understand that it is in their own enlightened self-interest to support the really good works of Hampton University. I think a lot of people make mistakes by going in and presenting a proposal or a figure they think they'd like for a corporation, a foundation or even an individual to contribute. I don't think that pays dividends. One has to establish relationships, to make sure that some of the officers of that corporation or foundation become involved with a Hampton, or with any institution, to be able to serve on advisory boards, to come to speak to students, to do a number of kinds of things. I raise a lot of money, very honestly, on the golf course and on my boat. There'll be people who have an interest in yachting or an interest in golf, and I've been able to do very well with that."[3] Since most of the money will come from corporations and foundations, he reminds his Fund-raising Leadership Team to "learn how corporate America works."

Supporters of Hampton University describe the King Midas of fund-raising as the "master of making friends for his University, from the newest alumni to the biggest corporations."[4] He is interested in building relationships with "those persons who have influence and affluence—people who can afford to partner with the University in something that's dear to their hearts. It may be a board member. It may be someone else," Harvey was quoted as saying in the *Daily Press*.[5]

Charles Wilson, member of the Board of Trustees, cited an example of that someone else whom the master friendmaker counted on to build connections. In 1989, when Harvey and Wilson attended the funeral of Jack Dorrance, then CEO of Campbell Soup and Board of Trustees member, Wilson gave this account:

> Bill and I were invited to go to [Dorrance's] estate after
> the funeral. Well, we walked into the estate and here come

his two sons and a daughter. Bill [President Harvey] said, "Which one do you think would make a good member of the Board of Trustees?" I said, "Gut reaction, I like the one to the right." A little black lady came through and said "Hello." And I said "How are you?" Now I have not seen many people of color except Bill and a guy up at the church. And she says, "Oh my God, Dr. Harvey! My granddaughter just finished Hampton." And I say, "Wow!" Here we are at a funeral and here's a lady who has been with the family for almost forty years, and she sees Dr. Harvey. There were multi-million-aires, perhaps billionaires, and a lady of reason and we asked her what was her opinion on which one we should invite. So she gave us the background on who we should and who we shouldn't.

John Dorrance left $5 million in his estate for the University, the largest donation of any individual or corporation.

Though most of the money comes from corporations and foundations, individuals give larger donations. "It is unlikely that we will get $5 million from a corporation, but will get it from an individual," noted Harvey. Other examples are contributors like Edward Hamm, Jr., president of E. L. Hamm and Associates and a Hampton alumnus, who donated $1 million to the $200 million campaign; Robert Hiden, an attorney with Sullivan & Cromwell donated $50,000; Ernest Drew, the president and CEO of Hoechst Celanese Corporation, who gave $100,000; Clarence Lockett, a vice president at Johnson and Johnson, who gave $100,000 and pledged $100,000; George Lewis, an alumnus and Trustee donated $100,000. Sometimes a donation may come from those without "influence or affluence." When Harvey first became president, he can clearly recall the heartwarming letter that he received from an 85-year-old lady in Connecticut. She commended him on his belief in excellence from all constituents of the college and she enclosed a check for $2000, nearly half of her annual pension.

Historically, Hampton has always built relationships. Harvey noted that "Hampton has always had the movers and shakers of the nation" associated with Hampton—individuals like John D. Rockefeller, former Chief Justice of the United States T. Coleman DuPont, and former President William Howard Taft. But prior to his arrival, that tradition had waned. Harvey, along with other members of the Board, again exposed Hampton to "some of the captains of industry and politics and business." William Ellinghaus, former Board member and chair of AT&T and later executive vice-chairman (chairman) of the New York Stock Exchange, was one such person. He spearheaded Hampton's five-year, $30 million capital campaign in the 1980s, which exceeded its goal and reached $46 million by its 1986 target date. At the conclusion of the campaign, he stated: "Working with Dr. Harvey was a great inspiration. He is a man of vision who works tirelessly on behalf of Hampton. He interacts very well with the corporate sector and has that rare quality of continually looking and planning ahead."[6] Harvey has also been able to attract other powerful people to serve as trustees, such as former Governors Chuck Robb (also former senator) and Linwood Holton, John Duncan of St. Joe Minerals, former Secretary of Housing and Urban Development Sam Pierce, the actress Elizabeth Taylor, Pepsi Cola chairman and CEO Roger Enrico, to name a few. He is always looking to bring on board members who clearly understand one of their functions is fund-raising—"People who can open doors I can't open," said Harvey.

The President has also developed relationships with those in the government at the federal, state, and local levels. He had direct ties with the presidential administrations of Jimmy Carter, Ronald Reagan, and George Herbert Walker Bush. He had ties to the Clinton administration, as well, through friends like Vernon Jordan and former Energy Secretary Hazel O'Leary, and the late Secretary of Commerce Ron Brown. Furthermore, he brings to campus prominent individuals, such as the poet, Maya Angelou; the journalist, Tony Brown; and the American Express President/CEO, Kenneth Chenault. These friends become the connecting bridge to other individuals and institutions. New acquaintances and trustees constantly promote the school and make new contacts for the University—"the more far-flung the better," said Harvey. Now and then, a benefactor will gather large groups of his compeers in the corporate world in one place to listen to the President.

Building an Internal Management Structure

Building networks for fund-raising require planning. Thus, having an internal management structure, one which stresses teamwork and performance, is critical. This structure has a two-pronged approach: 1) an efficient fiscal management team, steered by Doretha Spells, vice president for business affairs and treasurer [From 1978–1991, this position was held by Lucius Wyatt, the former vice president for business affairs and treasurer, who was a member of Harvey's first team, and from 1991–2000 by Leon Scott.]; and 2) a strong fund-raising team led by Leron Clark, vice president for development. The fiscal management team keeps a close eye on both sides of the ledger. Harvey was quoted as telling James Schultz, in the June 1988 *Virginia Business* magazine, "When you run a place like Hampton University, you've got to look at both sides of the ledger. I am absolutely convinced that is the best way a university should be run." So, in 1978, Harvey decided to change the way the institution operated. Based on a lesson he picked up at Tuskegee University as an administrator, one which still forms the basis for his leadership philosophy, he posited that universities are like businesses. Therefore, they should be run with a careful eye on the bottom line. "If you have a dollar," Harvey said, explaining the basis of his belief, "You can't spend a dollar and twenty-five cents." "We can't run colleges like we did in the '50s. We have to run them like a business," he asserted. In 1978, no doubt, this sounded like New Wave thinking in some educational circles, but he persevered. He employed what he called "supply-side economics at the University level" or better still, his mother's fiscal mother wit, and again concluded, "You cannot have a dollar and purchase a dollar and a half worth of groceries." Unarguably, he would agree that his philosophy of managing money can be summed up in the words of Beaconsfield, who said that, "There can be no economy where there is no efficiency," and in the wisdom of Confucius, who proclaimed that, "He who will not economize will have to agonize." The school, which had run at a deficit every year since 1970 save one, appeared an ideal place for Harvey's corporate approach to university management. So he tightened the fiscal and administrative belts at the University. He demanded a balanced budget, instituted presidential line-item budget review, eliminated excessive overtime, issued all contracts himself, and switched to quarterly allocations to guard against deficit spending. That is, instead of allocating money to departments for an entire year at a time, Harvey switched to funding them on a quarterly basis. He said that would avoid problems where a department might spend the majority of its annual budget in the first few months of the year and then come to the administration asking for more money. To implement his belief, he was not afraid to take risks. "I never have been. I believed in myself. I believed in my philosophy. I believed the plans and the programs I had for running Hampton as a business were correct," he said.

Lucius Wyatt, who was then the fiscal officer responsible for balancing the ledger said, there was "a lot of complaining about it. But we stuck with it. We maintained the course, and he did not let us deviate from it, although there [were] some very justifiable needs. But he stuck with it, and of course, after doing that for a few years, we were able to operate on an even budget." Not only did the University have a surplus, "we were able to do many things that we would not have normally done with funds from operations, like improvements to buildings and new equipment. In doing that in his early years, really and truly, some departments and programs had to operate on a shoestring." Harvey admitted, too, that some people didn't like his approach. "That was a departure," he said. "Anytime you do something different, there are going to be people who don't understand or don't like it, and we had both of those."

Similarly, about fifteen years later, at a February 19, 1993 Board of Trustees meeting, Harvey reported that Leon Scott, then vice president for business affairs and treasurer, had "initiated a system wherein all student accounts/bills must be paid before a student could enroll." He pointed out that this process had his approval and the approval of the Chairman of the Board. "This may initially create a few problems (i.e., enrollment may drop a little bit), but it is felt that this is necessary and better for Hampton University as a business entity in the long run." He also noted that because of the "economy and other things, the private gifts and grants received were not as much as they had been, and therefore, the University was continuing efforts to tighten the budget."

Harvey is interested not only in tightening the budget, but he expects the endowment fund to be well-managed. So in the 1993–1994 time period, the Investment Committee was formed, and advisors were changed to Cambridge Associates. One year after changing advisors, the endowment value, which was in the range of $86–87 million, increased to $97.4 million and increased significantly thereafter. When the Investment Committee was formed, Hampton was in the 83 percent quartile, meaning that 83 percent of the institutions were performing better. After changing advisors, Hampton got up to the 43 percent quartile, and by 1996 it had risen to the top 25 percent in the United States. In 1997, the University was at the top 21 percent of all institutions as ranked by the National Association of College and University Business Officers Endowment Study.[7]

While the President, along with Board members, is in pursuit of the highest return on the University's investment, it is not at the expense of human "dignity, decency, and fair play."

In the semi-annual meeting of the Board of Trustees, April 26, 1985, for example, the President introduced for discussion the issue of South Africa. In a subsequent lengthy discourse on the pros and cons of divestiture, the President argued that there was the need for Hampton University to assume a leadership role. Because of the President's persuasivness, the Board voted to support the following motion:

That the Board support in principle the President's ex-
pressions and that the Board authorize the Chairman to draft
a strong resolution in concurrence with the President's recommendations which were as follows: That our proxies and
managers subscribe to the Sullivan Principles and that they
be instructed that all Hampton University votes on issues
relating to South Africa should be in concert with the Sullivan
Principles; that our managers and proxies be advised that
Hampton University's position is to direct all companies to
discontinue sales of all motor vehicles and components to
the South African military and police until the government
commits itself to ending apartheid; and that a committee be
appointed by the Chairman in cooperation with the President
to look into ramifications that would come out of divestiture.

The University's endowment grows through reinvestment and by adding to it. So on the other side of the ledger, with the support of his
development team, Harvey toils tirelessly in fund-raising vineyards to
produce a bountiful cash crop for endowment and capital funds. In his
fund-raising labor, the President seeks the support of University constituents from trustees to students and alumni. Speaking before
alumni in Dallas, Texas on November 12, 1983, Harvey declared: "We
need our alumni; you are our largest constituents group; you not only
contribute to the college, but you also perform many other important
tasks in your communities and in your professional life which have
positive impacts for all concerned. . . . Alumni of the college have been
a consistent bridge linking past, present, and future." He understands
that in soliciting funds, donors want corporations to know the percentage of their contribution. In the semi-annual meeting of the
Board of Trustees, April 27, 1990, the President said that he shared
Trustee Edward E. Elson's idea that "if you cannot make a contribution to the University, you should not be on the Board." He reiterated
that there should be a 100 percent level of contributions from the
Board of Trustees. The President further stated that everyone should
give something, even the Student Trustees, and if you could not give,
you should get off the Board. The President's deed matches his creed.
As the CEO, William R. Harvey and his wife, Norma Harvey, have contributed significantly to the University. For example, they gave $1 mil-
lion to the University in 2000 to create a scholarship for aspiring

teachers and $125,000 for the $125 million campaign and the 125th Anniversary of Hampton University.

To promote results-oriented activities, the salaries and pro-motions for his development staff are linked directly to meeting fund-raising quotas. Team members are expected each year to get donors to raise up to at least two and one-half times their individual salaries. One-third of the University budget is expected to be raised by the President and the development staff, one-third by deans, and the remainder comes from tuition.

Harvey said of his development team, "We would plan the trip, write ahead, identify prospects and get on their calendars." For him, it is crucial that one's homework is done, so he arms himself with "A prospect research profile," a dense portfolio of facts, before meeting with corporate executives. He knows the types of grants the corporation had expended in previous years; in what areas those grants were given; and some information about the background of primary principals of the corporation. Harvey also knows what the sales of that corporation were last year; how many employees it has; how many Hampton University graduates are there; what, if any, possible connection it has with Hampton trustees and alumni; what are its activities and inter-ests; how much money it gave to charitable causes last year; what it gave the money to; what the size of its gifts were; where its cor-porate executives went to school; which fraternity they pledged; what were its company's sales revenues; who buys its products. Harvey said when he goes in to "talk to an AT&T or a Campbell's Soup, I know quite a bit about them and I know their giving pat-terns."[8] He tries to fit that with something at the University. This means that beyond delivering an in-depth presentation to the legions of corporate executives, foundation chairs, individuals and alumni, Harvey, sometimes, along with his developmental team, will come back to campus and confer with faculty members whose activities and interests might meld with those of the com-pany. In a typical scenario, the development staff will then carefully craft a detailed proposal and present it to the company. Harvey understands that the majority of benefactors favor giving along the lines of their interests. They want to make an impact in the form of a new program or building. The team has never been turned down flat.

Harvey has a war chest of stories of his strategies for raising funds. In one account, he was on the phone with a representative of a major national corporation. When the other party mentioned that the firm had donated a tennis court to the College of William and Mary, he "whipped out his ace in the hole." "Well, we happen to have a pretty good tennis team," he said. "They won the national championship several times and they just happened to beat William and Mary and all the other Virginia college teams. So, if you want to be associated with quality, then you should perhaps donate a tennis court to us." The corporate officers' attitude changed. "Quality—that's what I stress in all aspects of this University," said Harvey.[9]

Another anecdote claimed that when Robert Abboud was chairman of First National Bank of Chicago, in the 1980s, Harvey was aware that he and his company had money. So the President developed a strategy for Abboud to give Hampton a donation. "I try to go with connection," Harvey said. He knew that "Abboud's father was Hampton University's superintendent of building and grounds when the well-known bank chairman's family left the area. When Abboud asked if the old family home was still standing, Harvey knew the answer, and he said he came away with money."[10]

Still in other accounts, Harvey has also been courageous enough to tell corporations to increase their donations or take their money elsewhere. One large corporation, for example, was giving the school $10,000 a year. Smaller companies used that contribution as a guideline. "It would do me more good not to accept your $10,000 than for you to continue to give that," Harvey told the company executives. They gave him more money.

"I wasn't bluffing," Harvey says. "You got to be prepared not to accept the $10,000, but thus far, everybody has increased."[11]

Sometimes, corporation presidents have asked him, "If you're so successful, why do you need money from us?" Harvey has a stock reply. "Do you ask Harvard that when they come in?" Because of Hampton's sizeable endowment, the President has heard grumblings that it was "too rich," usually from people who don't understand why a University needs large amounts in the bank for a rainy day. By the same token, no one complains that the publicly-funded University of Virginia has more than $1 billion invested for inclement weather. Though Harvey's primary concern is to increase the University's coffers, some donors are unacceptable.

Harvey says, "The line is always drawn at the point where one has to compromise one's dignity or integrity and decency. . . . There are a lot of people for a lot of reasons that I wouldn't accept money from for the college," he told Stacy Burling of the *Newport News Daily Press*. A company once talked with college officials about donating two expensive buses to the campus; the company also wanted an honorary doctorate for its chairman. Harvey, who has authorized less than a dozen honorary doctorates, refused. "We are not for sale," he told the company officials. So the buses went to another college.

Marketing a Quality Product

How does the entrepreneur market his merchandise to the movers and shakers? First and foremost, Harvey believes in himself and his product; he believes in what he is doing and works hard at doing it. Even though for some, he makes fund-raising appear effortless because he convinces others to believe with him and in his commodity—Hampton University. Hampton University and Harvey are conjoined, so the entrepreneur delights in fund-raising. Although some university presidents play down their fund-raising activity as something of a sideshow, Harvey views it as his main show and has no problem holding center stage. Second, he has been described as approaching the task of fund-raising with all the "skill and verve of a corporate takeover specialist."[12] While many HBCUs have traditionally employed the hat-in-hand approach to fund-raising or the "guilt syndrome to repay past injustices," quality has been Harvey's principal selling point. He tells the story of Hampton University's successes. "Corporations are coming more and more to realize the importance of supporting higher education," he said. "But no one wants to support a loser. We have a product—quality—that we work very hard to sell. We are by any measure the best black school in the country and a fine small university—period! We show companies where we came from and what we're doing—and they've been very kind."[13] "My theory is that we've got an excellent [university] here and that if the money is received it can make a major impact," he contended. Moreover, Harvey maintained, "We've learned that most donors give to and support ideas; they want to hear and become part of an exciting plan. I have told my faculty that their involvement and expertise were needed to develop proposals which will provide for program enrichment; provide research/development activities; provide educational equipment; provide staff, and finally facilities."

At the beginning of his presidency, Harvey sold Hampton University's "solid past" and its "solid history. Its alumni, its Board and other factors in the past made Hampton really a strong institution," he noted. "When you are selling quality, it's an easier task." But it was not that way back in 1978 when he inherited a $482,516 deficit, backed up by five consecutive deficit budget years and the discontinuation of a five-year $700,000 Ford Foundation grant. In his first Board of Trustees meeting on October 27, 1978, Harvey said, "While the incurrence of a deficit does not signal impending financial collapse, it is a warning that deserves heeding. . . .'Not quite perfect' financial planning is the warning note of the downfall of even the most stable institutions." Besides, "corporations, foundations, and other entities are always anxious to know if they are making sound investments," Harvey stated. He clearly remembered this concern on one occasion, as he recalled during the Fall Faculty Institute of 1979, when he visited the Kresge Foundation in Michigan during the summer of 1978. "After making my presentation to the President of the corporation, he asked if we were operating on a balanced budget. Truthfully, I had to say to him that we are not. He then said that the Kresge Foundation might be willing to help [then] Hampton Institute again after we got out of our deficit spending situation. Needless to say, I will be visiting him again soon."[14] Harvey continued, saying, "Businesses are not going to put money in a losing venture. If their $100,000 has to go to make up a deficit, they can't see the real good it does. . . . People need to know that they're not giving money to support red ink, that they're not supporting ineffectual programs, that they aren't giving money to some shabby, run-down college. They are giving money to a place where it is doing some good, where it is making an impact."

Harvey was disappointed, yet undaunted, by being turned down for a donation, for he understood that "practically everything flows from a stable financial picture. Funds to obtain and retain quality faculty members, support for student scholarships, money for extra-curricular and support services are all dependent on the financial good health of an institution." In his first year as president, the builder set forth a plan to dig a solid financial footing. After balancing the University's budget, then, he once again told the story of Hampton's financial plight to the Kresge corporate executive. And he repeated his success story to other corporations, foundations, alumni, and individuals. The fund-raising increased by significant percentages. Corporate giving, for example, which stood at $225,000 for 1978, increased by 53 percent in his first year and reached $465,000 during 1980–81. In 1978–79, a Bush Foundation grant encouraged increased alumni giving. Similarly, alumni giving rose by $40,000 during Harvey's first year, and the following year, it reached $400,200. By 1982 corporate contributions had increased by 200 percent, foundation giving by 400 percent, and alumni contributions by 89 percent. Harvey noted that, "These things don't just happen. You don't just throw things up in the air. It takes planning. You have to have goals, and strategies for reaching them." Thus, a major part of

Harvey's fund-raising strategy, then and now, is to get potential benefactors to visit the campus for a firsthand look at Hampton's academic success. "It works," says Harvey. After more than twenty years from Harvey's arrival on campus, $25,577,458 worth of federal grants and contracts were garnered in 1999 in comparison to the $3,805,348 before his arrival in July 1978. (See figure 3.) Similarly, private gifts, grants and contracts increased to $14,895,582, up from $1,767,289 before his presidency. (See figure 4.) In 2002, Hampton University's Center for Atmospheric Science, under James Russell, co-director and principal investigator, received its largest grant ever—$92 million.

While Harvey, who was called a "money magnet" in a September 1985 edition of *Black Enterprise*, believes that individuals, corporations, foundations, and governments want to give money to successful operations, his fund-raising strategy is not only to sell quality but also to bring to the table a *quid pro quo* relationship in the fund-raising process, that is, showing donors that it is in their best interest to support the University.

The relationship between the Newport News Shipbuilding in Newport News, Virginia and the University serves as an example. When the company gave Hampton University $300,000 for its electrical engineering and naval architecture programs, the relationship was described by the Shipyard company's vice president of business and technology development as "natural" and also "mutual." Representatives of the Shipyard, where Harvey serves on its board, have not only visited the school but invited the University's scientists to learn more about the company's future projects. Maintaining an ongoing relationship assures the company and the University of how to mutually assist one another. "It does help to be understood. What do you bring to the table? How can we work together?" The shipyard's vice president of business and technology development was quoted as saying in the *Daily Press*, October 4, 1998. Some companies think it's enough to hire a school's students, but he believes they need to go further.

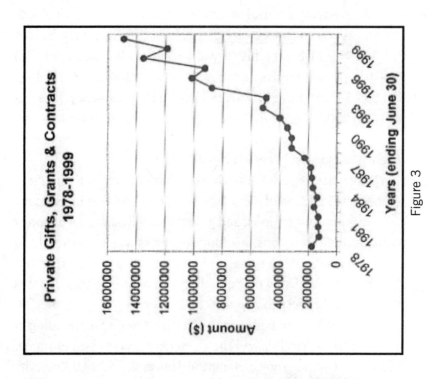

Figure 3

Year Ending June 30	Amount
1978	1767289
1979	1244621
1980	1293308
1981	1292832
1982	1601567
1983	1372137
1984	1676403
1985	1769592
1986	1837111
1987	2270900
1988	3192670
1989	3190357
1990	3489584
1991	4002293
1992	5202997
1993	4964632
1994	8761337
1995	10148639
1996	9268047
1997	13540260
1998	11881310
1999	14895582

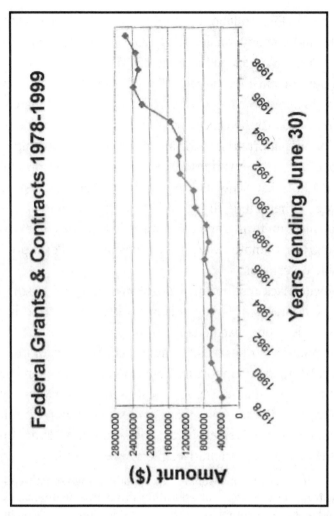

Figure 4

Year Ending June 30	Amount ($)
1978	3805348
1979	4524575
1980	6197266
1981	6459940
1982	6169783
1983	6234001
1984	6338601
1985	6687398
1986	7707181
1987	6792802
1988	7299898
1989	9792236
1990	100093726
1991	131335811
1992	134868883
1993	133823332
1994	154128802
1995	218158586
1996	237777807
1997	226801174
1998	233360571
1999	255774858

Working in close collaboration with universities like Hampton, he feels his company can get the kinds of graduates and cooperation it needs. "We're a public company. We have to be concerned about our bottom line," he said. "But I think that we take a longer view."[15] In another example of partnering, PepsiCo donated $4.1 million in 2000 to the University, of which $1 million of the contribution was appropriated for an endowed professorship in the School of Business. An additional $1 million was appropriated to initiate a Frito-Lay Scholars program in the fledgling Leadership Institute. Other funds are going towards the marching band scholarships, uniforms, and other athletic activities. In exchange for the grant, Hampton University is having only Pepsi products available on campus.

Since "black institutions have always had to fight the wolf from the door," said Harvey, it is in the best interest of the University to develop a partnership not only with the private sector but the public sector as well. His approach, as in corporate America, is to show that supporting Hampton or HBCUs is in its best interest. In a September 10, 1985 testimony on the Minority Science Program, for example, that he presented before the House Subcommittee on Postsecondary Education and Labor, United States House of Representatives, Harvey remarked:

> It is a distinct pleasure for me to address this committee's hearing on the status of education in science, mathematics and technology for minority citizens. . . . It is not surprising to find, as the National Science Foundation reported, that minority students in particular are conspicuously absent in careers in science and mathematics. . . . Currently, America is involved in an international competition for technological leadership. It is doubtful that today's average citizen and today's college student realize how the nation's economic progress and our national security are related to this specialized leadership. Moreover, American business and industry are relentlessly challenged by other nations who fully acknowledge the importance of a strong science and technology base to yield the collective competence and talent needed to compete at the international level. . . . As this committee and this administra-

tion consider appropriations for scientific research and training, they must be mindful of the fact that America can only maintain its important, albeit fragile, competitive edge if it unhesitatingly provides the resources to identify and to develop those individuals who possess the capabilities for and the interest in these critical disciplines. If America is to perform and to compete at peak capacity, it simply cannot ignore the largely untapped pool of minority students who remained unexposed to and untrained in vital areas that constitute one of its foremost priorities. The young men and women who comprise this untapped national resource must be prepared in learning environments that encourage and reward scientific research, creativity and, most importantly, hard work. . . . I would argue that the federal government and the American people at large have a clear and certain stake in the education of its minority students. I strongly support the wisdom of investing in this area, if for no other reason than the enormous and productive "human capital" it will yield.

Harvey then proposed the establishment of several programs which would serve to "attract minority students and to enhance the sciences for a generation of minority students."

A review of the October 27, 1978 minutes of the Board of Trustees reflected that shortly after Harvey's presidential appointment, he had already begun efforts to improve the University's federal grantsmanship program. He designated a special federal liaison officer as staff in the Office of Development through the Intergovernmental Personnel Loan Act. This person was responsible for enhancing the University's image in Washington, D. C., and securing funds for selected program thrusts. [In later years, Harvey appointed a vice president for research, which was changed to governmental relations.] At that time, the President was particularly interested in building bridges not only between the University's academic and research programs and the Departments of Education, Health and Human Services, but extending the linkage with the Departments of Transportation, Labor, and Housing and Urban Development. The political independent, having ties with both the Republican Party and Democratic Party, developed significant inroads into fund-raising not only for the University, but also other

HBCUs. He noted that, "Harvard has someone dealing all the time with whomever is in power and I think Hampton [University] should do no less." Maintaining his independence allows him to freely criticize any of the politicians; moreover, he believes that associating with leaders of both parties is part of his job. Under the Reagan Administration, Harvey visited the White House more than twenty-five times, though he was keenly aware of the skepticism by blacks of his relationship with the administration. "Blacks have traditionally been in the Democratic Party and when someone who has the visibility that I do is in and out of the White House as much as I am with a president that blacks have considered to be in many instances anti-black, that raises an eyebrow from their point of view," he acknowledged. During President Ronald Reagan's administration, for example, his staff asked Harvey for help in formulating positions on black colleges. So he led a delegation of four presidents of HBCUs to meet with then-Vice President George Bush for a very productive working session. "Without camera or lights," they developed proposals on student assistance programs, higher education budgets, CETA and other programs to improve the stature of these colleges and universities. In 1981, President Reagan signed, in the presence of Harvey and other CEOs of HBCUs, an executive order to help HBCUs to ameliorate their educational programs. The order directed federal department secretaries to increase support, where possible, to HBCUs. It also steered the Secretary of Education to monitor the agencies' increased support. Later, Harvey commented that the procedures the President wrote into the order "put teeth into it." He thought it was highly significant and historic that President Reagan had shown what he wanted done, and made sure that it was done. Noting that, "He has not left it to the discretion of each secretary to support black colleges."

Reagan's executive order increased funding to black colleges over the next few years, especially with reference to support for research contracts and grants. Moreover, the HBCUs saw greater involvement from departments such as Transportation, Interior and Commerce.[16] The Department of Transportation is a case in point. After the 1981 Air Traffic Controllers' strike, the Secretary of Transportation was quoted as saying that he would return to the country's colleges and universities for help in rebuilding the air traffic control system. Harvey saw this as an opportunity to increase the representation of minorities in science and to expand academic curriculum by developing an Airway Science program. Speaking before the Department of Transportation's Black History Month Program on February 4, 1987, Harvey told his audience in a speech entitled, "Black Colleges: Some Problems and Promise," "The commitment of America encompasses equal opportunity and a confidence in education to help promote upward mobility and, therefore, democracy. Vital in this process—though little heralded in the past—will be the black colleges. Historically, out of their bosoms has come strength for this nation over and beyond the thousands of students directly touched in the classroom and set on the road to solid citizenship—often to local, national, and worldwide distinction. The very concept of this nation and its origins has been made magnificently advanced by black colleges." He mentioned how Hampton could assist the Federal Aviation Administration in meeting the staffing needs of the air traffic system through its Airway Science Program. "It's truly time to turn to the colleges and universities and develop an alternate training source. Let's establish an Air Traffic School at Hampton. Why not an FAA Management School there as well?"

Reagan also signed into law, on September 26, 1983, the Higher Education Act Amendments of 1983, a bill that initiated the Endowment Grant Program, which allowed HBCUs and other institutions to receive matching endowment grants, and it also authorized $134 million for these institutions to bolster their academic programs. Harvey was convinced that his relationship with the administration helped the college get federal money. Shortly after the order, the government gave Hampton $4.5

million for a new dorm and $125,000 for a program to help small businesses. Hampton's allotment from Title 3, a program to strengthen college instruction, increased from $400,000 to $700,000 in three years. By 1983, under the Reagan Administration, the University had received $20.1 million in support from the federal government.

When President George Herbert Walker Bush was elected to office in 1988, Harvey was appointed by President Bush to an advisory board that oversaw the Department of Education's White House initiative on HBCUs. This program monitored the government's role in black institutions. Serving as the chair of a delegation of twenty-one presidents of HBCUs, he appealed to Bush to provide more federal support for these colleges and universities. Along with Bush, Harvey, in an hour-long White House discussion, met with Vice President Dan Quayle, Education Secretary Lauro Cavazos and Health and Human Services Secretary Louis Sullivan. Bush proposed to spend more funds to increase the endowments of black colleges. Under the proposal, institutions approved for the grants by the U. S. Department of Education would receive up to $1 million to match money raised on their own. Harvey noted that the federal money would provide incentive to the nation's 108 black colleges to raise their own money, and would give donors "an opportunity to see their money have a multiple effect."[17] As chair of the Legislative Advisory Board for Blacks in Higher Education, Harvey made a presentation before the U.S. House Committee on Education and Labor on December 10, 1990 in Washington, D. C. There he addressed the issue of federal endowment building assistance to black institutions and reiterated the need for continued federal support to "sustain and strengthen some of the nation's richest resources—our HBCUs." Harvey, who spoke as chair of a committee comprising delegates from three black college associations—NAFEO, the United Negro College Fund, and the Office for the Advancement of Public Black Colleges—contended: "Increased investment in these vital resources is an investment in our nation, for their value is indisputable. We cannot afford the immediate and long-term cost of relegating their continued viability to a place of lesser importance." The committee had asked Harvey to give his views on reauthorization of the Higher Education Act of 1965 and how black schools might be affected. This act was under consideration for the 1991 Congressional session. In his remarks, Harvey pointed out what he saw as a problem with the Endowment Grant Program, initiated in 1983 as an amendment to the Higher Education Act. He contended that federal grant programs aimed at black colleges and universities no longer met their intent. He called on lawmakers to repeal a 1986 change in the law that resulted in more federal aid to urban colleges that are not historically black but have large numbers of minority students. Initially, the Endowment Challenge Grant was a set-aside for HBCUs between 1984–86. These institutions received about 50 percent of the funds; however, between 1987–1990, the non-set-aside years, only 13 percent of the funds went to them. Harvey also noted that out of the $114.5 million distributed to 198 institutions between 1984 and 1990, only $32.9 million went to the 66 traditionally black schools across the nation. He proposed that "legislative changes need to be made in the reorganization of the Higher Education Act to restore the original intent."

Moreover, Harvey said that federal funds would instill an air of financial security that would help black schools to generate private resources.[18] He noted, too, that two universities, Coppin State College in Baltimore and Shaw University in Raleigh, North Carolina could link federal trust money with an increase in private donations. Harvey was encouraged by the government's commitment to enhancing the position of black schools, but in order to maximize the utilization of their resources and to improve programs and physical facilities, he suggested these changes: ensure that programs designed to aid black schools fill their intent; remove restrictions that penalize schools that have been more successful than others in building their endowments in the private sector;

provide a greater distribution of grant money based on the amount prohibited; reduce the hold-out period for large grant recipients. Harvey requested lawmakers to add six black graduate schools to the five that already received federal aid.

Clearly, Harvey works to improve Hampton University, but he is committed to helping other institutions. He once remarked when many HBCUs were experiencing a severe financial crisis in the late 1970s: "No one should get any joy from a sister institution experiencing some difficulties."

His generosity towards others is sometimes not reciprocated. In the annual meeting of the Board of Trustees, October 23, 1992, Harvey shared with trustees that his congressional activities included obtaining more funding for HBCUs in the field of science and technology. Though Harvey had been successful in getting Hampton University written into the legislation of the Higher Education Act, no money was specifically authorized. Yet, he still saw it as an accomplishment that the bill was passed and was signed by the President. He noted that Congressman Jefferson from Louisiana had been instrumental in these efforts, although there had been some opposition from some UNCF members on the inclusion of Hampton and other private schools in this legislation.

Any opposition has not hindered Harvey's success at "The Harvard of the South." He heard someone call Hampton University by that name, and it has become one of his favorite slogans. Under his leadership, the University has built a substantial war chest, increased both federal and private grants and contracts, and private gifts. He thinks, "The major difference, and probably the success at Hampton, is that a) we do have a lot of connections, and b) Hampton is viewed as a first-class, comprehensive University. And people tend to support winning endeavors." Yet, Harvey is cognizant that the University needs to change with the times. Thus, if the "Harvard of the South" is going to "compete with Harvard or MIT, it must have top-notch professors, Internet access in every classroom, and a museum that draws scholars from around the world. It must conduct research, as well as teach, and award doctorates as well as bachelor's and master's degrees," he added. Moreover, the University must renovate its historic buildings and provide added financial aid for young scholars, obtain more endowed professorial chairs, improve the athletic program, he said. For all these things, Harvey noted, Hampton University needs $200 million.

Dreaming No Small Dreams

On October 22, 1998, during his twentieth year at Hampton University, the President unveiled publicly his $200 Million Campaign for capital projects, which had already been in the silent phase for five years. By this time, it had raised $110 million and it will run for five more years. "That's a general rule of thumb—to be able to have a silent phase initially and then go public. The idea is to be able to raise money, announce the amount that you've raised before you publicly announce and create a snowballing effect," said Harvey. He noted that "the general rule of thumb is to raise about a third before you go public, and I can say to you that we've raised more than a third. I'm pleased that so many people have taken ownership of what we're trying to do here at Hampton. It's always a very difficult task. There are a lot of challenges. There are challenges every single day. But the fact is that so many people all over the country have taken ownership in what we are trying to do that it is very gratifying to me." The $200 Million Campaign is the largest fund-raising campaign in Hampton's history, and higher than any set by an HBCU. By 2000, the campaign had exceeded its goal, raising $216 million. Like the $30 Million Campaign, he started with a staff, a plan, and goals. As with most universities and colleges, he decided how much money is needed and how much the University can realistically raise. At the onset of the campaign, he told the *Daily Press* his development team must help him raise $200 million, and they won't get it by asking for favors. They will have to show donors that it is in their best interest to support Hampton. "We need to ask, 'What type of visibility best serves the corporate institution?'"[19]

Harvey was confident of reaching the fund-raising goal. His self-assurance was backed by alumni and supporters of the University who believed that Harvey could lead the institution to the $200 million finish line. When he meets with donors, he comes prepared to make his pitch, convincing them that Hampton University is a good investment. Then he listens, and artfully crafts a proposal from the donors' own suggestions, while pushing for a little more money. Harvey is quoted in the *Daily Press* as saying about his fund-raising technique, "What we do is first try to establish a gift table. We'll look at what gifts will be needed in order to raise the amount. For example, we have hopes of several gifts of $5 million, several gifts of $3 million, several gifts of $1 million, and then a number of other gifts. We'll look at corporations, foundations, individuals, our alumni. That's how we do it."[20] He is rarely turned down for a donation. Whatever Harvey does, it is his aim to raise the bar. But naysayers asked, "Could he raise $200 million—and how?" How could the University raise four times more than the last campaign, which raised $46 million? How could it raise more than the nearby College of William and Mary, which coughed up $150 million in 1993? How could it raise more than Spelman College, the historically black school in Atlanta, that set a record by raising $114 million? Harvey is not interested in comparison; he just wants to improve Hampton University. Those who know him believed that he would not undertake a campaign that was out of the University's reach.

The campaign kick-off, dubbed "Dreaming No Small Dreams," coincided with the celebration of Harvey's twenty years at the University. Kathleen Waltz, president and publisher of the *Daily Press*, along with William Fricks, chairman of Newport News Shipbuilding, and Herbert V. Kelly, a lawyer in Newport News, Virginia, co-chaired the black-tie dinner-dance.

The successful gala was hosted by actress Diahann Carroll, and speaker after speaker paid homage to the leader. JoAnn Haysbert said, "On many occasions I have listened as he has been described with an array of prose that rightly wove a tapestry of his character, his vision, his accomplishment, his style, his position, and his good fortune. However, tonight I would like to introduce our honoree as a wise master builder!" After a series of accolades, he stepped to the podium for the Kickoff of Hampton University's $200 Million Capital Campaign and Tribute to the President on his 20th Anniversary, and paid a special tribute to his "wonderful team," that is, all the constituents of the University for their past deeds, from the Board of Trustees to workers on the grounds and cafeteria personnel to corporate donors and friends. For Harvey, you cannot rest on your laurels. He said, "We must now look to the future, and that's what this $200 Million Campaign is all about. We must prepare students in all fields—in engineering, in science, in health, in education, in humanities—to sense and seize the new opportunities of a high-tech world. At the same time, we must hold true to our heritage—that heritage which emphasizes integrity and honesty and respect for oneself and respect for others, decency, dignity and responsible behavior . . . Therefore, this $200 Million Campaign is about making a great university greater."

Harvey reminded his audience, "Only a minor part of this campaign deals with new buildings. Other institutions seek to build bricks and mortar. We seek to build a world-class institution." The primary part of this campaign, he said, is "designed to enhance our curricular offerings with such programs as the new School of Pharmacy, Physical Therapy, Computer Engineering, Naval Architecture, Industrial Engineering, Bio-Medicine, and the Ph.D. in Physics. These programs, rarely found on historically black campuses and modest-sized white campuses, enable Hampton to expand its sphere of influence in science, technology, engineering, architecture, and health care delivery. Our goal is to put $100 million or half of the total proceeds for the entire campaign into these curricular enhancements."

Second, Harvey wants to use $25 million to "place Hampton on the cutting edge of new technology."

Third, Harvey wants to use $10 million to develop a Leadership Institute. "The Leadership Institute is designed to take potential leaders, train them in their chosen fields of endeavor, and return them to their communities fully prepared to make a positive impact and difference. Specifically, in addition to their major fields of concentration, students in the Leadership Institute are required to take a leadership course once a semester and, at some point during their matriculation at Hampton, spend a full session away from campus working in a service capacity." Hence, "in return for their leadership training and service requirements, those who are enrolled in the Leadership Institute will receive a full tuition scholarship."

Fourth, $10 million will be used for the museum, "which is a national treasure." Fifth, $15 million will be used for the endowment of professorships and chairs. Sixth, $15 million will be used for endowed student scholarships. Last, $15 million would be used for new construction and $10 million for renovations and improvements.

It is Harvey's style to sell his dreams and get others to buy into them. "Yes, we are the dreamers, but I don't mind being called that. And I hope you don't either because you are also dreamers. You dream not of what is, but what could be. Yes, we are dreamers, but we are also workers. We want those dreams to ensure that tomorrow's world is safe and secure. Our contribution to the next millennium—and the scores of centuries to follow—will be our students—the builders, the nurturers, the visionaries, the scientists, the spiritual leaders, the educators, the healers, the political trailblazers, the explorers, the craftsmen, the artists—the decision makers and the peacemakers. That's what this $200 Million Campaign is really about," Harvey said.

"It's about students who take risks and trample stereotypes; who knock down barriers and glass ceilings and venture into new and untried territories. Its about students who establish Hampton University's presence and influence in the White House, in the British Parliament, in Bangladesh, and in Sugar Ditch, Mississippi," he exhorted.

He challenged the audience, "Dream dreams for yourselves and your heritage. Dream dreams for those yet unborn who will one day walk, study, work and play on the beautiful shores of Hampton University, a place that I call one of God's little acres.

"The official journey of our 200-million-dollar trek begins officially tonight. Let's get on with it."

Designing a Master Facilities Plan

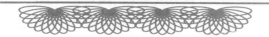

"Old buildings are not ours. They belong partly to those who built them, and partly to the generation of mankind who are to follow us. The dead still have their right to them: That which they labored for . . . we have no right to obliterate."

"What we ourselves have built, we are at liberty to throw down. But what other men gave their strength, and wealth and life to accomplish, their right over it does not pass away with their death."

—John Ruskin

President William R. Harvey drives around campus, surveying the buildings and the lay of the land with the eye of a landscape architect and the soul of a conservationist. Enter with him into this National Historic Landmark campus from the southeast shoreline, and behold the towering Emancipation Oak, with branches extending more than 98 feet in diameter. This exalted tree, one of the National Geographic Society's ten great trees in the world, is also part of fifteen acres designated as a National Historic site on the 254-acre, tree-lined, well-tended lawns of the Hampton campus. Under this great oak, an emblem of liberty, the Emancipation Proclamation was first read in 1863 to the African captives of the Hampton locality. The oral history, passed down through generations, alleges that the tree's wreath of oak leaves provided shade for the early classrooms of a newly-freed people thirsting for knowledge.

Now stroll along with the President to the western shoreline of the campus and espy the stately old buildings rising above the banks of the scenic Hampton River. Five of the 113 buildings on campus are imposing National Historic landmarks. The Mansion House, with its Southern Colonial architectural style, was built in 1828, and purchased as a part of Hampton Normal and Agriculture Institute. Originally, the structure housed teachers and the principal and his family. But now, the ten-bedroom mansion is home to Hampton's presidents and, since 1978, to President William R. Harvey and Norma B. Harvey and family. At this graceful estate, overlooking the river, Norma Harvey, the first lady of Hampton University, entertains the "Who's Who" lavishly and regally.

From the Mansion House, gaze upon the grand, symmetrical, three-story structure, Virginia Hall, surmounted by a two-story mansard regularly punctuated by chalet-gable dormers. The mass of the T-shaped building, now Virginia-Cleveland Hall, embraces both Second Empire and Victorian Gothic elements of style.[1] Designed by Richard Morris Hunt, renowned architect, this women's dormitory, "sung up" by the Hampton Singers, was constructed in 1874 at a cost of $98,000. Notice the less ornate and more solid look of the Academy Building, Hunt's other commission for the school. The ceiling is inlaid with a mosaic of Southern yellow pine and stained in natural color. It was constructed in 1882 after a fire destroyed the original, more decorative structure in 1879. Take heed also of the Italian Romanesque Revival-style Memorial Church. Erected in 1886, it has a 150-foot red brick tower and its interior has carvings of stone faces of African Americans and Native Americans. Near the anterior foyer is a coral stone from the foundation of Kawaiaho Church in Honolulu, built in 1842 by the Reverend Richard Armstrong, father of General Samuel C. Armstrong, and given to the University by Colonel William N. Armstrong in 1895. Take note, too, of the neo-Colonial general style Wigwam, with Georgian elements, which was built in 1878 as a dormitory for Native American students. "Wigwam" means "dwelling."

Each of these structures was planned by Hampton's faculty and built by the hands of its students. So these landmarks speak to us of a time past, beckoning to tell their rich and glorious history of those who gave their strength, wealth and sweat of brow to build these historic structures. As you saunter along with Harvey to the water's edge side of the campus, imagine how these edifices of learning link the past and present generations through the head, hand, and heart, the "wellspring of a quality education" and, at the same time, illuminate the bridge of knowledge and hope for future generations.

President Harvey must be credited with helping to preserve these landmarks and other edifices at Hampton University. When he arrived on the campus in 1978, he witnessed an institution with a glorious past in decline. These historic buildings, and much of the campus, were marred by ungraceful signs of aging, unpainted wood trim, crumbling streets, some asbestos-filled structures, and not-so-well-tended grounds. "It is important to maintain the beauty and dignity of this historic campus. This will be an on-going goal every year," Harvey said in 1978. The history buff understood, like John Ruskin, that these old buildings belong partly to those who built them and partly to those generations that follow them. While Harvey gazed upon the old buildings with reverence, he created new edifices that would blend with the old and, at the same time, meet the demands of a changing educational enterprise.

Accordingly, shortly after assuming his presidency, he commissioned and implemented a master facility plan, which is periodically updated. This blueprint provides for strategic growth and aesthetic enhancements, with a continuity of historical perspective, of the physical plant and grounds as necessary for a first-class university. In maintaining a celebrated coherence between the historic and modern, Harvey has, for example, chosen the "Harvey brick," a dark brownish-red one, to blend with the traditional red brick architecture, which contrasts with the yellow brick chosen by one of his predecessors, President Jerome H. Holland. As a student of history, it helped Harvey to see the urgency of protecting and preserving this institutional heritage—its buildings and its grounds. With history aside, perhaps his reasoning was something more ethereal—the search for excellence, of which pride is an element. "Excellence is pride. Pride in one's self, one's home, one's religion, one's work environment. Show me a person who has no pride in himself or his surroundings, and I will show you an example, at best, of mediocrity," Harvey is quick to reiterate. This ideal is in keeping with the tradition of Hampton's founder, Samuel Armstrong, who believed that students gathered at Hampton for a dauntless and momentous educational mission and having imposing buildings and an aesthetically pleasing environment would reflect that purpose.

Harvey regards his adopted "Home by the Sea," as "one of the most beautiful physical locations in the country." So in his *Annual Report of 1981–1982*, he wrote, "As I have stated in the past, one of my priorities as President is to continue to improve and upgrade our beautiful setting. A first-class appearance enhances academics, management, attitude, atmosphere, and just about everything else that we do." Lowell Middleton, the director of buildings and grounds since 1989, said that Harvey, who is meticulous about land management and conservation, is a "hands-on President." "He wants Hampton to look good at all times, as if the President of the United States is coming to visit. He might ride around in his car looking at the buildings and grounds on weekends or anytime. He will contact me about his observations. If, for example, there is a tree dying and must be replaced, he wants it replaced with two trees. He even planted pine trees and oak trees along the waterfront, so they could reflect the season, particularly fall." The groundsmen, with a work history at the University of 9 to 40 years, understand the importance of and the expectations of maintaining an aesthetically pleasing campus. One person is hired solely, for example, to pick up debris, and to make continuous rounds of cleaning the campus. Middleton stated that Harvey knows the groundsmen by name or sight, and he talks to them. "He is not so big, he can't talk with you. Little people are just as important as the big people. When Dr. Harvey asks housekeepers how they are doing or asks about their weekends, they are thrilled that he did so and can't stop talking about Dr. Harvey or saying nice things about him." Middleton added that a building captain, usually an administrator, is assigned to a building to report repairs or other maintenance concerns. He proudly pointed out that when he attends his regional and national conferences, he always receives compliments about the excellent maintenance of the campus. Some people have asked to visit the campus for ideas on vegetation and landscaping. Individuals, like Lowell Middleton and his team, under Leon Scott, and later Doretha Spells, and the former directors of buildings and grounds, Angle Owens and Alphonso King and their staffs, under Lucius Wyatt, have helped Harvey to make his dream a reality, because of their "innovation, dedication, and hard work."

Early in Harvey's presidency, the improvements in the physical plant were recognized. Robert C. Upton, who served as a member of the Board of Trustees and chaired the Buildings and Grounds Committee, commented, in a board meeting of April 27, 1979, on the "beauty and cleanliness of the campus, which had also favorably impressed visitors." He paid high commendation also to the staff, especially Lucius Wyatt and Angle Owens, for their diligence in this regard. Moreover, he noted that "the annual capital improvements budgets had been beneficial in avoiding deferred maintenance as well as renovating several structures which would have deteriorated beyond reasonable repair." Harvey agreed, too, that, indeed, the betterments of the physical plant, using the Facilities Master Plan as a guidebook for renovating buildings and increasing maintenance activity, has paid big dividends for the University.

Within the confines of Hampton's beautifully landscaped campus is the "storehouse of many treasures." Among them is what Harvey has built or renovated during his years at Hampton University. From 1978 to 1999, more than two decades under his presidency, the University accomplished unparalleled growth in new construction and major renovations. Between 1978–1999, fourteen new university structures were built on campus at a cost of $65,319,056 and twenty-two edifices underwent significant renovations at a cost of $29,905,471. (See figure 5.) The Facilities Master Plan, which included major renovations and new construction, correlated with fund-raising, program development, and other university goals. The $30 Million Campaign, outlined by Harvey to the board members in their semi-annual board meeting of April 27, 1979, proposed that $8 million would go toward new construction and renovations. Similarly, in the $200 Million Campaign in 1998, $15 million would go for new construction and $10 million for renovations and improvements. Under Harvey's tenure, from 1978–1999, the new construction included: four residence halls, a conference center, three academic buildings, a state-of- the-art university library, the Convocation Center, a maintenance warehouse and storeroom, grounds facility building, tennis stadium, and the Booker T. Washington Memorial Garden. The most impressive new construction project was the development of twenty acres to create the Hampton Harbor Shopping Village and Apartments, a for-profit undertaking, which generates more than $1 million each year to support scholarships and other University activities. The renovations are equally impressive, and include nine residence halls, four academic buildings, three administrative and student support facilities, Armstrong Stadium, the Memorial Church, and the Huntington Building.

Robert Binswanger, member of the Board of Trustees, said, "One could argue that Bill Harvey has an 'edifice' complex. I don't think that's his legacy. I think it is relatively easy for a president to be a bricks-and-mortar builder. Of course, it depends on the money they can raise to build, but that's something that occupies a lot of leaders in higher education." He knows that the President's vision is more expansive than building bricks and mortar or concrete and steel. Harvey views these structures as implements to help promote learning and living.

	New	Renovated
Cost	65319056	29905471

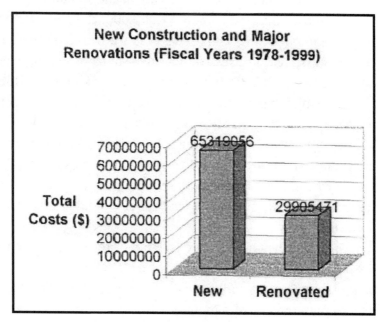

Figure 5

New Academic Edifices

Clearly, from Harvey's vision and actions, when he assumed his post at then Hampton Institute, he was interested in moving the institution to a comprehensive university, and its curricular emphasis to a scientific and professional one, with a strong liberal arts undergirding. In his first Board of Trustees meeting in 1978, he proposed the establishment of a center for marine science, in keeping with his vision to expand the science and technology fields for blacks. Since the University is near the Chesapeake Bay, it was a most likely place to implement his vision and to rectify the underrepresentation of blacks in marine science.

The Marine Science Center

In 1981, an old cinder block, diesel mechanic instructional building, which had been completely gutted with only the exterior cinder block remaining, was utilized for the new construction of a modern facility for the Marine and Coastal Environmental Studies.

At a cost of approximately $1,000,000, the contemporary center, equipped with a first- class laboratory, aquarium and classroom space, houses the marine science program, which began in September 1979. It is the first of its kind at an HBCU, and one which has a three-fold focus: teaching, research, and public service. "We want to reach out to the community and assist. . . We want to have a high level scientific research program," noted Harvey at his first Board of Trustees meeting. He aimed to have a first-class Marine Science program, where Hampton students and faculty could study the delicate balance between human and nature.

On September 10, 1985, when Harvey presented a testimony on the Minority Science Program before the House Subcommittee on Postsecondary Education, he discussed the implications of the underrepresentation of minorities in science, mathematics, and technology. And he noted that to build the scientific emphasis, it was important to obtain funds from various sources for programs, support services, and buildings. Thus, as academic programs were enhanced, facilities, such as the Science and Technology Building and Olin Engineering Building, were constructed to accommodate these programs.

Science and Technology Building

The Science and Technology Building, with a three-story contemporary modernist design, was completed in 1986 at a cost of $6,908,140. Once considered the university's high-tech hub, the building housed the university's main-frame computer. It has classroom, lecture and laboratory space for the computer science, communicative science and disorders, and airway science.

The Olin Engineering Building

Olin Engineering Building, designed by three Hampton alumni of Livas Group Architects and largely funded by the Olin Foundation, was completed in 1988. The contemporary-modernist style, five-story facility is used by Hampton students and faculty to carry out groundbreaking research in the fields of chemical and electrical engineering and nuclear and optical physics.

Speaking before the Olin Foundation on April 29, 1989, Harvey noted:

> Historically black colleges must receive the support necessary to continue to fulfill their unique role in addressing the issues of the 1990s and beyond. This support must include attention to the unequal funding to historically black colleges for research initiatives, for the implementation of graduate programs, for the full incorporation of new technologies, and for the erection of much needed new physical facilities. A history of limited resources and the struggle merely to survive have meant that funding for the latter has been necessarily diverted to a more compelling area. The result is that physical facilities at many historically black colleges have fallen into disrepair and are, therefore, in need of renovations and, in many instances, replacement. Given the crucial role which black colleges will play in the 1990s and beyond, this kind of support must be viewed as an investment in the future of higher education, in the salvation of young people, indeed, in the advancement of our nation.

Major Renovations of Academic Edifices

DuPont Hall

In the 1990s, several buildings, primarily in the sciences and technologies, were renovated as the academic curricular offerings expanded. DuPont Hall, constructed in 1928 and built by trade school students, costs $267,939 to renovate in 1990. Home to the Mathematics and Science Departments, the building provides individual offices equipped with laboratory computer workstations for the University faculty and staff. The four-story structure, with its neo-Colonial general style architecture, also features upgraded classroom, lecture and laboratory space and is currently used for biology.

Bemis Hall

Bemis Hall, built in 1933 by trade school students, is home to the University's Department of Architecture, the Naval Architecture Program, and the Art Department's ceramics laboratory. New windows, light fixtures, paint and floor coverings, as well as expansions to the architecture library, are among the additions completed in 1991 at a cost of $1,320,733. This modern building formerly housed the Department of Building Construction, maintenance department office, metal working shop, brick laying laboratory, and classrooms.

Phenix Hall, Kittrell Hall

With the expansion of the allied health fields of pharmacy and physical therapy, major renovations took place in Phenix Hall for the Department of Physical Therapy and Kittrell Hall for the School of Pharmacy, at a cost of $1,015,922 and $1,584,178, respectively. Constructed in 1931, Phenix's renovations included new heating and air conditioning, and upgrading existing classrooms, laboratory spaces, and office spaces. This edifice was originally operated by the college as a private elementary and secondary school, then leased to the City of Hampton for twenty-eight years as the only senior high school available to blacks. It was returned to the University in 1962. It also houses the School of Education, an upgraded laboratory for children, and several research centers. A contemporary modernist design, Kittrell Hall, built in 1968, was completely renovated to house the School of Pharmacy. Improvements include office spaces, laboratories, heating and air conditioning unit, added elevator, as well as a research center. Originally, this structure was used by two now-defunct departments: Home Economic (later Human Ecology) and Social Work.

Academic Support Services Structures

William R. Harvey and Norma B. Harvey Library

The William R. and Norma B. Harvey Library, the academic and intellectual crossroads of the campus, is named in honor of the President and his wife, Norma. Dedicated on Founder's Day, January 26, 1992, the 125,000-square-foot building, a modern U-shaped design with a five-story glass-enclosed atrium, is adorned with a two-paneled mural created by John Biggers, an alumnus and world-renowned artist. The "House of the Turtle" and the "Tree House" are "inspired by Hampton's past and future and stand as a metaphor for the human experience of growing, learning, thinking, and developing sensitivity and responsibility." The atrium can also serve as an exhibition lobby, as an area for special events, and as a spatial reference for each library floor. To have a first class institution, to increase the programs in the University, and to carry out research, a library is essential. Thus, it is designed "to promote diligent study and inspired research," said Harvey. It offers "physical facilities that are maximally conducive to living and learning." The $10,788,740 state-of-the-art library, designed by the late Hubert Taylor of Livas Group Architects, has the capacity for 600,000 volumes and seating for 1,000 and 24-hour study facilities. In addition, the library houses the Center for Teaching Excellence and the Academic Technology Mall, which is adaptable to the digital revolution.

Further, an impressive room contains the George Foster Peabody Collection of over 25,000 items by and about African Americans. This elegant room is specially "designed to ensure the long-term preservation of this highly valuable collection," noted Harvey.

Collis P. Huntington Building

The Huntington Building, conforming to Colonial architectural style, was built in 1903 at a cost of $60,000 as the University library. In 1997, it was renovated, at a cost of $6,159,397, to house the art museum, which has one of the best African American collections in the world, and the University archives, which contains over 8 million manuscript materials and 50,000 photographs. The archives is among the nation's most significant resources for research on the history of African American and Native American education. This brick structure, with an exterior trim of Indiana limestone and an interior trim of Tennessee marble, was a gift by Mrs. Collis P. Huntington as a memorial to her husband who served as a Trustee from 1890–1900.

Booker T. Washington Memorial Garden

While the Booker T. Washington Memorial Garden is not a supportive academic structure, it is indeed a supportive symbol of Hampton's mission—an "Education for Life." This memorial to Hampton's most illustrious graduate, which includes a bronze statue and meditation garden, was dedicated in 1984 at a cost of $250,000. It is a testimony to Washington's historical contributions to past and future generations. Washington, born in slavery in Franklin County, Virginia in 1856, graduated in 1875. He served in numerous positions before he founded Tuskegee Normal and Industrial Institute in 1881. During his 34-year tenure, he was principal of Tuskegee and achieved national prominence as a leader in education and as a spokesperson for Black Americans.

Building A Quality Student Life

As student enrollments increased under Harvey's leadership from 2,700 to 6,000, more dormitories were necessary to meet the demand for housing accommodations. Between 1978–1992, four new dormitories were constructed and eight dormitories underwent major renovations.

Modular Dormitories A, B, and C

Modular Dormitories A, B, and C consist of three semi-private dormitories, opened in 1978, at costs of $442,718. With their industrial design, they were the first new construction projects completed after Harvey became the President.

McGrew Towers Dormitory and Conference Center

McGrew Towers Dormitory and Conference Center, a modern nine-story dormitory designed by Livas Group Architects of Norfolk, towers above the Hampton River. Constructed in 1982 at a cost of $5,545,067, it serves as a residence hall for three hundred female students, and as a meeting facility for such prestigious annual gatherings as the Black Family and Black Ministers' conferences. Constructed of dark brownish-red brick and bands of stucco to blend in with the historic campus, the structure is organized into pods, each one with four bedrooms clustered around a central bathroom and a lounge. Named in honor of Hattie Smith McGrew, an alumna, this building was largely funded by the U.S. Department of Housing and Urban Development.

L. Douglas Wilder Hall

L. Douglas Wilder Hall was constructed in 1990 for $3,493,308. Named in honor of Virginia's first African American governor, this five-story structure houses two hundred male students. The dormitory's Victorian style blends with the adjacent historic Academy Building.

Thurgood Marshall Hall

This contemporary, two-story dormitory for male honors students was completed in 1991 at a cost of $855,708. Thurgood Marshall Hall, named in honor of the first African American Supreme Court Justice, was partly new construction and partly renovation, and it included new living quarters and upgraded parking facilities.

Queen Street Dormitory

Built in 1912, Queen Street Dormitory is nicknamed "Psych Hall," because it was converted from the former Peninsula Psychiatric Hospital to a dormitory. This facility was also used by the Old Dixie Hospital. This modern three-story facility, renovated in 1983 at a cost of $2,318,242, provided living, study, and office space for the University's female honor students. The facility, which was purchased for a mere $10.00 from the Hospital Corporation of America (HCA), houses about 225 students. Some added amenities of the dormitory include a swimming pool, a tennis court, a park, and a lower cost of renting. The President espoused that the lure of the extra accommodations would motivate more students to aspire to the honor roll.

Pierce Hall

Pierce Hall, an honors dormitory for males, was renovated in 1997 at a total cost of $238,980. Major improvements were made in the interior renovation and restoration of the floors. Fiber optic cabling was installed for access to the Academic Technology Mall and to the Internet prior to the installation in other dormitories. A computer was also placed in every room. Pierce, built by trade students, was originally erected in 1883 to house the Pierce Machine Shop, where Hampton students learned the machinist trades: iron work, steam boiler, and steam engine operation. When the trade school discontinued, it was renovated as a men's dormitory.

Kelsey Hall

Kelsey Hall, a women's dormitory, constructed in 1931 by trade school students, underwent major renovations in 1997 at a cost of $1,092,956. Major renovations included: refurbished lobby and replacement of plumbing fixtures—new toilets, shower stalls, and ceramic tiles on the walls and floors of every bathroom. Floors were painted, sanded, and finished. In addition, fiber optic cabling was also installed.

Kennedy Hall

Kennedy Hall, a female honors dormitory, was constructed in 1918. Significant repairs and upgrades were made in the student lounge, plumbing fixtures, and roof repairs. Fiber optic cabling was added at a cost of more than $1,411,820 in 1997.

James Hall

Built in 1914, James Hall, a male freshmen dormitory, had major renovations done in 1990 and 1999 that cost $383,734. In 1990, this five-story, neo-Colonial general style building with Georgian elements, included upgraded restroom and shower facilities, making it one of the most comfortable and alluring places to reside on campus. Additional renovations in 1999 made restrooms handicapped accessible and ADA compliant.

Winona Hall

Winona Hall, a women's dormitory, underwent major renovations in 1990. It costs $185,489 to refurbish the first floor of this building. Formerly the nurses' quarters, the University purchased this facility in the late 1960s from the Dixie Hospital.

Virginia-Cleveland Hall

Virginia-Cleveland Hall, originally constructed in 1874, is a five-story women's residence hall, which also houses the University's main student dining facilities. It was renovated in 1990 and 1996 at a cost of $4 million. Exterior restoration of Virginia Hall was completed in 1996. Upgrades and major renovations completed include: roof replacement; installation of new gutters and downspouts; cleaning, replacement and repair of the bricks, windows and doors; replacement and additional fire escapes; and painting and replacement of the masonry stoops and steps on the waterside. In 1990, new quarry tile floors, windows, restrooms, and student living quarters were added.

Du Bois Hall

Du Bois Hall, erected in 1970, was the first coeducational dormitory at the University. This structure is named for W. E. B. Du Bois, the scholar/activist, who was the first African American to receive his doctorate degree from Harvard University. This building was renovated at a cost of more than $238,653. Fiber optic cabling was installed in 1997 and a sprinkler system in 1999. In addition, a renovated penthouse houses the Honors College.

Student Support Services Edifices

Student Health Services Building

The contemporary-style structure, repaired in 1986 for the amount of $586,311, is an on-campus health-care facility that resulted from the growth in enrollment and the need for better care of students. It features examination rooms, laboratories and a dental suite, as well as offices for medical staff. The infirmary shares the building with the Hampton University Business Assistance Center, which provides technical assistance to small businesses. The Student Health Services Building was once the home of the St. Cyprian's Episcopal Church.

Athletic Support Facilities

The Tennis Stadium

The Tennis Stadium, constructed in 1992 for $615,985, is the place where the University's nationally ranked, intercollegiate tennis team practices and competes. This complex, with its contemporary Colonial style, features six courts for regulation competition, including one with locker rooms, a concession stand, and a grandstand that seats 400.

Armstrong Stadium

This colonial modern stadium was renovated and expanded in 1992 and 1999 at a total cost of $4,567,850. In 1992, the seating capacity was nearly doubled to accommodate more than 12,000 spectators who gather for sporting events at the University's main athletic facility. Enhancements also included two press boxes and a 400-meter, eight-lane cushioned Olympic track. In 1999, improvements included renovations to the facade and the entrance gate, additional grandstands, and office space for football coaches.

General Support Services and Auxiliary Utilitarian Buildings

Maintenance Warehouse and Storeroom

This two-story, 30,000-square-foot, utilitarian storehouse, completed in 1985 at a cost of $1,161,500, includes regular, combustible and security storage areas, as well as offices, lockers, and restrooms. It is the central shipping and receiving point for all goods and supplies that flow through the University.

Grounds Facility Building

Built in 1988 at a cost of $1,202,052, this industrial facility is the headquarters for the committed staff members that tend the attractive, 204-acre campus. It has maintenance and storage space for supplies, parts, tools, and University vehicles and equipment, as well as offices and locker rooms.

Computer Center

In 1986, renovations were completed at a cost of $115,470 to the Computer Center. This structure, constructed in 1944, was formerly the Grill, a snack bar for students and workers. It also once housed the University's book store. Now, the Computer Center provides office and work space for the University's data processing and computer services departments.

Armstrong-Slater Hall

A multipurpose facility, Armstrong-Slater Hall provides office and classroom space for the Department of Art and Department of Military Sciences, the Student Counseling Center, and the Office of Human Resources. Renovation of this two-story, Colonial modern-industrial building was completed in 1990 at a cost of $633,802. In 1896, under the administration of Hollis Burke Frissell, this edifice was constructed as Armstrong-Slater Memorial Trade School. It symbolized the change in the past mission of manual training at Hampton for character building and the economic support of the school's operations to training a skilled group of workers for agriculture and industry. Products from the student workshops were sold in the town of Hampton and exhibited at national and international expositions. In 1933, the Trade School was advanced to college level, and eleven years later the historic Division of Trades and Industries was closed. In 1955, the School of Agriculture and Engineering was discontinued, closing an era in Hampton's work in agricultural and industrial training.

Whipple Barn

Renovated Whipple Barn, featuring a two-story atrium, is the venue of the registrar, admissions, financial aid, campus police and airway science offices, as well as home to several units of the business office. This facility's facelift was completed in 1991 at a cost of $2,756,330. This Victorian style structure, built by trade school students in 1906, served as a farm horse and dairy barn, and was considered part of the laboratory equipment for agriculture students. Later, it was used as ROTC headquarters, maintenance storage areas, and other multipurpose usages.

Administration Building

Built in 1882, the structure, with a two-and-one-half story with part basement, houses the office of the President, offices of Provost, Vice President for Research, Vice President for Business Affairs and Treasurer, and Vice President for Development. A roof replacement was done in 1998 for $141,651. Originally built in 1882 and named in honor of General J. F. B. Marshall, first Treasurer of Hampton, the structure later became the Administration Building, with a portion added in 1918 known as Palmer Hall.

Renovating the Spiritual Sanctuary

Memorial Chapel

In 1998, the historic Memorial Chapel had major renovations at a cost of $715,963. The improvements included roof replacement and downspouts, refurbished floor, and a renovated ante room and two bathrooms. The church, with a seating capacity of 1,000, serves as the sanctuary for nondenominational religious services. Here President Harvey started the Sunday School after twenty years of its inactivity in early 1980s.

Building for Empowerment

Hampton Harbor Shopping Village and Apartments

Hampton Harbor Shopping Village and Apartments and the Convocation Center are admirable examples of how Harvey, as an academician and entrepreneur, can successfully blend his remarkable energy, skills, and talents. Hampton Harbor is comprised of a 60,000-square-foot shopping center and 246 luxury, two-bedroom apartments for Hampton residents. The complex employs over 200 and pays the local community an estimated $185,000 in taxes. The 20-acre development, completed in 1990 at a cost of $12,701,088, generates an annual profit of $1 million, which is used to fund scholarships.

Convocation Center

The dreamer might have had a doubt, but perhaps only for a moment, about building the $12.5 million Convocation Center, a modern, brick-and-glass domed structure, designed by three Hampton University graduates at Livas Group Architects in Norfolk, Virginia. There were times when Harvey wanted to jettison his plan for the 150,000-square-foot facility. But Lucius Wyatt, then vice president for fiscal and business affairs, encouraged him and reinforced Harvey's belief that the University needed a multipurpose center. This multifaceted facility, with a seating capacity of 8,000, was completed in 1993. It is used for concerts, sporting events, trade shows, exhibits, and conferences.

Building Beyond the Ivory Gates

The Hampton University Business Incubator

Under Harvey's leadership, building activities have not been confined to the main campus. In 1999, in partnership with the Hampton Community Development Corporation, a 4,000-square-foot structure was built in the Phoebus community on university-owned land. The Incubator provides a venue and core services for new businesses to start up at a substantially reduced rate.

Buying, Building, and Restoring in the New Millennium

Strawberry Banks

Harvey is continuing to buy, build, and renovate. In April 2000, Hampton University purchased the 26-acre tract, waterfront property of Strawberry Banks Inn, located near the campus, for $7.5 million cash as an investment in the future. This transaction is indicative of his well-thought out visionary planning. Of course, he had doubters saying that he could not do it, but he persevered. "I was able to make sure the discipline was there. I had groups come to me, that had nothing to do with the University, to say I think you are foolish because you are insisting on paying $7.5 million, which was a great buy for the University. They are being sent by the other side. But I stay my course, and I usually get what I want because it's well thought out from the beginning. Those that criticize, I respect that disagreement, but I don't let it persuade me from doing what I think is right and fair, and best for the University," asserted Harvey.

Student Center

In 2001, the 155,000-square-foot contemporary Student Center opened with fanfare. The $18.8 million three-story building includes a movie theater, an inside track, a food court, a six-lane bowling alley, a fitness center, a video arcade and several meeting and study rooms. In a groundbreaking ceremony that took place during the 1999 Homecoming, Harvey is quoted as saying in an October 31,

1999 article in the *Daily Press* that, "This came about as a result of listening to the students. They said they wanted more to do on campus, and this certainly means they will have more to do on campus." The new edifice replaced the original one-story C. H. Williams Student Union, which was built in 1884, and demolished in 1999.

White and Holmes Halls

In 2002, two new residence halls, designed by the Livas Group Architects and built at a cost of $13.5 million, was opened and both included the latest technological advancements. White Hall, a three-and-one-half story women's dormitory, with 48,059 square feet, is named in honor of Dr. Gladys Hope Franklin-White, a member of the class of 1939 and emeritus class leader.

Holmes Hall, a two-and-one-half story building, with 30,535 square feet, is named in honor of Dr. Wendell P. Holmes, Jr., a member of the class of 1943. He served as a member of the Hampton University Board of Trustees for 22 years, including serving as chair for nine years.

The Scripps Howard School of Journalism & Communications

In the fall of 2002, the two-story, 25,000-square foot center opened to journalism majors. The state-of-the-art journalism school was backed by a $6.3 million donation from the Scripps Howard Foundation. Harvey believes this partnership will increase the number of people of color in journalism and "revolutionize journalism and journalism education in this country. We want more minority reporters, editors, decision-makers, managers and owners," Harvey said. "They offer different points of view, which makes the media outlets stronger."

On the drawing board are plans for more structures, which include the School of Business and the field of allied health, and plans for the renovation of Odgen Hall and other edifices. In addition, the University also aims to commercially develop a 19-acre parcel that it owns in the City of Hampton. In fact, Harvey plans to continue his building until the "valley will rise up to meet the hill." As Harvey wrote of this allegory in his *President's Annual Report, 1987–88*, perhaps he, too, can see himself in the old man in the famous Chinese fable, who, like the rest of the people in the small village, had to cross an impeding hill every day to get to his fields.

> Each day he took a stone in his hands and carried it from the top of the hill to the bottom and placed it alongside previous stones he had carried down the hillside. Asked by a stranger why he did this, he replied, "I'm moving this hill. Not in my lifetime, or my son's lifetime, perhaps, but in time this valley will rise up to meet the hill.

"This is how we must view our work at the University. An institution such as ours emerges one stone at a time, building upon existing stones so carefully placed before us," said Harvey.

Restructuring the Academic Program

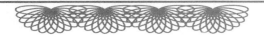

"Tradition has served us well and we must build on our proud heritage. We cannot become complacent, however. If this institution is to meet the challenges of social change and academic quality, we must affirm our resolve to continue our quest for excellence."

—William R. Harvey

For over twenty years, President William R. Harvey, like the old man in the Chinese fable, has, also, been crossing an impeding hill, carrying stones daily from the top of the hill to the bottom, building on each as a stepping stone, so he can move the Hampton hill toward a quality place of living and learning. Each mounted pebble aims toward academic excellence, his "cornerstone of institutional building." It is one way, John Gardner says, men like Harvey, "shape institutions to suit their purposes." And for Harvey that academic purpose is "to educate students; to encourage intellectual advancement and creativity; to promote and improve the economic and social condition of its constituent groups, as well as the wider society; and to promote individual and group self-renewal."[1]

Adding one stone at a time, the knoll of academics shifted to a place of distinction. Under Harvey's leadership, the University moved to become a comprehensive university, and added sixty-four new degree programs between 1978–2000, including four doctoral degree programs in physics, pharmacy, physical ther-

135

apy, and nursing. The faculty not only increased in quantity, from approximately 190 to 350, but also in quality. The professoriate scaled new heights of achievement in teaching, research, and service. Three faculty members have, for example, won the prestigious Virginia Council of Higher Education's Outstanding Faculty Awards. In research and sponsored programs, faculty generated $22 million in 1997–1998 compared to $3,796,792 in 1977–78 and over $25 million in 1998–1999. And, as previously noted, the university's Center for Atmospheric Sciences received a grant of $92 million in 2002. These university faculty members are involved in cutting-edge research, such as developing a cancer detection device, creating "touch" with fiber optics in artificial limbs, building a particle detector machine that could help scientists understand how the universe was created, experimenting with nuclear fusion as an alternative energy technology and studying nighttime clouds in the upper atmosphere. In public service, three faculty have been elected to serve as mayor.

Such milestones in "moving the hill" are having a salutary effect. *U.S. News and World Report* magazine has consistently ranked Hampton in the top 25 percent of the Southern regional universities categories. For example, in 2000, it ranked number 24 in this category; in 1999, it ranked number 29, and in 1993, it ranked number 14. The University continues to rank among the top five in Virginia universities (public or private) in the Southern regional universities category. Hampton University has also been ranked by *Black Enterprise* magazine as one of the best universities for black students in the country. In 2002, the University was listed by the magazine as second best.

The quality of a university is likewise measured by the number of its graduates and Hampton University is a known producer. According to *Black Issues in Higher Education*, Hampton ranks consistently in the top five U. S. universities and colleges in producing African American baccalaureates in all disciplines combined. In the July 19, 2001 edition of *Black Issues in Higher Edu-*

cation's "Special Report on the Top 100 Degree Producers," Hampton University ranked number two among U.S. universities and colleges in producing African American baccalaureates with degrees in biology. The University was also a top producer of African Americans with baccalaureate degrees in English, in business management, in communications, in psychology, and in health professions. In its August 19, 1999 edition, Hampton was also a top producer in physical sciences, in computer and information science, and in social science and history.[2]

According to the 1997 *Quality Education Minorities Network*'s "Weaving the Web of MSE Success for Minorities: Top Ten Colleges and Universities Report," Hampton ranked first in the state of Virginia for the largest number of degrees awarded to African Americans in mathematics, science, and engineering. Additionally, the National Network for Science Partnerships ranked Hampton as the third principal producer of African American medical school matriculants.

In his vision of excellence, what identifiable, well-thought-out goals, objectives, and strategies helped him to "move the hill"? In his address at the Fall Opening Convocation, September 10, 1978, President Harvey proposed a new academic direction for Hampton, which included the following goals:

First, he suggested "a core curriculum should be established which would enable every Hampton Institute student to read, write and do basic computations at a certain level. Additionally, a Hampton Institute student ought to have some knowledge and basic understanding of history, literature and the arts, as well as an opportunity to do some thinking about ethics and morals."

Second, he advanced that "business, one of the fastest growing disciplines at the college, needs to be strengthened in terms of faculty and program to provide a strong basis for a possible move into an MBA program. Contrary to most MBA programs, the Hampton MBA would require an internship for a specified period in the corporate/business community."

Third, he noted, "When I arrived at Hampton a year ago, I marveled at its waterfront location and the virtually limitless possibilities, which would augur well for a Marine Science Center here. Since the underrepresentation of minorities in the Marine Sciences is a national concern, it is my belief that Hampton can make a positive input as it is a 'natural' habitat for extensive research, seminars, and field trips related to marine life, ocean fisheries, coastal environmental research, fish food processing and management, and the like."

Fourth, he stated that "in keeping with its unique character and tradition, Hampton is well equipped to offer a four-year program in Building Technology, utilizing an interdisciplinary approach with a heavy concentration in clinical experiences."

Fifth, he submitted that since, "Continuing Education has also been one of Hampton's hallmarks from its founding, I feel that the college has an excellent opportunity to expand its curricular offerings to older adults, women and other special groups to enable them to meet changing societal demands in employment or other activities."[3]

Finally, to deal effectively with the new curriculum, he proposed the elimination of academic divisions and the establishment of academic schools.

The young president "hit the ground running," departing in a radical new direction from his predecessors. Even though the pride and tradition of the Hampton way was often in conflict with change, he was unstoppable. His friend, Arthur Greene, who from the beginning could see "leadership qualities of determination and forthrightness," said, so many people doubted the capacity of the "aggressive, very personable, charismatic person," who was "assuming the helm of a prestigious university with a long tradition, to lead." Because he was young, and this "historically black University has had so many strong leaders in the past that have been much older than himself, I would suspect that there were those who felt this would just be too much for him and would overwhelm him." But he differed from other predecessors "by virtue of style," said Greene. "By virtue of breaking up a preconception that you had to be older to be wise, you had to be older to understand the fundamentals of leadership and management. I think he prepared himself well from his previous exposure to be at the right place at the right time. It just happened to be in a younger body." Indeed, here was a man whose ideas and time had come. Harvey wanted to move Hampton beyond survival to a standard of excellence. He understood that the decade of the 1970s in higher education was facing central challenges of "purpose, objectives, strategies, resources, organization, and the need for leadership to ensure the survival of the college as a viable, effective and efficient entity."

As Harvey set about to achieve the goals he laid out, his first objective was to hire a competent administrator to carry out his vision for a new academic model. "This administrator was to transform the faculty and academic administration from a parochial vision of academics to one that was global in perspective, involving not only teaching and service, but also research and scholarly productivity,"[4] said Martha E. Dawson, whom Harvey chose as his first vice president of academic affairs in 1979. "The challenge of academic affairs was to find ways to unlock the hidden talent of faculty, so that they and Hampton itself could be more competitive. . . . Teaching had always been viewed as its *raison d'etre*, and to get more faculty to consider it in collaboration with research and other scholarly activities was a challenge,"[5] said Dawson. She credited Harvey with "changing the whole character of the institution," and noted, "It used to be that people could get tenure for breathing. But we said you had to have a doctorate, and then you have to continue to work. Some people were complacent; they did not try to compete. They would teach, give grades, and go home. I said something about doing research to faculty and being competitive, and one faculty member wrote me a note that this was a teaching institution. When you have to compete out here [in the larger society] and send in papers, that's hard. But this was a different world. Black schools just couldn't sit back in their corner and be ignored. You can't do that anymore, when the accrediting body looks at you and wants to know how much research does your faculty do? How many national committees are they on?" contended Dawson. Having previously served at the college for a decade, before returning from Virginia State University, she acknowledged that Hampton was a strong school. But, she said, "We did [research] if we wanted to, but now we had to do it. If you were going to stay, you had to do the same thing at a research university. That's how we got credibility. It took a lot of ideas and a leader who would allow you to do it."

To stimulate research, grantsmanship, and scholarly activities, faculty members were provided technical assistance through the development office, offered proposal-writing workshops by external and internal consultants, given a reduced teaching load of one-quarter release time, rewarded with merit pay, and promoted for tenure and promotion based on the criteria of not only teaching but research and grantsmanship. Clearly, this was not an attempt by the administration to negate teaching. For Harvey made it apparent in his Opening Convocation speech during 1978–1979 that, "Good teaching has highest priority at Hampton Institute, for we believe our society needs citizens who can lead, who have high personal and moral standards, who are problem-solvers, and who desire to improve the quality of life for their fellowman. We are concerned with providing the best possible environment for learning for the 3,000 students who come to us from diverse backgrounds—both in terms of prior learning experiences and geography." It is a theme that he has reiterated throughout his tenure. In the August 13, 1995 Annual Retreat of administrators at Hilton Head, South Carolina, using the theme "Promoting and Insuring Teaching Excellence," Harvey remarked that, "For Hampton University to continue to survive and thrive in the twenty-first century, we must be known for the highest academic quality possible. And that begins with good teaching. . . . All associated with us must realize that good teaching is one of the important foundation cornerstones of our institutional building. . . . Research enhances teaching, but the operative word is 'enhances.' We can continue to do millions of dollars of research as we are doing, but if our reputation for teaching excellence is not solid, then we will have failed."

Under Dawson's able leadership, she carried out this charge of integrating research and grantsmanship, and service with teaching excellence until her retirement in July 1991. This daunting task of recasting the culture of faculty and administrators for a new paradigmatic shift helped to pave the way for the institution's move to a comprehensive university. And to acquire such status, Dawson noted that "team building, professional development, and fiscal support would be pivotal to the transformation of the academic unit."

Team Building

Harvey and Dawson were harmonizing on the same chord of academic team building. In the *President's Annual Report, 1980–1981*, he reaffirmed: "It is my belief that leadership requires collective competence and that leadership demands responsibility and accountability more than ever before. Instruction is one area in the operation of any college or university which needs greater attention in terms of improved management; and academic leadership today involves extensive consultation, communication and information." Shortly after assuming the duties of the vice president of academic affairs, Dawson visualized a way to increase communication within the academic unit. She created her brainchild, the Academic Leadership Team (ALT), a networking cabinet. It consisted of deans and directors who met weekly to carry out the President's vision. Monthly, she met with the Council of Academic Chairpersons (CAC). This planning was the impetus for the new direction in greater professional development, which included effective teaching, research, and grantsmanship among faculty.

Professional Development

So successful was Dawson's concept that in the 1980–1981 academic year, Harvey appropriated special funds to establish a professional development program called Special Administrative Leadership Training (SALT), designed to "train top level academic administrators to be effective managers." Dawson said the President wanted to have a team of people who would make a difference. "We had changed from directors to deans, but we didn't want deans, as he and I both agreed, just to have the title. So he was extremely supportive of SALT." This program allowed the administration to broaden the series of workshops held during the academic year for deans, directors, and chairs. "An effort is being made to develop deans who do not 'upbuck' decisions that they should make," said Harvey. In the program, managers were trained by nationally known speakers and consultants in topics involving budgeting, planning, grantsmanship, law, responsibility of middle and top-level administrators, and time management. "These changes were designed to chart a deliberate course of action, which would keep Hampton in the forefront of the higher education enterprise," he noted.

Team building and professional development were also essential to get faculty to buy into the shared vision. Along with the Special Academic Leadership Training for the professoriate during post-commencement, faculty development included fall and winter institutes, designed to promote academic excellence in teaching, research and scholarly activities, and service. SALT for academic administrators and the winter and fall institutes for faculty, along with other professional development workshops and conferences for academic administrators and faculty, have continued under the leadership of individuals who have followed Dawson and who have been responsible for academic affairs. These individuals have included Elnora D. Daniel, Marshall Grisby, Demetrius Venable, and JoAnn Haysbert, who assumed Elnora D. Daniel's position. Daniel served twice in this capacity, before accepting a position as President of Chicago State University in 1998.

Each year a new theme is selected as a focus for all academic units. Although the theme of the institutes differs each year, critical issues are highlighted in higher education and in the area of professional development. For example, in the first five years, the themes focused on an internal evaluation of the academic unit. His first two years, though not given a theme, involved reviewing, evaluating, and planning, while the next three years emphasized qualitative growth, assessment, refinement and accountability, and enhancement of academic programs through instructional technology.

Unquestionably, Harvey understood, as he wrote in his *President's Annual Report, 1980–1981*, "The strength of Hampton Institute depends on the training, intelligence, and commitment of faculty and staff to the aims of the institution. It is a well-accepted fact that a college or university acquires prestige through the competence and performance of its faculty. Thus, one primary priority of the college is to attract and retain a faculty of excellent quality and high morale. Moreover, the college recognizes that the most competent faculty members are also the most mobile and that the most capable prospective faculty members have many choices."

Fiscal Support

While increasing competence through professional development is one avenue of retaining good faculty, another is having a good financial base. And for Harvey, "Everything flows from the financial base. A healthy financial base allows the college to obtain and retain quality professors" and "provide support for research and faculty development." Moreover, he contended, in the *President's Annual Report, 1980–1981*, that, "It has been proven that academic leadership must be based upon an adequate and sound program of income development." Hence, it becomes increasingly infeasible to regard financial matters as discrete from academic policy. "Responsible academic administrators owe it both to themselves and the college to be able to separate the wheat from the chaff in an institution's finances. There is a direct line of accountability between those who provide funds and how such funds are spent. The need to develop program objectives and departmental budgets in consonance is being emphasized over and over at Hampton."

So in 1984, Harvey announced that the schools' deans would be accountable for generating external funds to cover one-third of the operating budget for their school. In addition, grantsmanship would support academic research, help to build existing programs, and to expand curricular offerings.

Indeed, as stated in the *President's Report, 1980–1981*, Harvey was "committed to providing effective leadership" and to "building a strong institutional framework in academics, governance and student life to enhance the college's role as a model in higher education." He was sailing against the tide of a gloomy projection for higher education in the eighties, but through well-thought-out planning, he steered his course into a bright forecast of successes and accomplishments in his first five years.

Harvey's First Five Years
A Time of Introspection and New Academic Direction

During Harvey's first year as President, which he characterized as "one of excitement, innovation, quality, growth, and stability," the academic unit, in 1978–79, initiated a sequence of internal academic evaluations. It was important to look inward in the late 1970s and the 1980s, because higher education was undergoing critical challenges and Hampton University was intricately connected to this trend. So Harvey, the prognosticator of trends, began an "intense reevaluation and a series of innovations." As his friend Arthur Greene reminds us, Harvey has a "knack for vision, the ability to know what's going to happen before it happens. He can basically convince you or me that something is going to happen. And whether it's by his hand or by fate, it happens. It has happened more than it hasn't." To make those innovations happen, "whether it's by his hand or by fate," Harvey said that it was essential to assess, for example, "matters such as consideration of a core curriculum, the desire to take advantage of our waterfront campus and establish a marine science program, an effort to boost the underrepresentation of minorities and women in the sciences, and a look at our internal academic structure to ascertain if it were sufficient to meet the challenges of the 1980s." Moreover, he appointed task forces to engage in reviewing and planning the instructional program, which related to the needs of a changing student population and the job market. This self-analysis resulted in a myriad of changes, including numerous curricular initiatives, one of which was the initiation of a marine science program. Another milestone in the 1978–1979 academic year was the action by the Board of Trustees and faculty to restructure the undergraduate program into five undergraduate schools "to facilitate more responsible management procedures; clarify lines of communication; enhance administrative leadership for curriculum development, implementation and evaluation; and maximize academic freedom for faculty and students."[6] Beyond the classroom, the First Annual Black Family Conference and the First Annual Young Authors Conference began during his first year of tenure as the President.

In the academic year of 1979–1980, after appointing Martha Dawson as the vice president for academic affairs in July 1979, the evaluation and review continued under her academic leadership. An outcome of the assessment was the marine science program, the first new degree program under Harvey's administration, which was instituted in the fall of 1979, and the first of its kind at an HBCU. Cognizant of the changing technology, computer-assisted instruction was also implemented in the School of Pure and Applied Sciences (now School of Science). In search of other innovative educational approaches, a touring ensemble began in the Department of Speech and Theatre Arts (now Fine and Performing Arts). Harvey noted that the "1979–1980 academic year might well be captioned the Year of Innovations." The first two years of reviewing, planning, and innovation worked to maximize the "effectiveness of our administrative structure through reorganization," contended Harvey.

As the decade of the 1980's approached, the President discerned that the school did not have the physical nor human resources to be "all things to all people," so the institution employed a "system of selective academic excellence." Hampton had to, therefore, "consider reordering of programs and priorities," to strengthen educational processes, to adapt to new social needs and audiences, and to make prudent use of scarce resources. Harvey wrote in the *President's Annual Report, 1980–1981*, "One of the most important indicators that must be judged is the educational program." And he wanted academics at Hampton University to be in the forefront of the American educational enterprise. Recognizing "real strengths in business, mathematics, biology, physics, and chemistry, as well as mass media, communication disorders, architecture, psychology, [and] nursing," he wanted to build on them.

The decade of the 1980s, particularly from 1980–1983, would prove to be a time of "inner growth, development, and educational enrichment." In 1980–1981, with an emergent theme of *qualitative growth*, faculty, staff, and administration worked collaboratively, along with external consultants, as Harvey wrote in his *President's Annual Report, 1980–1981,* "to examine our leadership structure, to identify troublesome issues, to reemphasize the educational purposes of Hampton Institute, and to establish role models for academic administrators." During that year, the restructured academic unit from divisions into schools was implemented. "Instead of only departments and divisions, we now have departments, divisions, and schools headed by deans," said Harvey. The schools, at that time, were Arts and Letters, Business, Education, Nursing, and Pure and Applied Sciences. Moreover, academic deans for each of the schools were appointed. Seemingly, the organization of the academic units into schools had a "salubrious effect" on the departments as evidenced by increased faculty activity, wider participation in proposal writing, the desire to complete requirements for the doctorate, and by an increased sense of community, the President said. Particularly impressive was the amount of grants generated in the School of Pure and Applied Sciences under Robert D. Bonner, the dean, whom the President also credits with building the sciences at Hampton. Writing in his *President's Annual Report, 1980– 1981*, he said: "The research/development activities of the faculty and administrative staff for the past biennium have given reliable data about the college and its potential, intrinsically and extrinsically. Guided by these data and with improved communication at every level, the '80s at Hampton will reflect the direction the college will take in its second century of service."

Academic year 1981–1982 was "our year of 'Assessment, Refinement and Accountability,'" Harvey claimed. The focus shifted to the "needs of college students in a changing society. In response to current trends, we conducted an internal review of past as well as current programs at Hampton and began to explore the implications of high technology for program refinement," he stated. In keeping with the subject, the Assessment and Learning Support Center had its genesis in the fall of 1981. Since its commencement, the center has given indispensable support for the overall academic aims of the University and the specific academic and career goals of individual students. It has generated a profile on each student and developed an efficient method for monitoring students' academic progress, providing academic counseling and tutorial programs, and promoting the successful integration of students into the academic milieu. In addition, the center has achieved outstanding results for the placement of students in honors classes, the reduction of academic probation, and the increase in the student retention rate.

In 1982–1983, the theme, "Enhancement of Academic Programs Through Instructional Technology," helped to facilitate Hampton's administrators, faculty, and staff in the development of an "integrated approach to the use of instructional technology."

Under the auspices of the Office of the Vice President for Academic Affairs, the first University-wide "hands-on" demonstration of microcomputers as a teaching tool was planned and implemented. This venture promoted the fusion of new technology into "teaching, administrative and research processes."

With Martha Dawson at the helm of leadership of the academic team, the academic years of 1980–1981 to 1982–1983 were times of both qualitative and quantitative growth in terms of programmatic offerings. Though the decade of the 1980s, as noted, was a time of retrenchment in academic course offerings for most institutions, at Hampton, it was a time of advancement. A cooperative program in engineering was established with Old Dominion University during the academic year of 1980–1981. And by 1981–1982, six new master's degree programs were approved and three bachelor's degree programs, along with a Navy ROTC program. In fact, under Harvey's leadership during his first five years, Hampton had increased the number of offerings by fifteen new degree-granting major fields of concentration. They included: Bachelor's degree in Computer Science, Marine Science, Criminal Justice, Building Construction Technology, Naval Science, Chemical Engineering, Electronic Engineering; and Master of Business Administration, and Master of Science in Management, Nursing, Physics, Chemistry, Museum Studies. The Master's degree in Nursing achieved accreditation by the National League for Nursing in only two and one-half years. Another example of the cutting edge philosophy under Harvey's leadership was the development of a Navy ROTC program. Hampton had been the first black school in the nation to receive a naval program during World War II. Thus, the program, a reinstitution of an old concept, was designed to attract highly motivated minority students interested in pursuing some area of the natural sciences. These sundry enterprises offered students opportunities to explore and expand career possibilities, as well as gain useful hands-on experiences and greater competency in a special academic area.

The redesigned Continuing Education program reached out to the growing military and other adult populations during the first five years of Harvey's presidency. For example, classes were held on board the *USS Atlanta* submarine, which allowed personnel to continue their education. The Elderhostel program was also held at Hampton for the first time in 1980–81. Two graduate degree programs in business were initiated at off-campus locations during the 1982–1983 year—the Master of Business Administration and the Master of Science in Management.

Harvey felt these new academic directions of marine science, building construction technology, computer science, naval science, and a redesigned continuing education program offered excitement, purpose, and promise. Moreover, to enrich academic offerings on campus life and in the local community, various segments of the college brought outstanding consultants, artists, local, national and international speakers to the campus. Hence, the existing offerings, along with the new directions in the classroom and beyond, convinced him at that time to say, "Hampton Institute is educating its students for today's world." The institution rode the crested waves of retrenchment in the early 1980s and remained on the cutting edge of education via planning for new directions in higher education.

With these new academic offerings, faculty increased by 10.5 percent by the 1982–1983 academic year and their salaries by an average of 25 percent. In the previous year, Harvey said, "We are pleased that Hampton Institute has been able to secure and/or maintain a distinguished faculty which continues to initiate and project new uses of our electronic technology, to enrich programs in the creative and performing arts and to exemplify academic and administrative excellence through their achievements."

At the end of his fifth year, Harvey reminded us that the following goals he set for Hampton in 1978 had been met: development of an MBA program; implementation of a marine science program; initiation of a building technology program; the reorganization of the academic program from the concept of divisions to schools; and, the expansion of the Continuing Education program.

Forging New Links
Academic Years of 1983–1984 to 1987–1988

While the first five years of Harvey's administration were looking inwardly to achieve excellence, the next five were looking outwardly, with the anticipation of forging new links and partnerships beyond the campus to facilitate this end. The introspection and self-analysis were crucial in laying the foundation for university status that would make that linkage a reality. It happened in the 1983–1984 academic year. After a two-year deliberation, the Board of Trustees voted unanimously to establish an umbrella unit for the institution with the name of Hampton University. Upon becoming a university, Harvey wrote in his *Annual Report, 1983–1984*: "I want Hampton University to be a place such as one described by John Masefield, poet laureate of England," who said:

> *There are few earthly things*
> *more beautiful than a university*
> *It is a place where*
> *those who hate ignorance*
> *may strive to know. . .*
> *Where those who perceive truth*
> *may strive to make others see. . .*
> *Where seekers and learners alike,*
> *bonded together in search for knowledge*
> *will honor thought in all its finer ways. . .*
> *Will welcome thinkers in distress or exile,*
> *Will uphold ever the dignity of thought and learning,*
> *and exact standards in all these things. . .*
> *There are few earthly things*
> *more splendid than a university. . .*
> *In these days of broken frontiers*
> *and collapsing values. . .*
> *When dams are down*

and the floods are making misery. . .
When every future looks somewhat grim. . .
And every ancient foothold. . .
Has become a quagmire.
Wherever a university stands it stands
and shines. . .
Wherever it exists, the free minds of men
urged on to full and fair inquiry,
may still bring wisdom into human affairs.

To create a university like John Masefield's, the President indicated that he would accept full obligation for how it unfolded. "As President of Hampton University, ultimately I have the responsibility for whatever happens or does not happen to assure that we offer high quality programs to our students; to establish and maintain high standards of students and institutional performance; to promote excellence and to shepherd our limited resources, keeping in mind cost effectiveness in our operations. We know that excellence costs, but over the long haul mediocrity costs much more."

The strengthening of academic programs and the significant surge in research and grantsmanship during the previous five years led to the name change in July 1984. Harvey pointed out in his *President's Annual Report, 1983–1984* that, "The institution had the structures, facilities, programs, finances, and diversified student body required for an undergraduate college, a graduate college, a college of continuing education. Thus, the governing body, the administration, and faculty, maintained that flexibility under a university umbrella was mandated in terms of offerings, in terms of opportunity for research by faculty and students, in terms of facilities, and in terms of resources." To retain its history and heritage, the undergraduate college continued as Hampton Institute. At the same time, the university status provided for the expansion of opportunities.

In the quest for excellence, Harvey, the perennial visionary, provided the momentum for perpetually reassessing the internal operation of the organization. It is an essential obligation and task of an effective manager. Harvey said in his *President's Annual Report, 1984–1985*, "Every enterprise takes into account the initiatives of individuals and of the organization which results in innovation, coordination and flexibility so that new opportunities may be seized and adjustments to change may be continual and orderly." The leader and his academic team "perceived the need to reassess and reconfigure academic affairs at Hampton from a global rather than a parochial perspective." Accordingly, in 1983–84, "Academic Restructuring for the Twenty-First Century" was the theme. Ten task force committees were appointed by Dawson to generate ten futuristic documents: *Task Force I—Admission of Undergraduate Students; Task Force II—Accountability for Our Graduates; Task Force III—Retrenchment of Programs and Faculty; Task Force IV—Common Freshman Year; Task Force V—Establishment of a Lower and Upper Division; Task Force VI—Hampton Institute Scholar Program; Task Force VII—Graduate Studies and Research; Task Force VIII—High Technology Across the Curriculum; Task Force IX—Writing Across the Curriculum; Task Force X—Hampton Institute: Today and Tomorrow*. These folios explicitly enunciated how then Hampton Institute as an academy of higher education should respond to the emerging needs of their students in future decades. Emanating from *Task Force X—Hampton Institute: Today and Tomorrow* was the recommendation of renaming the institution. Furthermore, the Honors College was a by-product of that forward-thinking document, Hampton Institute Student Scholars Program. Invariably solicitous of the special need to focus on high achieving students, in the 1983–1984 academic year, the President unveiled a plan at the Faculty Institute to establish an Honors College. However, even as early as July 17, 1980, he had established an Honors Task Force committee, and charged it with the responsibility of developing an Honors College and of giving consideration to an honors dormitory. When the committee did not develop the idea as quickly as he hoped, he charged Martha Dawson to expedite the concept in 1983–1984.

While focusing on the academic needs of high achieving students, Harvey did not overlook the 10–20 percent of those who were unprepared in the basic skills of reading, writing, and mathematics. He deemed the University as accountable for rectifying their unpreparedness; therefore, the University instituted basic skills proficiency undertakings to address these issues.

Whether addressing the high-achieving student or one of the 10 to 20 percent with special needs, the President has always put forth the idea that decency is just as important as degrees. At the 1983 Opening Convocation, he proposed the idea for an honor code. "Primarily, the function of such an honor system is to educate—to instill a sense of honor in our student body. Morality is not inborn. It is learned in a specific environment. It is my belief that an Honor System helps to create an environment that is conducive not only to the individual's awareness and development of honorable traits and behavior, but would check against those who would deviate from the established accepted code," he wrote in *The President's Annual Report, 1983–1984*. Feeling that society was losing its sense of "decency, dignity, integrity and self-respect," he reaffirmed that, "We must restore these values in our society, and in the Hampton University community, which is both a reflection of and a contributor to that society."

Other innovative initiatives were implemented. For example, Hampton was one of the first universities in the United States to offer the Investment Banking program. It was designed to provide minority students with increased employment opportunities in the industry.

Harvey proposed future directions of the University, which included emphasizing Hampton's treasures in the arts and humanities; promoting efforts to increase social science research; and championing international education and the concept of distance learning. In the 1983–1984 academic year, the University extended its outreach program with the military by adding a Distance Learning Center at Guantanamo Naval Base in Cuba. Furthermore, the international connection was energized, when in August 1984, Harvey headed a delegation of six other college presidents to the People's Republic of China, a trip sponsored by the United States Government. They were invited to visit the People's Republic of China in an effort to build linkages between American universities and Chinese institutions of higher education.

"Maintaining the Standard of Excellence During a Period of Transition" was Hampton University's goal during the 1984–1985 school year. Harvey pointed out four notable tasks that were accomplished: (1) Hampton's Board of Trustees, recognizing the growth and development of the institution, created three colleges under the umbrella of Hampton University. These colleges were Hampton Institute as the Undergraduate College, the Graduate College, and the College of Continuing Education. (2) "The faculty and staff of the three newly created colleges accepted the challenge to maintain the critical standards congruent with university status." (3) "The Office of the Vice President for Academic Affairs established criteria to be used for the implementation of differential salary increments based on meritorious performance"; and (4) "development of an assessment/ accountability model for student outcome, such as senior seminars, senior theses, standardized testing, and test-taking seminars."

"Enhancing the Quality of Education Through Comprehensive Assessment and Instructional Media," the academic theme for 1985–1986, was the conveyor to improve teaching and learning. Desiring to keep Hampton on the cutting edge of educational change, Harvey recognized that, despite specific disciplines, "students and faculty must have the essential skills and knowledge to employ computers, media, and other high technology in the current information society." So he spoke to that issue, noting that "various constituencies of the University have addressed themselves to the singularly important task of curricular expansion and reform. However, throughout this endeavor, we have remained cognizant of the fact that excellence in

education cannot be achieved exclusively within the rigid structures of the curricula and/or within the narrow confines of the
classroom. Rather, sustained excellence is to be achieved
through continuous assessment of the impact of our curricula
and through the implementation of special programs to complement the curricula." In accordance with that aim and the 1985–86
theme, the University established a Teaching, Learning Technology Center, consisting of three components: (1) production and
equipment; (2) engineering and maintenance; and (3) learning
resources. Moreover, in keeping with the theme of comprehensive assessment, the University also initiated a special program
for Army ROTC Cadets, a project designed to enhance the basic
skills proficiency of minority ROTC Cadets who plan to become
commissioned officers.

The academic year 1986–1987, denoted as the "Year of
Renewal," was designed to assist faculty members in employing
critical thinking skills as a part of the learning process in all disciplines. Harvey stated, "One of the major hurdles facing the University is making the successful transition to the twenty-first
century while maintaining its superior standards of academics
and character. We at Hampton have accepted this challenge by
honing our teaching skills, implementing accountability strategies, and utilizing critical thinking." The Honors College, fully
implemented during the academic year of 1986–1987, serves as a
centerpiece for excellence and as a model for promoting critical
thinking skills. The program is fashioned, said the President, to
encourage "gifted students to pursue academic excellence more
rigorously and to place high moral and ethical standards among
their top priorities." In implementing the Honors College, the
University also fulfilled its inaugural challenge to the faculty.

The academic year 1987–1988 emphasized the subject of
"Moving Forward to a New Era of Excellence." "The theme was
most fitting in that faculty and staff joined with others in the
nation in taking a critical look at the relevance of our curriculum,

the quality of our instruction, and the integrity of our degrees," said Harvey. The establishment of a Center for Teaching Excellence was congruent with this topical direction.

The aforementioned thematic topics were not disparate, pointless exercises in futility, starting and stopping at the end of the academic year, like a stagnant lagoon. Rather, each continued to flow along, aiming for excellence—the larger blueprint of his vision—like perpetual waves in the water of the river seeking their terminus into the vast ocean. And these thematic tributaries were connected to the goal of forging new links and partnerships and to the larger vision of excellence in teaching, research, and service in the promotion of learning and building character. Moreover, they produce results. Academically, from 1983–1984 to 1987–1988, many progressive, pioneering ventures transpired. Although the University is "cognizant of its historical stature, there continues to be a pioneer spirit within the academic community to introduce innovative programs," said Harvey in his *President's Annual Report, 1987–1988*. One such endeavor was the establishment of the Airway Science program at a traditionally black institution. This program, approved by the Federal Aviation Administration and the University Aviation Association, prepares students to enter aviation fields and it offers concentrations in airway science administration, airway computer science, and airway electronics systems. In addition to Airway Science, the curriculum, for example, added a total of twenty-eight new academic programs, including undergraduate programs in financial management, economics, computer systems; and graduate programs in museum studies, applied mathematics, computer education, nutrition; and in the College of Continuing Education, a bachelor's degree in systems organization and management and fire administration. In the College of Continuing Education, for example, when the Fire Administration program was established in 1985, the National Fire Academy in Emmitsburg, Maryland, recognized the Fire Administration Degree program at Hampton University as the most successful program in that region. Moreover, the International

University Consortium for Telecommunications in Learning selected the College of Continuing Education's Baccalaureate Degree program in Systems Organization and Management as the outstanding External Degree program in 1986. Under Harvey's leadership, from 1978 to 1988, the curricula extended by twenty-four new academic programs. The President believed these new programs, together with the existing ones, clearly kept and placed Hampton on the competitive edge of the knowledge explosion in all of higher education. Furthermore, the number of faculty holding the Ph.D. increased from 83 to 132. The number of actual faculty slots increased over a ten-year period from 191 in 1977–1978 to 274 in 1987–1988.

The results of forging links with both public and private sectors, as well as the community, brought more funding to the University. The amount of federally-sponsored research dollars brought in by Hampton's faculty increased from $1,873,529 in 1977–78 to $6,860,352 in 1987–1988. These grants permitted faculty to augment substantially their research activities, which resulted in publications of books and of articles in refereed journals. Similarly, they increased their number of scholarly paper presentations at regional, national, and international conferences. "Since research and scholarly activities enhance teaching, our students have indeed been the beneficiaries of these and other faculty efforts," the President said.

During this period, the University continued to fashion new ties with the community. The School of Nursing, for example, established the Hampton University Interdisciplinary Nursing Center for Health and Wellness, which has become a major source of health care within the Virginia Peninsula.

Although the classroom is the center of education, Hampton University looks at formalized curricula as only one of many venues for educating the total student. According to the *President's Annual Report, 1987–1988*, a ten-year review, vigorous efforts were made, during the 1980s, to provide the campus community with numerous and diverse academic and cultural enrichment projects. The University brought to campus distinguished writers, such as Sonia Sanchez, Toni Cade Bambara, Tony Ardizonne, Gwendolyn Brooks, Toni Morrison, Ernest Gaines, and James Baldwin. Moreover, an annual campus-wide "Read-In," designed to involve all administrators, faculty, students, and staff in the reading, analysis, and discussion of a selected text, was implemented in 1987–88 academic year.

In addition to literary initiatives, a concerted effort was undertaken to bring to the campus special consultants, visiting scholars, such as Vincent Harding, and programs to enhance academic disciplines. Other examples of illuminaries to visit the campus included: Thomas Tobi, 1981 Nobel Laureate in economics; Eric Lincoln, noted author, lecturer, and professor; Mary Hatwood Futrell, then President of National Education Association; Richard P. Keeling, an internationally recognized expert on AIDS; Jesse Lewis Jackson, who delivered the 118th Commencement Address; and L. Douglas Wilder, then Lieutenant Governor of Virginia and later the first African American governor in the nation, who delivered the 119th Opening Convocation Address. In addition to on-campus events, opportunities were available for faculty and students to attend and/or to participate in a variety of off-campus cultural/enrichment activities. Of particular note, during the 1980s, was the frequency of off-campus student excursions to libraries, museums, theatrical productions, operas, seminars, workshops, lectures, and foreign countries. These aforementioned programs and other similar ones supplemented classroom instruction and supported Hampton's original philosophy of an "Education for Life."

Addressing the Educational Imperatives
of the 1990s and Beyond
1988–89 to 1992–93

"As we approached the final decade of the twentieth century, we continued to reject the paralysis of stasis and the indulgence of mediocrity. Instead, we demonstrated our acceptance of change, our boldness of vision, and our courage to address the educational imperatives of the 1990s and beyond," Harvey proclaimed in the *President's Annual Report, 1988–1989*. He began his message to constituents by noting that the

> academic year 1988–1989 marked the beginning of the second decade of my presidency at Hampton University. That this new beginning should roughly coincide with the final decade of this century seemed a most propitious time for assessing the past and anticipating the future. This spirit was evident throughout 1988–89, as we seized upon this moment in the University's history to refine curricula, to inspire faculty and students to greater achievements, and to increase our financial resources. In short, we used this time to build bridges which would facilitate the University's smooth transition into the 1990s and beyond.

Utilizing the theme, "Innovations in Teaching and Learning" for the 1988–1989 academic year, academic administrators and faculty linked internal bridges in a collective venture to reevaluate curricula, the freshman year experience, and instruction in relation to student outcomes. In response to Harvey's charge to develop a core curriculum, and under Martha Dawson's leadership, task forces were established for this initiative. The conscientious efforts of administrators, deans, and faculty members to the charge resulted in a proposed new General Education Curriculum. It required students to complete a common core of courses which constitutes the General Education sequence for the undergraduate college. This proposed core of courses included six (6) hours each of English, humanities, mathematics, social and behavioral sciences, and natural and physical sciences; three (3) hours each of speech and history (World Civilization): and two (2) hours of health and physical education. The most ingenious characteristic of this General Curriculum included a Common Freshman Year Program. "At the heart of this program is an orientation course, 'The Individual and Life,' designed to facilitate the successful transition of freshman students into the University experience," Harvey noted. "This model includes a unique set of common experiences which will begin with the admissions process."

In assisting the University to meet the educational demands of the future, each school and department, during the academic year of 1988–1989, was rife with enterprises and explored innovations in teaching and learning by engaging in a comprehensive reassessment of its particular programs and curricula. Based on these reassessments, the departments restructured their academic programs. For example, the senior thesis or an exit examination became a requirement for graduation in most departments.

"Maintaining Educational Excellence Through General Education" was the focus for the 1989–1990 academic year. Consistent with the University's academic theme for 1989–90, the "New General Education Curriculum with Common Freshman Year" was adopted. Specifically, the model required all freshmen to enroll in the orientation course, "The Individual and Life," implemented as a pilot project during the 1989–1990 academic year and fully instituted in the 1990–1991 academic year. Harvey viewed "University 101" as a radical departure from the models on which orientation courses are primarily based; that is, because its subject matter stems from students' own experiences as young African Americans and from larger issues impacting society as a whole. Thus, the subject matter in certain aspects serves as a segue to the new General Education Core Curriculum. At the same time, the course also gives students a common core of experiences to facilitate their transition to the University environment. University 101 consists of a coordinated series of units that include such topics as "Hampton University: Its History, Legacy, and Future," "African American Art," and "Learning as Innovation." The course format includes plenary sessions and small group sessions. Plenary session presentations are given by Hampton University administrators, senior professors, distinguished scholars from other institutions and prominent individuals with expertise in one of the subject areas that encompass the course. This course continues to enrich the quality of life for entering freshmen by assisting them to understand the value of higher education, to learn more about Hampton University, and to cultivate affirmative attitudes and coping skills indispensable for a productive college experience. Harvey reminded his constituents in his *President's Annual Report, 1989–1990* that his dream of a core curriculum had become a shared reality.

> In my first public address at Hampton University, I called for development of a core curriculum which, among other objectives, would provide every Hampton University student with proficiency in reading, writing, and basic computations; a knowledge and appreciation of history, literature, and the arts; and the infusion of ethical and moral dimensions throughout the curriculum. This charge was based on my belief that there are a set of skills and a body of knowledge which all students should master, regardless of their chosen areas of specialization. During the academic year 1989–90, with the adoption of the core curriculum, my mandate was fulfilled.

The 1989–1990 academic year represented also the transition to a new decade where the emphasis extended to fashioning links with diverse cultures, while reclaiming Hampton's legacy to promote the teaching and learning process. The initiation of the American Educational Opportunities Program serves as an example. Native Americans had matriculated at Hampton from 1878 to 1923, so it was an educational opportunity to resurrect Hampton's historical commitment to educating this group.

This multicultural emphasis expanded and the 1990–1991 academic year focused on "Implementing International and Multi-Cultural Programs" into the curricular offerings. "Reclaiming Our International Legacy" was, for example, the motif of the Winter

Faculty Institute. In Harvey's opening remarks at the 1991 Winter
Faculty Institute, he stated:

> At Hampton we are cognizant of the fact that the world
> continues to become smaller in terms of the extent that the
> various cultures impact on one another. We recognize the
> need to know and understand that our neighbors increase
> daily and that as an institution of higher learning we have an
> obligation to help solve world problems and to contribute to
> the world's progress. Today, international issues touch us
> more than at any other time in our history, perhaps. We are
> affected by the many events that have occurred, particularly
> in Europe, Asia, and Africa. Therefore, we must actively
> reclaim our international legacy.[7]

Dawson, who retired during that year, was instrumental in providing
the leadership initiative in this direction. Consistent with this international focus, the faculty workshop included Linda Terry, an African
American Russian scholar and linguist. In addition, a SALT workshop
on implementing international and multicultural programs laid the
foundation for the International Programs. Throughout the semester,
other departments hosted seminars with an international focus. For
example, during the First Gulf War, the Department of Political Science hosted a conference on "The Middle East: Past, Present, and
Future." The area of Modern Foreign Languages presented a foreign
language month celebration, focusing on four topics: "Contemporary
Afro- American-Brazilian Women Writers," "Political Developments in
the New Germany," "The Black Man's Plight in American-Cuban Perspective" and "Racial Pride Expressed in Afro-Hispanic Poetry." The
highlight of the academic year was the world leader, United States
President George Herbert Walker Bush, who delivered the Commencement Address and received an honorary degree.

In addition to the workshops and speakers focusing on international issues, the University Museum, a chief resource for
research and learning, continued to augment its collections and
to display major exhibitions which contained international collections from Africa. As Harvey indicated, "These efforts were
designed to achieve more integrated teaching and learning and

to ensure the preparation of our students to compete success-fully in a world where knowledge and understanding of world cultures is imperative."

The 1990–1991 academic year also was a time of internal restructuring. The former School of Arts and Letters merged with the School of Education to form the School of Liberal Arts and Edu-cation, which had a two-fold effect—an increased enrollment and an improvement in the quality of students who aspired to teacher education. The President noted, too, that this incorporation has "greatly facilitated increased collaborative academic initiatives at the University. The merging of Special Education and—when pre-ferred by the student—Early Childhood Education with Psychol-ogy is an excellent example of such an initiative."

The 1991–1992 academic year had as its focus, under the new Vice President for Academic Affairs, Elnora D. Daniel, the former dean of nursing, "Creating Partnerships in the Academic Enterprise." While continuing to highlight multiculturalism and the internationalizing of the curriculum, the academic unit stressed developing internal program partnerships among dis-ciplines, developing internal program partnerships with ele-mentary/secondary schools, and with corporate and community agencies. In this vein, faculty members participated in external consultation visits to foreign countries, such as Tanzania and Belgium. These activities were connected to the University ini-tiative of creating academic, economic, cultural, and other part-nerships which empowered the community. Improving teaching through the implementation of an institutional-wide advise-ment model was also a focus for 1991–92.

A much-needed additional academic support unit was the dedication of the William R. and Norma B. Harvey Library. He said, "The dedication of the new William R. and Norma B. Harvey Library was a particular highlight, for which Mrs. Harvey and I are humbly grateful. Over and beyond the personal fulfillment deriv-ing from such an honor, there is the satisfaction that this truly state-of-the-art library will greatly advance the intellectual life of the University."

The academic year of 1992–1993 was a time of celebration of the 125th Anniversary of Hampton's founding. It was also a time to reassess the past and prepare for the next century. So it was appropriate to have the theme "Shifting Paradigms: Reshaping the Future of Hampton University Through Strategic Planning" as its focus. Harvey remarked, "The future challenge to Hampton University is the challenge to all institutions of higher education: to achieve financial stability, to maintain excellence, and to remain relevant in a changing world." Accepting the challenge, he charged the University community to engage in a year-long strategic planning process, which brought under intense scrutiny its total operation: academic programs, institutional culture and values, the educational environment, the student body facilities, academic support, finances, and administrative efficiency and effectiveness. While some academic departments like building technology, human ecology, and social work were recommended to be phased out, others like the Department of Art and Department of Speech Communication and Theatre Arts merged to become the Fine and Performing Arts. Other new programs were endorsed, such as pharmacy and physical therapy, to meet the demands of a changing workplace. The outcome of the planning was implemented in the 1994–1995 academic year.

Again the themes were an integral component of Harvey's aim-toward-excellence philosophy, one which is results-oriented. Growth and change continued in the expansion of the academic curriculum. In a period of retrenchment in higher education, Hampton's Department of Engineering received accreditation in 1991–92. Harvey noted that the "very able" leadership was provided by Adeyinka Adeyiga, chair of the department, and Trustee Ernest Drew, who chaired the Engineering Advisory Board. To keep Hampton on the cutting edge of the higher education enterprise, eight new academic programs were introduced, including the first Ph.D. degree granting program, which was in physics. It was introduced in 1992–93. Demetrius Venable, then chair of the physics department and later a provost, played a significant role in this development. By Harvey's fifteenth year, fifty-one new academic programs had been introduced, although many were eventually phased out.

Faculty continued also to be involved in significant research centers. The three most important were the Minority Research Center of Excellence in Nuclear High Energy Physics, funded by the National Science Foundation; the Research Center for Optical Physics, funded by the National Aeronautics and Space Center; the Center for Fusion Research and Training, funded by the Department of Energy and housed in the Department of Mathematics.

Preparing for Twenty-First Century
1993–1994 to 1997–1998

"Confronting and Resolving Ethical Dilemmas in the Academy: Revitalizing the Institutional Culture and Values of Hampton University," the motif for the 1993–1994 academic year, was a fitting focus for the afterglow of the previous year-long 125th Anniversary Celebration and the implementation of the strategic plan. The academic year 1993–1994 marked a crucial turning point for Hampton University; that is, a renewed shared vision by all constituents emerged as a result of the execution of the strategic plan initiatives. Harvey reiterated that, "These initiatives were a part of a continuing effort to improve the total Hampton University culture. Emphasizing academic excellence, character-building, and efficiency and excellence in all things, this newly emerging culture was evident in every aspect of the University's programs, events, and operations. . ."

Academically, in 1993–1994, Hampton University had a banner year. In the fall of 1993, *U.S. News and World Report* identified Hampton as number fourteen among the top fifteen regional universities in the South. To this honor, the President responded: "Such an accolade is not easily won and is impossible to achieve without a shared vision of where we are and of what we can and must become in the years ahead."

The University set in motion a series of academic changes and innovations. These innovations were designed to improve the quality of academic programs and to ensure their relevancy in a global political economy. First and foremost, as a result of the strategic plan in 1993, the University adopted a new mission, stressing that it is now a "comprehensive institution of higher education, dedicated to the promotion of learning, building of character, and preparation of promising students for positions of leadership and service. Its curricular emphasis was scientific and professional, with a strong liberal arts undergirding." In line with the new mission, there was a restructuring of the sciences and engineering. Harvey argued that "in order to leverage its considerable strength in engineering and the sciences and to address the underrepresentation of minorities in these fields, the University established a School of Engineering and Technology. The establishment or reconfiguration of these schools is consistent with the University's professional and scientific curricular emphases."

With funding from the Kellogg Foundation and Hampton's long-standing commitment to minority entrepreneurship and economic development, the University also established a Center for Entrepreneurial Studies. It was designed to "increase the quantity and quality of minority entrepreneurs; to improve the ownership/investor share of capital resources for minority populations; to contribute to a literature flowing from applied research and practical experience; to provide educational programming and technical assistance to minority individuals, organizations, and colleges and universities; and to develop and phase in an entrepreneurship major in Hampton's School of Business and, hopefully, to be replicated at other historically black colleges and universities. The Center for Entrepreneurial Studies positions the University to become a leader and authority in the areas of entrepreneurship, intrapreneurship, and related ventures," the President noted.

A new grading system was approved and the Code of Conduct for students and University personnel was inaugurated. Congruous with that component of the strategic plan, which calls for more rigorous academic standards, the University adopted the use of plus and minus letter grades and approved a new grading scale, which increases the requirements for an A by three points. The President noted that, "These initiatives are designed to challenge more rigorously our increasingly more capable student body."

With the adoption of the Code of Conduct, which underscores the values of honesty, decency, integrity, dignity and respect for oneself and one's fellow man, the President fulfilled another vision that he presented at the Opening Convocation in 1983. He proclaimed that, "At Hampton, we believe strongly that the building of character and the teaching of moral values are as important as the teaching of academic disciplines and that they should be an integral part of the total teaching-learning process."

Finally, arising from the University's strategic plan was the implementation of programs/activities designed to promote the muticulturalism and globalization throughout the curricula. Almost from its beginning, Hampton University has encouraged the participation of its students in an international exchange program.

The 1994–1995 academic year's theme, "Improving the Hampton University Culture: From Rhetoric to Reality: Implementing the Strategic Plan" was, as Harvey noted, a pivotal year in "the life of Hampton University, a year characterized by immense energy, motion, and change, a turning point which concretized elements of the University's new mission, which emerged from our 1993 strategic planning process. Prominent among these elements was phase-one implementation of initiatives which undergird the University's new scientific and technological emphases." As an example, that academic year saw the commencement of a partnership among the government, private industry, and the University that catapulted the Hampton University/Hughes Aeroscience Center, now known as the Hampton University/Raytheon Aeroscience Center, into existence. The center is designed to prepare minorities, women and the economically disadvantaged for career positions in the commercial aviation industry. It offers fully accredited programs in aviation maintenance training; professional pilot training; aviation management; air traffic control; aviation safety; meteorology; and advanced training, research and development. Additionally, the reaccreditation/accreditation of programs in the sciences and engineering, and a restructuring of programs in these fields positioned the University to remain competitive on the higher education landscape in training well prepared minorities in these career fields.

"The Hampton Renaissance: Promoting and Ensuring Teaching Excellence" was the focus for the academic year 1995–1996. "The University renewed its emphasis on effective and responsible teaching while strengthening the value of 'community,'" said Harvey. Exemplary of this effort of teaching excellence was the Department of Communicative Sciences and Disorders, which achieved national visibility as one of only six historically black colleges and universities with an accredited Master's degree program in the discipline of speech, language, and hearing. Moreover, the graduates of the program passed the National Examination in Speech-Language Pathology at 95 percent pass rate, which was much higher than the national average for African Americans (65 percent) who passed this examination on their first attempt. Furthermore, the program has graduated more African-American speech-language pathologists than any university in America.

Faculty members and students extended the learning process beyond the classroom and focused on international education. For example, the Department of Chemistry expanded its Research and Study Abroad Program in Tanzania for biology and chemistry majors through the Minority Institution Research Training (MIRT)

Program. Other students in the MIRT Program began a Research and Study Abroad Program in Helsinki, Finland.

The Department of Physics continued its outstanding work with the Thomas Jefferson National Accelerator Facility. Harvey pointed out that Hampton University, the first large partnership with the world-renown Jefferson Lab, helped not only to strengthen the Ph.D. program in Physics, but also resulted in many pivotal collaborative projects. The Center's director, Hermann Grunder, praised the great accomplishments of Hampton's Nuclear and High Energy Physics (NUHEP) Center of Excellence as noted in the *President's Annual Report, 1995–96*. According to Dr. Grunder, Hampton University has made "one of the greatest contributions of any university group. . . to the successful completion of the first Jefferson Lab physics experiments."

During the academic year of 1995–96, the University continued to diversify the curricular offerings and activities, which integrally related to the promoting and insuring of teaching excellence. In that vein, a two-year Pre-Pharmacy program was instituted. Additionally, in response to the technological revolution and what it portends for the future of education, the University opened a state-of-the-art Academic Technology Mall (ATM) to "facilitate the design of teaching models for the campus of the future and to prepare our students to meet the educational and technological demands of the twenty-first century and beyond," said Harvey. He noted, too, that, "While the faculty are at the heart of the educational process, the institution has worked arduously to provide the structure and climate to support, promote, and reward effective teaching. Thus, the Academic Technology Mall (ATM), which opened in 1995–96, facilitated the goal of obtaining excellence by involving students and faculty in long distance learning through means of telecommunications and other multimedia equipment. "I wanted all Hampton students to have an appreciation for the role of technology in the global economy," the President said. "The Academic Technology Mall holds enormous potential for enhancing the University's teaching, research, distance learning, and administrative functions. By infusing process learning and information literacy across the curriculum, these technologies promise to revolutionize the educational process at Hampton."

"Building the Educational Enterprise: The Business of Vision, Leadership, Ownership and Advocacy," the focus for the theme for the 1996–1997 academic year, continued with the idea of raising the bar in the teaching and learning process. To this end, the University developed a model for teaching excellence, defined in student outcome. The President stated, "The goals of the Hampton University Model for Teaching Excellence are designed to strengthen the teaching and learning process by focusing on the teaching behavior of the instructor. The Hampton University model emphasized a systematic program of faculty for: 1) enhancing curriculum objectives and content; 2) identifying and implementing characteristics of effective teaching; 3) retaining outstanding faculty." The model requires changes in the course requirements, which reflect "the technological, economic, and social influences of a futuristic society." Such changes include a minimum foreign language requirement; the addition of required professional development courses for all students; increased opportunities for international travel; the requirement of a business-related sport; the expansion of English 101–102 composition and literature requirements; and expanded choices of electives in the social science discipline. All departments are required to review their curriculum.

In keeping abreast of the changes in the workplace, the president appointed a task force and charged it with the responsibility to review the tenure process. The perusal of the literature indicated that a five-year post-tenure review was the best way to maintain the high standards of faculty productivity. Responding to the finding, the President asserted: "We must incorporate a mechanism for the continuous review of senior faculty by exploring measures that have the potential for supporting resilient careers and promoting the adaptability of faculty for what should be the capstone of their professional lives."

"Hampton University: Advancing the Learning Revolution Through Human Resources Development, Fund-raising, Accreditation and Technology Enhancement" was the theme for 1997–1998. The year was focused on assessing teaching quality, integrating technology into the classroom, developing proposals, and clarifying issues in ethics. It also marked another five-year milestone of Harvey's presidency, a time to take stock of his numerous achievements. Among his attainments, six new programs were added between 1993–1998. In the 1992–1993 academic year, the university's first Ph.D. program (in physics) was established and its first Ph.D. degree (in Physics) was awarded at the Commencement in 1998. Two more doctoral programs were added in 1997 and 1998, respectively— one in pharmacy and one in physical therapy. A fourth program in nursing was approved by the State Council of Higher Education for Virginia. One outcome of these enterprising and prescient changes is that Hampton has one of the highest graduation rates of African American undergraduates with science degrees. At the same time, increased opportunities are occurring at the graduate level. Grant activities also multiplied during the 1997–98 academic year. Faculty brought in over $23 million worth of federal grants and contracts, compared to $13 millions five years earlier and $3.8 million in 1978.

Moving Into the Twenty-First Century
The Focus on Globalism, Technology, and Teaching
The Academic Years 1998–99 to 2002–03

In the 1998–1999 academic year, the Faculty Institute theme, "Beyond 2000: Curriculum, Technology, and Globalization," presignified Hampton's readiness for the new millennium. The University, therefore, continued to assess curriculum and to examine ways to integrate technology and globalization in the teaching and learning process within and beyond classroom walls. To facilitate this process, a university-wide distance learning think tank was established to develop innovative ways to articulate the teaching-learning undertaking. The College of Continuing Education, which offered the university's first on-line academic course in business finance during the year, served as an example for other web-based courses.

Though Harvey sees technology as an effective tool in the teaching process, it is not a replacement for effective teaching. He reminded new faculty in his opening remarks on August 24, 1998 that:

> As a new faculty member, you have an important responsibility in this community of scholars. First and foremost, you have an obligation to be a good teacher, thereby ensuring the students are not short-changed. At Hampton University, it is not enough to be well-informed of their respective discipline and to remain abreast of current trends. . . . Teaching excellence. . . requires that faculty take a personal interest in the lives of our students. It means that you make the effort to enhance not only the mind of the student, but the spirit and character as well. . . . Interacting with students only within the confines of the classroom is not the best example of excellent teaching. Certainly it is necessary for you to make the effort to attend their presentations, assemblies, and other activities which take place during the evenings and on weekends. As well, it is appropriate to invite them into your home and space. Not only will this show them that they are more than a means to a paycheck for you, it shows that you do take a personal interest in them. It is also the best way I can think of to serve the role of role model for them, a role very many of them desperately need to be played in their lives.

Since teaching is considered the highest priority for the President, the 1999–2000 academic year began with the theme, "Institutional Change: Preparing for the Future Through Teaching Standards, Tenure Options, and Technology-Based Instruction." The emphasis was on advancing the learning revolution through technology enhancement and refining curriculum in a world dominated by technology. Each department was required to submit a three-year long-range plan for integrating technology into the classroom. Issues of accountability, curriculum, faculty evaluation, and tenure options were also topics for discussion. To ensure teaching effectiveness, the instructional and administrative assessment and accountability model, designed to safeguard the national reputation of the University, was implemented in 1999. All faculty members are, henceforth, required to comply with minimum standards for delivery of instructions.

With the implementation of a Ph.D. in nursing in the fall of 1999, students increased their professional career opportunities in the health fields. In addition, the Ph.D. program in nursing, which focuses on research to advance knowledge and to promote effective health care policies and practices, launched an on-line distance education component to its program.

In the academic year of 2000–2001, the teaching theme continued. "Profile of the Hampton Faculty for the New Millennium," focused on different teaching and learning styles, strategies and student outcomes. Specifically, the fall Faculty Institute emphasized the faculty's responsibility in fostering student leadership. It underscored the launching of the Leadership Institute in the fall of 2000. As Harvey has emphasized repeatedly, in leadership, having a good ethical grounding is as essential as having a degree. Therefore, students selected for the Leadership Institute, regardless of the major field of study, are required to take a course in ethics and leadership each semester. In addition, they are required to perform community service. The Institute has become another one of Harvey's dreams translated into reality.

As previously noted, President Harvey's visions are not doled out as piecemeal plans. Rather, they are connected to a larger strategic one. In this grand design, each department and school must submit an annual five-year operational plan to the Provost, which includes projected budget, curriculum changes, student enrollment and retention, faculty recruitment, grantsmanship, and a technology plan.

During the 2001–2002 academic year, the motif, "HU Strategic Planning: Maintaining the Competitive Edge," reminded faculty and administrators of the importance of planning in implementing Harvey's vision. At the Faculty Institute, teachers participated in workshops demonstrating the application and integration of technology to the teaching process. The advances in technology are not only changing styles of learning, but how and what students learn. "A World in Transition: The Role of Academic Affairs," the theme for the 2002–2003 academic year, focused on global issues and on the role of international affairs on academic programs in ensuring the proficiency of students to meet future challenges. In addition, the Faculty Institute addressed the transitions in technology and the challenges they posed for students, such as maintaining competence in reading and writing skills across the curriculum.

Since Harvey believes teaching excellence is priority in the mission of the University, he understands that to maintain the competitive edge on the higher education landscape, it is important to connect the campus to the global community through technology, through expanding curriculum, through research and grantsmanship, and through capital improvements. During the past five years, Harvey added seven new programs, such as computer engineering, Spanish, management information systems, medical science and nursing, as well as enhanced old ones. The Scripps Howard School of Journalism and Communications opened in the fall of 2002. "Students will benefit from all our hard work," Harvey said at the groundbreaking ceremony held in September 2000. "We will revolutionize journalism and journalism education in this country. We want to move people of color into newsrooms, executive suites, and boardrooms. We have a long way to go and that's why this partnership is important."

Other academic programs have been initiated during the past five years, such as a five-year MBA program in the School of Business. A value-added equestrian course was offered for the first time in 2002. The College of Continuing Education, in 2000–2001, also began offering classes at the Roanoke Higher Education Center in Roanoke, Virginia. In addition to the new programs, the

School of Pharmacy, under the leadership of Arcelia Johnson-Fannin, received its accreditation in 2002 and conferred twenty-eight doctorates at the 2002 Commencement exercises—its first graduating class in pharmacy. Likewise, the Department of Physical Therapy, under Marilys Randolph, graduated its first class with thirteen doctorates in physical therapy, and, in 2002, the School of Nursing also granted its first doctoral degree.

Hampton's faculty members also increased their grantsmanship activities. In 2002, as previously noted, Hampton received a $92 million grant, under the leadership of James Russell and his team, to study nighttime clouds. Hampton, with five other institutions, is taking the lead role in the project. In competing for this grant, Hampton won out over universities such as the University of California at Berkeley, Stanford University, The Johns Hopkins University, the University of Colorado, and Washington University at St. Louis.

With its mission to develop an "Education for Life," over the past twenty-five years, the energetic master builder keeps adding stones to build up Hampton's valley. And he has shouldered more boulders to build academic programs than any of his predecessors.

Anchoring Art
An Education for Life

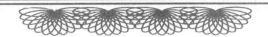

"Art is man's expression of his joy in labor."
—William Morris

The mission of Hampton University is to infuse its students with an "Education for Life." Art, like athletics, is an exemplary mooring for this calling—an enterprise where the head, hand, and the heart are welded together. Under President Harvey's leadership, he has not only balanced symmetrically the visual arts and athletics, he has angled them toward a crown of excellence. Between 1978–1992, for example, more than 1,700 pieces of art were added to the Hampton University Museum collection, increasing the total holdings to over 9,000 artifacts and works of art.

The University's museum collection is one of the largest and strongest of its kind in the United States. Acknowledged as one of the United States' outstanding cultural resources, and as one of the leading repositories of African and African American art in the country, the museum's corpus of paintings, works on paper, and sculpture is among the *crème de la crème* of collections in African American art internationally. It is by far the choicest collection affiliated with any HBCU or with any African American museum. Approximately three hundred and eighty-six significant pieces were added to the museum's fine arts collection between 1978–1991, bringing the total number of works to over 1,700.

The museum also houses the archives, which contains over 8 million manuscript materials and 50,000 photographs. The archives is among the nation's most important resources for research on the history of African American and Native American education. Here one can find the nation's first African American Poetry Archive, which was established under Harvey's administration. In recognizing the contributions of African American notables such as Phyllis Wheatley, W. E. B. Du Bois, and Langston Hughes, the President felt that it was crucial to establish Hampton University as a "cultural mecca for the exhibition and study of African American art, artifacts, and poetry."

In art, Harvey's philosophy is to strive toward excellence. "Excellence is sought by Hampton University in every area of its programs and operations. However, to achieve distinction is only the beginning, for excellence is a continuing process of maintaining quality and superiority," Harvey wrote in his *President's Annual Report, 1990–1991*. And with obtaining such distinction, how did the anchor blocks of art come to be framed so successfully?

Framing Art

The successful framing of art is the result of the vision of one man, along with a supportive team. Harvey wanted "Hampton to be a place where art can flourish again." It is what he said to John Biggers in the late 1980s when Harvey commissioned him to paint the murals for the William R. Harvey and Norma B. Harvey Library. A decade earlier, in 1978, his eyesight was focused on that path, when he toured the museum, then located in the Academy Building, and saw a cache of valuable art stored away and concealed from public viewing. "What he initially saw and understood was the value of these collections, how important they were, what quality they were, and how they could be used more widely. They should be known more widely and they could make a real contribution on this campus to the teaching program, to the cultural environment, and beyond that to the scholarly world and to the community in general," said Jeanne Zeidler, former director of the museum. What Harvey also saw that day in 1978 was the oldest African American museum in this country, established in 1868, and one of the first two museums to be established in the Commonwealth of Virginia. He also saw two paintings by Henry O. Tanner, procured in 1894, which resulted in Hampton University becoming the first institution in the United States to establish a collection of African American art. One of these acclaimed paintings, *The Banjo Lesson*, is recognized as perhaps the most revered of any work by an African American artist. Understanding the value of this collection, and in order to facilitate the growth of art at Hampton University, he hired Jeanne Zeidler in 1980 and a support staff to reclaim the University's legacy of preserving and promoting art.

Almost from its commencement in 1868, the school's faculty, staff, and students regarded the collecting of art, artifacts, and folklore of peoples of color as a consequential ingredient of their mission and as an integral component of Hampton's curricular and extracurricular undertakings. General Samuel Chapman Armstrong, Hampton Institute's founder and first principal, proclaimed the centrality and relevance of African American and American Indian art forms to the greater cultural enterprise when he avowed that "the Negro has the only American music; the Indian has the only American art."[1]

While Harvey, like Armstrong, viewed Hampton as a place where art could grow, Richard J. Powell in "Seeing and Thinking About the Unexpected in American Art," reminds us that "Teaching, collecting and exhibiting the visual arts at HBCUs has been a labor-intensive enterprise not entirely supported by these institutions. Rather than becoming established as a long-range agenda by administrators and trustee boards, the collecting and exhibiting of art at HBCUs has occurred when someone acts as a catalyst to make things happen."[2]

That catalyst stemmed from Harvey's own values and views, and his vision about and strong support of the arts. Arguably, he contended, an educated person is one who is "exposed to, understands, and appreciates many aspects of life." Therefore, the individual "needs to know something about not only art, but African American art." Harvey believes that, "Interest in any kind of art should be for its beauty, its functionality, the enhancement of its surroundings, and its investment. Interest by African Americans in African American art is social, aesthetic and cultural." Paraphrasing Samella Lewis, he asserted, "The interest is also for self-discovery, self-understanding, and cultural identity." And "for both blacks and whites," he maintained that "it is important to know that blacks have been contributing in this medium for a long time." Drawing upon the inspiration of Jacob Lawrence, renowned artist, Harvey quoted him, saying: "There is a need to make known the uniquely creative, artistic and philosophical aspirations, social motivations, and scope of black artists throughout the development of arts in the United States."[3] In sum, art for Harvey, particularly African American art, "is a labor of love, a thing of beauty, and a source of investment." Jeanne Zeidler noted that Harvey indicated to her that "one of the motivations for his own collection, that is prominently displayed in his home, was to create an environment where his children could see some cultural figments and role models through the art on the walls."

For over thirty years, he and his wife, Norma, have been collecting art by African Americans. Their interest was kindled when he purchased his first piece from David Driscoll, renowned artist and then Chair of the Department of Art at Fisk University in the late 1970s. Since that time, they have acquired one of the largest personal collections of works in "private hands" by African Americans in the United States. It includes such artists of the nineteenth century as Robert Scott Duncanson, Edward M. Bannister, and Henry O. Tanner; in the twentieth century such artists as Stephanie Pogue, Walter Williams, Mal Gray Johnson, Romare Bearden, Aaron Douglas, David Driscoll, Lois Mailou Jones, William Tolliver, Palmer Hayden, Paul Keene, Claude Fiddler, and Jacob Lawrence; and artists affiliated with Hampton University, such as John Biggers, Samella Sanders Lewis, Elizabeth Catlett, Charles White, and Loraine W. Bolton.

Whether it is a nineteenth- or a twentieth-century artist or a Hampton-affiliated artist, the President speaks knowledgeably about his collection. Such was the case when he spoke before the newly initiated University 101 class at Hampton in 1989, a course in which a coordinated series of modules included a focus on African American art and the University history. Both units stemmed from his idea that it is important for Hampton students to "understand their culture and heritage." That day Harvey conversed easily about nineteenth century and other contemporary artists, such as Joshua Johnson, and Samella Sanders Lewis. He discussed with finesse two of Lewis' oil on board paintings in his collection, which were done in 1943. "There is a story surrounding them that you might find interesting. She was first asked to do the paintings by the chaplain of then Camp Lee here in Virginia. Both are scenes depicting soldiers, one called *The Preaching* and one *Returning Home*. When the officer saw the paintings and saw that the subjects were African Americans, they asked her to change the faces. She refused, and the chairman of the Department [of Art], Dr. [Leo] Lowenthal, supported her in this matter. Therefore, Camp Lee refused to accept the paintings. They were then just placed in a storage for most of the time since she painted them in 1943. I saw them and liked them and bought them," he revealed.

With his genuine appreciation for the "work of fine artists and their ability to convey not only beauty but strength of character and a very positive message through their work," Harvey thinks that is "something to be nurtured and to be encouraged as an important part of this campus environment," stated Zeidler. Accordingly, the museum has become an important teaching and learning resource for one's "history and heritage," because, in the best sense, it has combined "two separate entities as part of a cultural whole," Zeidler asserted. "The way we interpret both our

African, and actually all of our collections, is in part through the history and how and why these collections came to be here over a hundred-and-thirty-some-year period."

Unarguably, for Harvey, no dialectical tensions exist between his aspirations for preserving and promoting the rich history and heritage of artists of African and Native American descent for himself and his family, and his dreams of having a museum that houses the best art collection, not only as a "thing of beauty," but as a teaching, learning, and research tool for students, for the Hampton family, and for public viewing. Zeidler surmised that Harvey views the museum as a learning resource for "art and production of artists, the vision of artists, and the way artists communicate as part of the richness of life and the richness of what is offered on this campus in terms of the learning environment. Students may be pursuing careers in science or medicine or education or politics, or anything else, but to be well-rounded and thoughtful and caring individuals, they need exposure. And they need understanding of the arts and humanities and their own history."

Such a teaching and learning tool was not the case when Harvey toured the museum in 1978, and found, as Zeidler noted, that "most of the collections in storage had very low usage." But early in his tenure at the University, she stated that:

> Dr. Harvey, along with Dr. Martha Dawson, came up with this vision to create what they called a cultural center—a combining of the holdings of the museum and the archives or cultural resources to make a center that could better be used for teaching, learning, and research. They applied in 1980 for a Challenge grant from the National Endowment for the Humanities, and went about to make this a reality. He set this as a goal to improve the facilities and the operations of both the museum and the archives. I think it's really important to say that from the beginning, it was his vision and his real understanding of the importance of these materials that made it possible in the next fifteen years to bring the kind of recognition to this museum.

As Zeidler claimed, Harvey made enormous contributions to the growth of art on campus, along with the supportive role of Martha Dawson during those early years. Clearly, Dawson can recall talking with Harvey about the museum, to which she refers as a "national treasure." "He had a little drawing that he kept in his armoire. 'When we get the money, Dr. Dawson,' [we will build a museum] he would say. We talked about it and he kept on and would be encouraging you to bring in your ideas, so they finally got the money [to renovate a building for the museum]."

Before obtaining the money, however, to properly house the art collections in the $6 million renovated Huntington Building in 1997, Harvey worked on the University's acquisitions. Collecting was a way to meet the museum's primary goal. As then in 1868 and now, the aim is "to provide knowledge and understanding of, and respect for, diverse cultures and artistic traditions," said Harvey. Such a goal is achieved "through the collection, preservation, research, and interpretation of significant works of art and artifacts," which "supports the University's tradition of national and international leadership in multicultural education." Therefore, through a combination of carefully considered purchases and gifts from numerous donors, the museum's acquisitions grew significantly during the twenty-five years of his presidency. It especially grew from 1978 to 1991 by 1,756 artifacts and works of art. In the fine arts, 395 pieces of African American art were collected; in African art, 818; Native American, 94; Hampton University History, 302; Asian Pacific, 147.

African American Art

In 1986, Harvey "put the first sizeable amount of money toward acquisitions, so that we could continue to build the collection. It was important to not only recognize the importance of what we had was valuable, and significant beyond this campus, but the thought that you don't keep a collection strong and important without constantly improving it and adding to it. That was something he was aware of from the beginning," said Zeidler. Twenty-nine works were obtained from Ida Mae Cullen, widow of the renowned Harlem Renaissance poet, Countee Cullen. These paintings and sculptures are the productions of six major twentieth century artists, most of whom were part of his innermost circle of friends. Always building on the vitality of the institution, Harvey was keenly aware that this collection would merge well with the other works created during, and inspired by the Harlem Renaissance. A 1967 gift from the Harmon Foundation donated hundreds of inestimable pieces from the Harlem Renaissance. After purchasing the rare group of works from Cullen's widow, the museum added other artists' works of the Harlem Renaissance period, such artists as Lois Mailou Jones and Walter Ellison.

Cognizant that African American artists made significant contributions a century prior to the Harlem Renaissance era, one aim of the museum was to obtain exemplary works by the major African American artists of the nineteenth century. A religious painting by Henry O. Tanner was the first work purchased in 1984, which increased the Museum's Tanner holdings to a collection of nine. In 1991, two Tanner etchings were procured to show the range of his work. In 1989, other works purchased of nineteenth century artists included paintings by Joshua Johnson, Robert Scott Duncanson, and Edward Mitchell Bannister. The 1991 purchase of a landscape by James Ethan Porter added to this impressive nineteenth-century group.

While the 1980s focused on the collection of nineteenth century pieces, and at the same time filled in voids from the University's Harlem Renaissance collection, the 1990s turned to acquiring works by renowned contemporary artists like Ron Adams's superb self-portrait, *Profile in Blue*, and three works by William Tolliver, and procuring the most extensive collection of works by Jacob Lawrence. Harvey remarked, "At Hampton University, the persistent support of African American artists and the continued nurturing of the development of an African American art tradition is an important institutional priority. This commitment is reflected in the acquisition of prime works by notable contemporary artists." Some of these outstanding artists, whose works have been acquired by the museum, have a Hampton connection or were trained there as a student, such as Charles White and Elizabeth Catlett. In the 1990s, Elizabeth Catlett, who has a Hampton connection, designated Hampton as her archives for her works on paper. Her generosity was the result of improvements in the museum's physical facilities, its collection storage, its reputation, and its staff. Zeidler noted that Catlett is also working with the University to acquire each of her best works on paper. According to Zeidler:

> We are now up to about 109 pieces in that collection. So this is becoming an incredible repository. For the same reason [1999], Samella Lewis offered through a gift and a purchase arrangement to make available to Hampton twenty-one sculptures by Richmond Barthe. Its just an incredible collection, the largest collection of his work in any museum. We've got the largest collection of Elizabeth Catlett's work; the largest of John Biggers' work, with over one hundred pieces acquired through a gift and purchase; the largest of Samella Lewis' work, and these are all pretty recent developments because these artists and collectors recognize that to put work in Hampton's collection is to put them not only in good company and a great collection, but also that Hampton has the knowledge, the desire, and the ability to care for these pieces and to make them available to researchers and to the general public. These are residual benefits of the sort of sustained commitment and support for the arts that Dr. Harvey has demonstrated over the period of years he's been here.

These residual advantages include, not only a permanent exhibition—*Soul and Spirit: Two Centuries of African American Art*—organized from Hampton's African American fine arts collection and the only one of its kind on permanent display in any American museum of African American artists from various periods, but a periodic Artists-in-Residence program of African Americans at Hampton University, which was initiated in 1988–1989. To offer a different perspective and a fresh vision, accomplished artists like Ron Adams, the printmaker, Claude Fiddler, and William Tolliver are brought to the campus to work with students in the visual arts. John Biggers, renown artist and a Hampton alumnus, was also an artist-in-residence for 14 months while he painted the two 20' x 10' mural panels that hang in the atrium of the Harvey library. These murals also exemplify the President's commitment to public art. According to Biggers, "The paintings are a metaphor for the human experience of growing, learning, thinking and developing sensitivity and responsibility." One panel is called *House of the Turtle*, and the other panel is called *Tree House*. Both panels illustrate the strength of the "Great Mother," as Biggers stated that the mural is dedicated to women. Both panels are inspired by the past and the future of Hampton University.

In the early 1980s, through the encouragement of Biggers, Harvey provided the support to restore the long-neglected Charles White mural, painted in 1943. It was brought back to visibility on campus in a 1981 rededication ceremony. Included in this panoramic mural, along with such great people as Harriet Tubman, Booker T. Washington, George Washington Carver and Paul Robeson, is the common man, with his wife and child, fighting for a better life.

The Booker T. Washington Memorial further illustrates Harvey's commitment to public art. Zeidler noted that Harvey convinced the State of Virginia that "here was an illustrious graduate of our school who made such an impact on this nation that he deserved to have a real monument on the campus. That was the first piece of sculpture not only on the campus but in the City of Hampton when that piece was commissioned and dedicated in 1984."

Zeidler noted that:

> The President has encouraged people to look at the arts as an important part of life and has supported it in different ways. The fact that he has continuously built his own collection and that it is displayed very prominently in his residence, which is a place that is used for so many public functions, that people who go into the Mansion House understand that art is an important part of the environment on this campus. He certainly has encouraged students in the art department to

pursue their talents and their studies by visits to the art department and by talking with them and encouraging them. He purchases works that they have done, and what could be more encouraging to a fledgling artist than having somebody show their approval and support of your work by purchasing a piece of your work and wanting to own it?

Harvey's support of the arts, like Samuel Armstrong's, also embraces a multicultural perspective, an important tool for learning and appreciating different cultures.

Native American Art

The heritage of Native Americans is integrally connected to Hampton. Between 1878 and 1923, an American Indian Education program, which was initiated by Samuel Armstrong, enrolled more than 1,300 students from sixty-five tribes. During that forty-five-year period, Hampton University's Native American art and artifacts were developed to heighten awareness and greater appreciation for Native American cultures and to conserve a peoples' heritage that was in rapid transition. According to the *President's Annual Report, 1990– 1991*, ninety-four pieces have been added since 1978 to supplement the original crux of this collection, including the gift by collectors, the A. Harvey Schreters, of a group of rare pre-Columbian textiles. In 1986, a significant contribution of American Indian textiles and works of art on paper was received from Helen Farr Sloan, the wife of a noted artist, illustrator, and educator, who was instrumental in furthering the preservation and appreciation of Native American arts. These works helped to place "Hampton's long-standing interest in Native American art in a national and an historical context."

Additional acquisitions since 1978 reflect the University's sustaining dedication to Native American education and to the conservation and documentation of Native American cultures, particularly those pieces that are related to Hampton's historic program. Perhaps most notable in this grouping is a collection of contemporary pots made in the traditional method by members of the Pamunkey Indian Pottery Guild.

The University is building its collection of representative contemporary pieces by prominent living Native American artists that show the continuity of cultural traditions. Beginning in 1999, the University began maintaining a permanent exhibit for Native Americans, "Enduring Legacy: Native Peoples, Native Arts at Hampton." This exemplifies a time capsule of items collected, bought or used by Hampton students, teachers and patrons during their boarding school years between 1878 and 1923. Using objects, pictures and primary commentaries, the exhibit offers a glimpse into how a Hampton education prepared Native Americans for their return to reservations as "cultural missionaries." Furthermore, the exhibit also illuminates the policy of assimilation, the federal policy dictating that Native Americans adopt the language, dress, and culture of white Americans.

African Art

"Collecting at Hampton University not only looks to preserve heritage, but is equally committed to forging links with the global community," Harvey said in his *President's Annual Report, 1990–1991*. Thus, building on an outstanding tradition of collecting valuable African art, the museum has acquired the largest number of works since 1978 and established links with other nations and peoples. Eight hundred and eighteen works of traditional art between 1978–1991, for example, have come to the Museum through gifts from private donors, or through purchase by the University, which represented an increase of over forty percent. Hampton University's African collection, widely praised for its age and the quality of its individual pieces and documentation, is distinguished as one of the earliest collections of African art to be established in any American museum. The first African artifacts arrived at Hampton in the 1870s to support the school's African studies program, and groups of objects from several cultures were added in the following decades.

In 1911, the most important sub-collection of African material was purchased by the Hampton Normal and Agricultural Institute from the collector, William H. Sheppard, one of Hampton's most distinguished alumni, who was a missionary, explorer, author, lecturer, and internationally-known advocate for the rights of Africans. While living in the Congo Free State (now Zaire) between 1890 and 1910, he collected four hundred pieces, which the institution purchased from him in 1911. According to the *President's Annual Report 1990–1991*, "This collection, predominantly from the Kuba people among whom Sheppard lived and worked, is known as the first of the world's three early Kuba collections and is equally distinguished as the first collection of African art to be gathered by an African American. William Sheppard's purpose in building his collection was to educate African Americans about Africa and its cultures." In 1984, the Hampton University Museum received as gifts several additions to the Sheppard Collection, given by Sheppard to members of his family. "The value of the pieces is further increased by the fact that Sheppard was the first foreigner to enter the Kuba kingdom. He developed a strong relationship with the royal family, and he carefully documented what he observed and collected." Since 1987, Hampton University has made a major commitment to complete the Kuba collection, adding pieces of the age and quality of the Sheppard Collection. Dozens of major works of art, including textiles, masks, objects of personal adornment, musical instruments, sculptures, weapons, and hats have been acquired. Most of these pieces have a strong association with the Kuba royal court. In 1991, Hampton's ties with the reigning Kuba royal family were renewed, and several pieces were acquired from the royal treasury of the monarch, Nyimi Kwete Mabeeky III.

Beside Kuba art, and collecting in countries of West Africa, the museum began, in 1988, to strengthen its Kenya collection. Hampton received some artifacts from donors' materials which complement the school's historic Koinange Collection, acquired by the school from the Kikuyu student Mbiyu Koinange in 1929. Jean Zeidler said, "We have been acquiring a lot of pieces from the Democratic Republic of Congo in the 1990s. In particular, we acquired all of the gold collection from Ghana—maybe more like forty [pieces], and the textiles from Ghana." Many of these pieces, especially from the Kuba people, are in a permanent exhibit, *Power, Beauty, Community: African Art at Hampton University*, which was installed in 1998.

Asian Pacific Art

From the continent of Africa to the Asian Pacific, Hampton has been collecting art and artifacts since 1868, when General Samuel Chapman Armstrong founded the museum collection at Hampton. In 1868, he contacted his mother in Hawaii and requested her to send him the first collections. From this association, Hampton developed a strong group of materials from the Pacific and Asian regions. Between 1978–1991, 141 pieces were procured for the Asian Pacific collection. Most noteworthy among this collection is a group of more than one hundred works of traditional ceremonies and everyday life from New Guinea, a gift of A. Harvey Schreter. Equally paralleled are acquisitions from Japan, such as a rare, centuries-old Kabuto helmet presented by Margery C. Raymond, which complements an important collection brought from that country at the turn of the twentieth century. This early collection was gathered by Hampton faculty member Alice Bacon, who established Hampton's historical links with the Japanese people in 1888. These contacts were renewed when the President and his wife, Norma Harvey, visited Japan in the spring of 1991. Plans are underway for a permanent Asian Pacific gallery.

Hampton University History Collection

Cognizant of the significant role of Hampton University in the history of this nation, a Hampton University History collection was established in 1980. The President said, in his *Annual Report, 1990–91*, that it was "designed to complement the documentary materials preserved in the University Archives. This collection of diverse three-dimensional materials reflects the changing instructional programs, the accomplishments of faculty and students, and the institution's contributions to American history." Thus, materials collected have included those related to the agricultural, trade school, and academic programs, as well as to individual graduates whose careers have exemplified Hampton's mission of leadership and service. A sword belonging to General Armstrong and a collection of historic scientific equipment used in classrooms and laboratories from the early- to mid-twentieth century are among the major acquisitions. Since 1978, two hundred eighty-eight pieces have been acquired for the Hampton University History Collection. A most significant item was the 1991 purchase at auction of *The Pen of Liberty*, the writing instrument that was used by President Abraham Lincoln on April 16, 1862 to sign the document emancipating the slaves in the District of Columbia. This pen, along with other artifacts will be displayed in a permanent exhibit. Additionally, in 1987–1988, the University funded the archaeological excavation of a pre-historic Woodland Native American site and an early seventeenth-century domestic site on campus. Thousands of artifacts were recovered by the archaeologists, and are now part of the of the museum's collections. Understanding excellence as a continual process has "guided a very significant and very successful program of collection development at the Hampton University Museum," said Harvey.

A Hampton History Collection Acquired During the Harvey Administration

As noted, while the Hampton University Museum has three permanent exhibits and expects to install an additional two, Zeidler, for whom Harvey has high praise for helping to build a first-class museum, said, "For most of my twenty years here we have done four or five temporary exhibitions a year." She selected the following temporary exhibits as being among the most prominent: *View from the Upper Room: The Art of John Biggers*—a nationally traveling retrospective exhibition containing 125 works of art; *Countee and Ida Cullen Art Collection*—twenty-nine works of art collected by the noted Harlem Renaissance poet Countee Cullen and his wife, Ida. The collection was purchased from the widow in 1986 and was the first major purchase of art by the museum; *The Art of Samella Lewis*—

approximately fifty works of art in a variety of media representing the fifty-year span of the artist's career; *To Lead and To Serve: American Indian Education at Hampton Institute 1878–1923*—a traveling photographic exhibition organized by the Hampton University Museum; *Five Decades: John Biggers and the Hampton Tradition in the Arts*—organized by the Hampton University Museum, the exhibition focused on the history and development of the Hampton Art Department and featured works by former students and faculty; *Elizabeth Catlett Works on Paper, 1944–1992*—seventy-five works on paper by this renowned artist spanning the length of her print-making career. The works were subsequently purchased by Hampton; *Jacob Lawrence: The Frederick Douglass and Harriet Tubman Series of Narrative Paintings*—sixty-three paintings, owned by Hampton, tell the stories of Frederick Douglass and Harriet Tubman, and were organized into a national traveling exhibition with a full-scale catalogue. According to Harvey, the goal of the exhibition was to "disseminate to a broad audience the concepts, values and visions embodied in Hampton's rich collection;" *Faithful Voices: Five Decades of African American Art*—thirty-five works by nine artists selected by President Harvey from his personal collection. The exhibition was organized in celebration of the President and Norma Harvey's twentieth anniversary of service to Hampton; *The Sculpture of Richmond Barthe*—organized from a collection of twenty-one sculptures by this noted artist acquired in the 1990s.

In addition to the exhibits, President Harvey has expressed his support of the arts through the museum's publication program, which includes: *Jacob Lawrence: The Frederick Douglass and Harriet Tubman Series of 1938–1940* by Ellen Harkins Wheat, in association with the University of Washington Press; *A Taste for the Beautiful: Zairian Art from the Hampton University Museum*, a 116-page book that documents the Kuba collection and William Sheppard's journey into Central Africa; and *Elizabeth Catlett's Works on Paper, 1944–1992*. The Hampton University Museum also publishes *The International Review of African-American Art*.

The glossy, full-color quarterly, that combines scholarly criticism with high-quality display of artwork, was started by **Samella Lewis**, a Hampton alumna, and the ownership was transferred to Hampton University in 1994. Its circulation of 12,000 to 14,000 includes major libraries and museums. Zeidler, who acted as publisher for the quarterly until 2001, said the magazine, the only one of its kind, serves as an important scholarly journal for scholarship on North and South American art derived from African traditions. Moreover, she pointed out that the fact that the President seized the opportunity "to accept the responsibility for the *National Review of African American Art* when Samella Lewis offered to transfer the ownership and responsibility of that important journal to Hampton, was no small commitment to art. I mean that is a publication that it takes serious support to get it produced; it is the only publication devoted solely to African American art, and it is very well respected. It probably would have been significantly altered had it not come to Hampton. It would probably not have survived, so I think that is another indication of very, very strong support. Samella Lewis could no longer sustain the operation. She needed institutional support for this journal." Not wanting to see the journal discontinued or altered, Lewis offered it to Hampton. "But I see Dr. Harvey's part in it in recognizing how important it was that this journal continues and what a significant contribution it makes in the art world. It is no small thing to publish it," said Zeidler

These publications, along with other extensions of the museum collection, can be purchased in the museum shop, which began in the late 1980s. This shop is a source of revenue for the operation of the museum.

Building Relationships for Learning, Teaching, and Enriching Lives

The President has further supported the arts by creating a milieu for individuals who have a genuine interest in the subject to connect through the museum's membership program, which started in 1991, as a way to closely connect with people who have a real interest in the museum and its collections. "If we could identify them, we could invite them here and find ways to solicit information from them about what their interests are and how we can serve them better," Zeidler said. With a membership of approximately 950 people, Zeidler also noted that "it is designed to strengthen our relationship with a primary group of people. It could also resolve into bringing support to us in a number of instances. Fund-raising comes from people who know you best and value your services. But it was not designed primarily to be a fund-raising group."

Forging partnerships has also become an important vehicle for extending service and visibility of the Hampton University Museum to a wider audience, nationally, regionally, and locally. Within the past several years, productive relationships have developed with other universities, museums, libraries, school systems, city governments, and other organizations which have enabled the museum to participate in off-campus programs and to attract more people to on-campus programs. To illustrate, a consortium of institutions organized the Studio Museum of Harlem and the Addison Gallery of American Art at Philips Andover Academy; it included the following HBCUs: Hampton, Fisk, Tuskegee, Howard, North Carolina Central, and Clark Atlanta. Together this group organized a major exhibition, *To Conserve a Legacy: Art from Historically Black Colleges and Universities*, which traveled in the East, South, and Midwest from 2000 until 2001. Work on this show resulted in the conservation of numerous works in Hampton's collection, including hundreds of photographs, and invaluable summer internships for two Hampton students interested in museum careers. When the University shares its collections in this way, it not only makes them accessible to a wider audience, but also helps to further the understanding of art and history in this country and abroad.

While the Museum attracts off-campus activities, it is also a resource center for learning. It brings to the campus everyone from school children to scholars to "learn from the exhibits and take whatever knowledge they can from studying the works of art," said Zeidler. Culturally, with the President's support and enthusiasm for collecting and preserving art, he has helped to catapult Hampton University into a position of eminence, along with the National Museum of American Art, as the leading holder of African American art.

Given the preeminent role Harvey has played in collecting and preserving the works of celebrated and uncelebrated African American artists and other people of color, he is assuring that Hampton University continues as "a place where art can grow." He wants the University as a place to discover and nurture new talent, whether young or old. Take the example of David Meade, the 52-year-old hourly-wage carpenter at Hampton University, who was making only nine dollars an hour when his creative talent was discovered. Harvey noticed the carpenter's artistic flair after requesting the worker to carve animal figures to put on the wall of the new nursery of his granddaughter, Taylor, at the Mansion House. When Harvey observed how lifelike the characters were, he encouraged Meade to paint, so he purchased paint, brush, canvas, and easel for the carpenter who had never attempted a brush stroke. He gave Meade an hour off each day to paint any scene around campus, including the oil portrait of Taylor that hangs in Harvey's office. With the President acting as his agent, he has sold over $5,000 worth of paintings for Meade. In 2002, Meade exhibited his first show at the Hampton University Museum.

7
Anchoring Athletics
An Education for Life

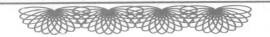

*"I see athletics and other extracurricular activities as just
another learning tool. They prepare people for the game
of life—not just a specific sport or activity."*
—William R. Harvey

Like art, the anchor block of athletics was also successfully framed from the vision of one man. Both speak to the duality of Harvey's existential being: the compassionate and the competitive. Collecting African American art with his wife, Norma, and golfing and boating help to keep fresh winds in his sails and help to invigorate his mind, body, and spirit, especially since his demanding work to strengthen Hampton University leaves him little time to enjoy his own pursuits. But athletics have always propelled him forward and sharpened his competitive spirit, from his days of Little League baseball during summer vacation to his days of football at Southern Normal in Brewton, Alabama and on to his basketball seasons at Talledega College as well as during his stint in the U. S. Army. This is also true of his passion for playing tennis. To Harvey, who is one of the owners of an Arena Football Team, athletics means more than a game; it is part of life and the learning process. "Athletics prepares people for life, conditioning the mind and body," he contended. "It helps you to develop strategies, goals, and objectives, and to execute them whether on the tennis and basketball courts, or on the football field. In life, if you are clean in mind and body with goals and objectives, and work toward them, you can be successful anywhere. Thus, athletics is an integral part of the learning process, which is the *raison d'etre* for academics."

This learning process, supported by his own experience, is also in keeping with the mission of the University, which "subscribes to the philosophy that a sound education involves the development of the total person."[1] It is a process that goes beyond the classroom. And, therefore, he regards the athletic program as essential to this holistic development. "Competitive sports play an important role in developing school spirit, attracting students, and providing other benefits to the community," Harvey acknowledged in his *President's Annual Report, 1978–1979*. Like academics, Hampton has a tradition of excellence in athletics and, also, winning numerous national and conference championships since the inception of competitive sports, starting with football in 1902. But championship cheers fell silent from 1968 to 1978, save for the Pirates tennis team that netted five consecutive CIAA titles and an NCAA National Championship. So Harvey's vision was again to rebuild a strong intercollegiate athletic program. Since 1978, under Harvey's leadership, the Hampton University Pirates and Lady Pirates have continued the tradition of achievement that their founders established in the early part of the twentieth century.

From 1978 to 2000, the intercollegiate athletics program distinguished itself, winning fifty-seven championships, including two NCAA National Championships, seven Black College National Championships, and seven Conference All-Sports titles. The outstanding tennis team alone earned eighteen of these victories. Since its successful move from Division II, CIAA Conference, to Division I, Mid-Eastern Athletic Conference (MEAC), in the academic year 1995–1996, the University has won eight MEAC championships. Additionally, in 1999, Hampton was the winner of the Heritage Bowl, which was televised on NBC. For Harvey, "The University acquitted itself in excellent fashion before a world-wide audience. For that to be the last Heritage Bowl of the twentieth century, the University, its football team, and band showed a great deal of class in winning the football game and the half-time competition." Hampton University, in the 1999–2000 academic year, was voted by the Virginia Sports Hall of Fame and Museum as "The Winningest Division I Athletic Program in the State of Virginia."

During the first decade, 1978–1988, the Hampton tennis team raised the Pirates' championship banner most proudly and repeatedly. From 1978–1981, the men's tennis team won three consecutive CIAA championships, the only titles for the school during that time. In the 1981–1982 season, men's basketball appended its logo to Hampton's championship banner, along with men's tennis, winning its first CIAA crown. The succeeding year (1983–1984) men's basketball and men's tennis recaptured conference championships, leading Hampton to the C. H. Williams All-Sports Trophy, which is given to the best all-around sports program in the CIAA. Men's and women's basketball also held the distinction of having the highest GPA in the CIAA.

These seasons of success continued through the next decade as women's and men's basketball, football, and tennis shone brightly in CIAA competition. Women's volleyball entered the fray in 1986, winning its championship, and the success of Hampton's athletic teams thrived during the 1980s and early 1990s in the CIAA, with the men's and women's cross-country teams and women's track staking their claims on championship trophies.

In 1995 Hampton University moved up to Division I and joined the Mid-Eastern Athletic Conference, but that did not quash Hampton's winning tradition. Men's and women's (first year) tennis and softball captured all-MEAC titles the first time around the conference. The men's golf team won Minority Collegiate National Championship, their first national title ever. In the 1996–1997 season, men's cross-country and men's tennis won MEAC titles. The 1997 academic season was Hampton's most glorious since joining the MEAC. Football and men's and women's tennis won MEAC championships, and women's basketball tied for the regular season MEAC title. In the 1998–1999 season, the winning tradition expanded to include not only all of the previous championship teams, but added to the list the men's indoor and outdoor track team. In 1999, the University was lifted to international prominence when the football team, under coach Joe Taylor, who was selected in 2001 as president of the American Football Coaches Association, defeated Southern University 24–3 and was crowned the Heritage Bowl Champions. This game was televised on NBC before a world-wide audience. The football team also won the MEAC All-Sports Trophy. The total number of MEAC championship teams stood at eight in 1999.

Hampton University's championship banners continue to wave at the crest of the twenty-first century, as the Lady Pirates basketball team took the MEAC championship in 2000. In 2001, the men's basketball team, under Coach Steve Merfield, won the MEAC championship. The team created "Hampton Hysteria" in its first trip to the NCAA tournament when the number fifteen-seeded Pirates surprised the nation with an upset over the number two seed, Iowa State University, by a score of 58–57. The Richmond *Times-Dispatch*, in its March 17, 2001 edition, reported, "Four days before the Pirates and Iowa State met, Hampton's President offered this analysis: 'I think we have a good chance of shocking the nation. We may not be that kid on the block everybody beats up. If we have our game, we're going to beat Iowa State.'" Again in 2002, the Pirates won the MEAC championship and headed for the NCAA tournament, but lost in the first round.

The Pirate hoopsters were not alone in their championships. While the men's and women's tennis teams won the MEAC championship in 2002, in 2001, the men's tennis team claimed the victory, under its long-time successful coach, Robert Screen. The women's track and field team nabbed the MEAC outdoor championship, while the women's track and field indoor team claimed the MEAC title in 2001.

As a result of these victories, the Virginia Sports Hall of Fame honored the Hampton University Department of Athletics for attaining the highest overall athletics winning percentage in Division I for 1999–2000 and 2000–2001.

Winning championships is the prize, and Harvey, who is very competitive, wants student athletes to win. His friend, Arthur Greene, told this story to illustrate his competitive nature. "I once bet him that he couldn't beat me in a race and rather than just talk about it, he wanted to go outside and race. So we went outside in the middle of the night and raced. He won. And, of course, I never heard the end of it, and that was about ten years ago. He's extremely competitive. He hates to lose—absolutely hates it." Though he loves to prevail in competitive sports, he stresses the total development of students, said Dennis Thomas, the former director of athletics. "It is important not only to win championships and be winners, but we also want to educate our student athletes for life, to obtain their degrees and to be good solid citizens and [Harvey] expects us as coaches and administrators to do those kinds of things."

The President, an ardent supporter of college athletics, reiterated clearly that it is "for a purpose more than just entertainment." It is another learning tool, which prepares people for the game of life, not just the specific sport that is being played. It promotes a culture of excellence. "It teaches organization, fundamentals, teamwork, setting goals, strategy to meet those goals, and the satisfaction of making them if you work hard." Moreover, this "game of life" not only teaches the conditioning of the body and mind to the athlete, but Harvey reminds us, also to the student watching him or her play. He believes "if you do all those things, you're going to have a successful athletic program and also you're going to be successful at whatever you venture into in life."

Yet, he doesn't want people to overlook the reality that a successful athletic program and a successful life require college sports figures to understand they are student athletes, not athletes who just happen to be students. "[There are those] who feel that because a student, high school or college, has some outstanding extracurricular ability,[he or she] should be allowed to slide in their academic course work. I am not of that opinion. As a matter of fact, I am on record as saying that a high schooler or college student ought not to be allowed to play football, basketball, sing in the choir, act in the Little Theatre or participate in any other extracurricular activity unless the student has an overall C average and is in good standing with the school," said Harvey. And Dennis Thomas added, "Hampton is committed and sincere about developing scholar athletes and that, in my judgment, sets us apart from other institutions of higher learning. We go about developing our students academically, and they are here to receive a degree and athletics is a means to an end for them to achieve that." With a graduation rate of 65 percent, Hampton is above the national norm. Perhaps, there is a link between being above the national average and the number of Hampton University student athletes who have distinguished themselves. Between 1978–1999. twenty one student athletes received the MEAC Commissioners' All-Academic Award in the same year. The awards are given to student athletes with a cumulative grade-point average of 3.0 or higher over a two-semester period. Other all-academic awards won by Hampton athletes include Sports Scholar Award, Black College Football All-American first team, five Burger King Scholar Athlete Awards, three National Football Foundation and College Hall of Fame Scholar Athletes Post Graduate Fellowships, two 100 percent Wrong Club Eddie Robinson Academic and Athletic Achievement Awards, Sheridan Black College Poll Scholar Athlete of the Year Award and a full medical scholarship from the University of Buffalo, College Division GTE/CoSida Academic All-American National Award. Students have also received Toyota/BET Player of the Game Award, and the Toyota/BET National Leader of the Year Award. Many student athletes have gone on to medical school, law school, graduate school, and are employed in Fortune 500 companies. The athletic program takes credit for that success.

Adhering to a philosophy of aim-for-excellence in all aspects of its operations, under Harvey's leadership, the Hampton University athletic program, certified without condition by the NCAA Division I athletic certification program, has blended a model of academic and athletic success. He did it through his leadership, vision, teamwork, philosophy of excellence and holding people accountable, said Dennis Thomas, whom Harvey hired in 1990 as the director of athletics, "to maintain the highest of integrity," of the program. "I want to emphasize the impact Dr. Harvey has had upon athletics. All we have accomplished athletically would not have been achieved without his support, without his vision, without his involvement, and that's critical to have a CEO support." Thomas even noted that Harvey's involvement with athletics extends from "words of encouragement to student athletes and to their coaches, to attending most of the games, even those out of town. When he meets with student athletes or their coaches, Harvey encourages student athletes to do their best, whether they win or lose the game. "He always indicates to them there is another day and the next time we'll do better. Dr. Harvey is a competitive person and he gives his critiques, pluses and minuses, the good things we do and the things we have to improve on. He talks about the games in reference to our evaluation process every year. Dr. Harvey meets with our head coaches for football and basketball, and he has a year-end review and talks about what our improvements should be, what we did well. He talks about strategies, personnel, facilities, market and promotion, fund-raising. He is well versed in basketball, tennis, football, and other sports."

As with other components of his building programs, Harvey began with a team who bought into his vision. And Thomas not only believed with him, as athletic director, he assisted the President in carrying out the dream during the second decade of his presidency. In the first decade of Harvey's presidency, Wilbert Lovett served in that capacity, where the competitive sports made significant improvements and won championships in the Central Intercollegiate Athletic Association. Beginning in 1990, under the dynamic leadership of Dennis Thomas, who has also served as chair of the MEAC Directors of Athletics Association, the Hampton University Pirates were also propelled to CIAA championships and, moreover, took a giant leap into Division I athletics. Furthermore, Hampton added several intercollegiate athletic programs, namely: coed sailing, women's tennis; men's golf, women's golf, and women's bowling. Perhaps more importantly, Thomas has shared in Harvey's vision of building a culture of excellence, which begins with developing scholar athletes as part of the learning process and which involves providing a supportive milieu where athletics can thrive.

Like Harvey, Thomas feels, too, the "participants of athletes in athletics mirror life."

> When I say it mirrors life, it teaches one respect of self; it teaches one respect for others; it teaches one to work with others, which is known as teamwork; it teaches one how to persevere; it teaches one to lose and to see that's not the end of the world; it teaches one to get back up and go about another good effort in trying to achieve a goal or objectives; it teaches one about communication; it teaches one about understanding fair play, and playing by the rules. Those things are what life is about. In terms of how it amalgamates with the University mission, it's an "Education for Life." This tool to promote learning also involves the head, heart, and the hand. I think it fits perfectly, simply because in athletics you have to use your hands, and your head in terms of strategy, making the right decisions during competition. You have to have a competitive heart and a drive and determination and that's what we teach. That's what our coaches teach. That's what we believe in. And that's why it matches the mission of the University in terms of the hands, the head, and the heart.

Thomas said that Harvey strongly expresses the feelings that "there is good in participating in athletics and that one can learn not only in the classroom but that they can learn in different environments and different settings. And I think that's one of the reasons that sets Dr. Harvey apart from a lot of people—presidents and administrators and successful people alike. He has a vision that is unique and that uniqueness is about excellence in all that we do. Not only does he expect it, but it is a clear vision that is given to us athletically. There is no ambiguity in terms of his approach. It is clear, it is well-defined and he expects results." When Thomas thinks of Harvey, he remarked: "I've been exposed to a lot of college presidents; I've been exposed to a lot of corporate people; and he has the right stuff in terms of what it takes to be successful. He is steadfast in his convictions about doing the right thing and treating people fairly, then giving you the resources to get a job done and holding you accountable for getting it done. That's why I said there's a uniqueness to him. He can be very gregarious, very affable, on the one hand, and in the next second, he can be the taskmaster, asking: Why are we not accomplishing our goals? Why are we not providing the students with very positive experiences? Why are we not being held accountable for our actions? He has that versatility and you don't find that in a lot of successful people."

A true believer in the President, Thomas contended that, "Dr. Harvey has been the catalyst for all that we do here in the athletic department. He sets the goals for what we want to do and then we go about the business of achieving those goals."

In executing the vision, Thomas, whose duties entailed but were not limited to, staffing, budgetary concerns, hiring of coaches, facilities, fund-raising, game management, alumni relations, and a potpourri of other activities, said "We don't leave anything to assumption. When we hire people, we review what our purpose and goals and mission are. We evaluate that sometimes on a monthly, weekly, and daily basis." Citing an example, he pointed out that, "During the year, we meet with all of our student athletes every semester and really impress upon them what the goal is—what the mission is of not only the University, but the athletic department." Thomas indicated that "we have the standard of excellence that is part of that and is well-defined. The Code of Conduct is clearly defined as to what the expectations are for everyone—students, faculty, staff. Student athletes are expected to abide by the Hampton University Code of Conduct, and to be the best that they can be academically, athletically, socially, and intellectually. And when we talk about the head, which is the intellect, and the hands, being able to do, and the heart to have compassion and determination and zeal for what you do, that's what we try to do in our athletic department. I think that is the education for life. [Dr. Harvey] expects us to make a positive impression upon our student athletes."

Making a positive self-presentation implies that each person must be held accountable for his or her actions collectively and individually. "Accountability is held in the classes that students take and on the team that they participate," noted Thomas. To be accountable to scholar athletes, Hampton University started the Athletic Academic Support program, which monitors the academic progress of student-athletes. The program makes sure athletes meet the NCAA and the Hampton University requirements. "They are monitored in terms of their academic progress, class attendance, and grades every week, every month, every semester by an academic support unit that is housed in the athletic department. We have study halls, we have tutorials three nights a week, and if you don't have a cumulative 2.20 GPA, then it is mandatory that you have to go to study hall and you have to be involved in our program," Thomas claimed.

Additionally, another component of the program is called S.A.L.L.S. (Student Athletes Involved in Learning, Leadership and Service). It is geared toward the total development of the student-athlete through athletics, academics, career development, personal development, and community service. The service component of the program is considered an important element in character building. As with the general student body, the University is committed to providing its student-athletes with opportunities to develop the foundation for a lifelong commitment of service to others. The leadership qualities of the student-athlete have been prominently demonstrated in the community as tutors in elementary schools, middle schools, and junior high schools, as participants in community read-ins, as helpers of the needy during Thanksgiving and Christmas holidays, and as inspirers of the community. The football team has an inspirational choir that performs for the community. In addition to these activities, student-athletes are required to participate in a Life Skills Program, which also covers community service and reinforces the learning process.

At Hampton University, in 1998, 65 percent of athletes graduated within six years, which was the best in the MEAC. Compared nationally, this graduation rate exceeds the national norm of Division I teams. Harvey was always clear about the priority of academics in the life of the student-athlete. When most black college presidents felt the rules adopted by the NCAA, which stiffened eligibility requirements for athletic scholarships and went into effect in 1986, were discriminatory, he disagreed. He told Tom Foster, a reporter for the *Daily Press*, January 23, 1983, that he believed that the new eligibility rules for Division I schools would lessen some of "the exploitation of black athletes" in major colleges for two reasons. "I think most people realize that there are cases where an athlete uses up his eligibility and then the school does not support him in an attempt to get a degree. There have been celebrated cases of porters and garbage men who played four years of major college ball and then the only thing they could do was work of a menial kind. I don't think it will eliminate the exploitation because the major colleges are still going to hire ball players, but it should help reduce it." Second, "I think the rule will assist most of the black colleges because they are Division II and the rule only applies to Division I. Historically, black colleges have taken students who are disadvantaged for whatever reason and have given them programs of a supplemental nature to improve their standing educationally. Programs have been developed to help the marginal student in the Division II schools. I hope that this rule will get many of the Division I schools who want to attract the better black players into offering such supplemental programs. If they really want a great player who doesn't have great grades, they have the money to put him in a special program and allow him to sit out a year to bring up his grades." In sum, he stressed that an education is supposed to be the number one goal of college students and not training grounds for pro teams.[2]

Moreover, he was not opposed to supporting a requirement that all student athletes take a specific set of basic college courses and that a school must have a specific percentage of its athletes graduate to remain a member of the NCAA.

Supporting the University's notion of putting students at the center of the learning process is not incompatible with the President's perspective of viewing competitive sports as a means to increase *esprit de corps* and to raise school spirit among the various constituents of the University. Dennis Thomas would agree, noting that, "It also galvanizes the alumni, and the community in a way that I don't think other aspects can in relation to a university. When you are winning, or having success, people identify with an athletic program. And that program brings people to the University in a very positive manner. Dr. Harvey's position has always been that we can have an outstanding academic program and still have an outstanding athletic program. The two are not mutually exclusive. And Hampton has been able to do both. The academic reputation of this great University has not been sacrificed by the athletic department being successful."

Likewise, Robert Binswanger emphasized that the President is "smart enough to know that Hampton, if it is going to succeed as one of the top schools, must be strong enough in not just one area, but in seven or eight. One of them is athletics. Probably, it doesn't make sense to some people that he has made athletics one of the areas that is important, but I'll go back to Harvard.

Harvard puts a lot of money into its athletic program and has for centuries. Not simply because they feel students need to have some kind of outlet, but they do it because it is important to alumni; it is important to the community; it helps build a national reputation; it attracts money."

Harvey's vision, many years before Dennis Thomas arrived on campus, was to move to Division I, where greater opportunities would be available to students, and the University could market itself for revenue and recruitment, as Binswanger suggested, to a broader audience. Hence, athletics would become a *sine qua non.* "[Harvey] doesn't just come up with a vision today and say I want it done tomorrow. No! He has this vision years and years in advance and then he has that stick-to-itiveness to see it through to the end, that importunity to see it to the end. And he can say, okay, we're Division II now, but he can see ten years down the highway, and say we'll be Division I and this is what Division I will do for Hampton University. Moving to Division I has exposed us to the world. We were recently on NBC television. We would not have been on NBC had we not made the move from Division II to Division I. And the world knows about Hampton. We've been on regional television and we've been on ESPN. We have on our Board of Trustees the former president of ESPN, Mr. Steven Bornstein, and people want to know why he is on the Board. But years before he was appointed to the Board, Dr. Harvey had a vision that if we get this person on our Board, we will have more opportunities to be on TV—ESPN. And lo and behold, five or six years later, we are guaranteed one football game a year on ESPN; we are guaranteed one basketball game on ESPN. That's all the result of a vision that Dr. Harvey had. And it's tremendous."

Doubters hovered around him when he announced in the early 1990s that the University would be moving from Division II to Division I. Thomas recalled, "Constituents of the University, community people, alumni asked, why are we doing this?" Thomas compared Harvey to Martin Luther King, noting that

"King was a visionary, too. And people thought he was off base when he preached nonviolence. A lot of people didn't agree with that. But King had a vision to give us the best approach to end segregation. And ultimately, it proved itself right. So I would have to put Dr. Harvey in that same kind of company because what is ossificated [sic] now will be elucidated ten years down the highway. It will be clear. It's fuzzy and murky now but he knows the vision." Even Thomas admitted that when Harvey mentioned that he wanted to move to Division I, he scratched his head, and said, "What! I don't understand." Then he responded, "Okay, we can move to Division I, but there are things that have to happen in order for us to do it." And Harvey said, "Here's the game plan." "He has a way of helping us to understand his vision, step by step by step," noted Thomas.

Harvey does this by indicating to his administrative team members, "This is where we want to go. Now, these are the steps that are needed in order for us to reach our ultimate goal." So in moving to Division I, the University had to meet all the criteria—adding scholarships, adding teams, adding personnel, adding coaching staff, adding academic support, adding facilities. And Harvey would say, "Okay, we want to do this, this year; we want to do this, the next year; this is our long-range plan," Thomas contended. It is how he will "get people to buy into his vision. And once you buy into his vision and he develops those steps about how you're going to accomplish this, and then step by step it becomes clear to you. You say, 'Oh, yeah, I see what he is trying to accomplish now,'" said Thomas.

Building athletic facilities was one phase in moving the goal line closer to Division I. The President's impact is matched only by Thomas' enthusiasm for his efforts in this process. "My God, not only have we done renovations to Armstrong Stadium, we have new press boxes on both sides, renovations underneath the stadium for the dressing rooms, and put in more seats in the north end of the stadium where it seats two thousand more people now. The stadium has state-of-the-art offices, media production, team meeting room, players' lounge, and a fabulous trophy case. We have a new tennis stadium, which has dressing rooms, concession area, lighted tennis courts. We have a brilliant, beautiful convocation center which seats 8,200 for basketball games; it houses the coaches' offices, visiting locker rooms, home locker rooms, an entertainers' dressing room, and it houses the convocation center staff. It is a tremendous facility. We hold concerts; we hold fashion fairs; we hold conventions; we have meetings."

In addition to building adequate facilities and adding new programs for men and women, the University had to increase the number of scholarships to attract outstanding student-athletes, as well as provide for the athletic department's operating budget. It is the athletic director's responsibility to produce these funds.

"We have to go out and generate as much revenue as possible. We go out and present programs to corporate managers, and we tell them about our program, and we also impress upon them the value of them becoming a partner in our athletic programs. And so far, we have Pepsi Cola, Alltel, Progressive Insurance, Papa John's Pizza, Holiday Inn, and the Marine Corps as corporate partners with whom we have a financial relationship."

In addition, funds are generated through Hampton University's football classics, which began in the early 1990s. According to Dennis Thomas, who was appointed "Director of Athletics of the Year" for Division I-AA, Southeast Region, 2001–2002, and was named chair of the NCAA Division I-AA Football Committee in 2001, it was another vision of the President. "Dr. Harvey indicated to me that he wanted exposure for the University, and to generate as much revenue as possible for the athletic program. One way to do that was the promotion of those classic football games and he charged me with that responsibility. I went out to speak with people about the classics all over the country before the board of directors and presented the Hampton story. They

got to know the Hampton story." Initially, the University participated in three classics and then five in 1999. "And that's another
part of Dr. Harvey's vision. He wanted us to really market and
expose the University around the country at professional venues
for professional football teams, like the RFK stadium in Washington, D.C." Other sites include the classic games, such as the
Washington Urban League Classic in Washington, D.C.; the Gate-
way Classic in St. Louis, Missouri; Urban League Classic in East
Rutherford, New Jersey; and Circle City Classic in Indianapolis,
Indiana. Thomas said that the Heritage Bowl was also a tremendous exposure for the University. "It goes back to Harvey's vision.
He uses athletics to promote the University and accomplish
things other than athletics. It gains exposure and enhances the
enrollment of Hampton University. When Hampton is getting
national and international exposure, playing in venues all over
the country, parents, principals, and counselors see this and they
will send top quality students to attend Hampton. It was good for
the University. We had the University [promotional materials]
there that tell the world about the University, our band, our academic program. It was a win-win situation for Hampton University in front of the world. And Hampton, as Dr. Harvey likes to say,
hit a home run."

Hitting home runs is a quality of this leader, whether in athletics, arts, or academics. Thomas would argue that his success is
predicated on vision, but he has "the ability to inspire, and that's
just great leadership. Great leaders are able to inspire people to
achieve a common goal."

Dennis Thomas believes he accomplishes this common goal
by creating "a supportive environment—an environment with
clear goals and objectives, an environment with everyone being
held accountable for achieving their goals and objectives, and
everybody focused on making Hampton the very best, not just in
black America, but the very best in America. And I think that if Dr.
Harvey had not been that visionary in terms of his approach to

what we can actually achieve, not just locally, not just regionally, not just nationally, but internationally, we would not have, in my humble opinion, achieved the internationally-known programs and the name that Hampton has."

Dennis Thomas would probably also say that if he had not been a participant in Harvey's vision, he probably would not have been appointed, in 2002, as the commissioner of the Mid-Eastern Athletic Conference. In a July 31, 2002 issue of the *Daily Press* (Newport News), Harvey is quoted as saying of Hampton's move into Division I and the MEAC, "I was the architect and he was the builder." "I had the plans but I needed someone to implement them. Dr. Thomas stepped up and implemented the plans unbelievably. He helped to build our program into a top-tier one."

President Harvey shares a lighthearted moment with a
Hampton football player during a ball game.

An early picture of the Harveys at their home on campus

Rev. Seymour Gaines and Rev. Michael Battle share a moment with the Harveys at daughter Leslie's christening.

Mrs. Claudis Harvey poses at Christmas dinner
with her four grandchildren

The Harveys at daughter Kelly's graduation

Dr. and Mrs. Harvey, Lionel Ritchie, and Gov. Doug Wilder celebrtate the opening of the $125 Million Campaign.

President William R. Harvey and
First Lady Norma B. Harvey

Dr. and Mrs. Harvey and his sister, Anne, celebrate
at the $200 Million Kick-off.

Grandaughter Taylor waives to her "Pa Pa" at Leslie's graduation.
Grandmother, father, and mother Valerie look on.

Dr. Harvey and son, Chris, pause during wedding reception.

Granddaughter Taylor smiles for the camera and her "Pa Pa" during a recent visit.

The Hampton University Board of Trustees

Science and Technology Building

Collis P. Huntington Building

William R. and Norma B. Harvey Library

McGrew Towers Dormitory and Conference Center

L. Douglas Wilder Hall

Hampton Harbor Apartments

Hampton Harbor Shopping Village

Convocation Center

Student Center

White Hall

Holmes Hall

Scripps Howard School of Journalism and Communication

Olin Engineering Building

Robert Scott Duncanson
Landscape with Hawk
1848/1849

Hampton University
Museum Collection

Joshua Johnson
*A Portrait of an
Unidentified Young Lady*
1805

Hampton University
Museum Collection

Jacob Lawrence
Street Peddlers
1943
Hampton University Museum Collection

Elizabeth Catlett
Red Cross Nurse
1944

Hampton
University
Museum
Collection

Henry Ossawa Tanner
In the Holy Land
ca. 1890
Hampton University Museum Collection

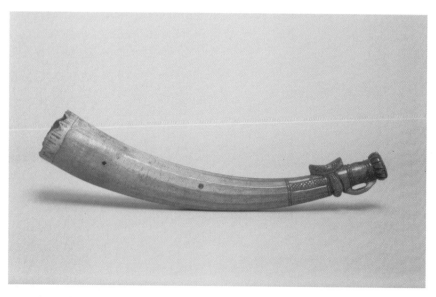

Ivory Trumpet, Mende people, Sierra Leone/Liberia, ca. 1837
Hampton University Museum Collection

Opening a Philanthropic
Window of Opportunity

"The Lord has given me the power to serve."
—William R. Harvey

President William R. Harvey's voice, filled with emotions, cracked as he strained to choke back the tears that flowed freely down his face when he presented Melvin Spurlock's Ph.D. degree and hood posthumously to Spurlock's four-year-old daughter, Olivia. Overcome with sorrow, he announced that the 31-year-old native of Richmond, Virginia had died suddenly of a heart attack two months earlier. Then, with Spurlock's widow, Dale, who was pregnant with their second child, standing nearby, he reached out and gracefully swept Olivia up into his arms, cradling her tightly as he wept. Few eyes were dry at that May 1999 Commencement as the announcement of his death sent shock waves rippling through the densely packed audience. In December 1998, Spurlock had just completed his doctoral studies in physics, the first African American to receive the Ph.D. degree in the history of Hampton University, and also in its first doctoral program, which began under Harvey's leadership.

But Harvey's compassion and empathy did not end there on the center stage. Adhering to his conviction that "the duty of man is not a wilderness of turnpike gates through which he is to pass by tickets from one to another. It is plain and simple and consists of two points—his duty to God, which every man must feel, and with respect to his neighbor, to do as he would be done by."[1]

215

Accordingly, he established a scholarship fund for Spurlock's children to attend Hampton University. In a letter to Dale Spurlock, he wrote: "Dr. Spurlock's example was one that personified ongoing work, ongoing service, and ongoing accomplishment which will continue to enlighten and inspire our graduates. It is my hope that your daughter, Olivia, and your unborn child adhere to the high academic standards set by their father."[2] The University will provide each of the children with $40,000 scholarships, payable over four years. But to receive the scholarships, the children must be admitted to Hampton, remain eligible for student status, and maintain a 2.8 grade point average. This stipulation is in keeping with his philosophy that individuals should be given an opportunity, but they must work for it.

A similar opportunity was extended to the children of the late Chris Harper, the University police chief. When he died unexpectedly in 1995, Harvey also set up a college scholarship fund for them. Likewise, on an individual and collective level, he has assisted a myriad of students, faculty, administrators, staff, citizens, and organizations beyond the University. Many accounts of his altruism remain unpublicized. Only a smattering of individuals know, for example, that he has given $12,000 to assist Carver Memorial Presbyterian Church in Newport News, Virginia, to purchase three lots that adjoined the church's property; that he has given $10,000 to First Baptist Church in Hampton, Virginia; or that he has given a van and $30,000 to his home church in Brewton, Alabama, all within a period of three or four years. Sidney Tucker, the minister of the church, Missionary Baptist, for thirty-four years, estimated that Harvey has contributed more than $50,000 dollars within a twenty-year time frame. "He calls you up to ask what you need," said Tucker. Moreover, whenever Harvey visited Brewton, particularly prior to his mother's death, Tucker noted that he always asked how we were getting along, and would say, "Reverend Tucker, what can I do for the church?" And Tucker would respond, "Doc, we need a couple of things that it looks like money is not available for, like a copy machine and a word processor." "I'll see what I can do about that," Harvey would say. So he sent funds to purchase the office equipment. The scenario has been repeated. When the minister wanted to erect a fence around the church's property line, to pave the parking lot, to purchase hymnals, to buy computers, or to install a ramp for the wheelchair-bound, he would ask for Harvey's assistance. "How much is it going to cost?" is Harvey's response. "Whatever amount, he would send me the money and we'd get it done," contended Tucker.

The minister was particularly animated when he told the following stories.

> One Sunday, Dr. Harvey came to church and I asked him, "Is there anyway you can help us look out for a van?" We had been talking about getting another one. And he said, "I'll see what I can do." And you know that year, coming up to Christmas, he came to Brewton, and he called me and said, "What are you doing?" And I said, "Not anything." He said, "Come down. I got something for you." And there was the bus parked in his mother's yard. I felt like I was somebody. I had to cry a little bit. That Sunday, I carried it to church, and parked it in the church yard. And I said, "This van is given to us by Dr. Harvey. We will write him a receipt showing the purchase of this van."

When Harvey's mother, claudis P. Harvey, the president of the Missionary Society and a staunch supporter of the church, died, Tucker said,

> He called me to ask if I would intercede in getting the educational building named after his mother. "I'm going to bring you $10,000," Harvey said. So I told the church that if we would let this building be named the claudis P. Harvey Educational Building, he would give us $10,000. Don't see nothing wrong with it. I called and said, "Doc, it's okay." He came to his mother's funeral and there were a number of resolutions and sympathy cards and he said, "I don't want but two read—one from the Board of Trustees at Hampton University and one from the church. And I have this check here for $10,000." And in that service, I had the resolutions read

from the trustees, and the one from the church, which stated that: "The annex from the church will be named from this day forward the Claudis P. Harvey Educational Annex."

Since Harvey's mother's death, Tucker stated that, "He has sent me a check around Christmas time for $1,000 to be used at my discretion for the church."

Harvey also invites his Brewton minister to attend the annual Hampton Ministers' Conference. "You come to Hampton and don't you worry about a thing," Harvey tells him. And for Tucker, he reiterated, "I admire the whole family for their concern and their Christianity, for their Christian hearts. Dr. Harvey can walk with kings and not lose the common touch."

Harvey's philanthropy goes beyond the church. At Hampton University and Virginia State University, he has set up endowment funds of $30,000 and $20,000, respectively, for the field of elementary education in honor of his wife, Norma, who was teaching elementary school when they met. The interest from the endowments will provide a modest scholarship for students entering elementary education. Harvey believes that K-12 teachers are "our precious resources," despite the fact that they are the lowest paid professionals and have scant scholarship support for teacher education. To support them and "make that one step for mankind," the President and his wife, Norma, donated one million dollars in honor of W. D. C. Harvey, the President's father and civil rights leader, for scholarships to support students in teacher education from Hampton and Newport News, Virginia. "It is important to be of service to others and everybody should give no matter their status in life. It may be with their time and talent or some other resources. Everybody can give. If someone wants to be great, they ought to be of service to others. This is another way of giving back to the community, uplifting the community, and trying to provide, in this instance, where there is little support," the President declared.

The President has also named an award in honor of his mother, the claudis P. Harvey Outstanding Staff Award. Noting that his mother was a very humble woman, he felt it was appropriate to pay tribute to her by annually recognizing a staff member who receives a plaque and $1,000. "I want to reward people who don't get rewarded. Everybody contributes and everybody is important—staff, administrators, faculty, and students. There are awards for faculty, students [and even an award for citizenship in the larger community], but we did not have one for groundskeepers, housekeepers, or the secretaries. It is a way of uplifting the downtrodden."

Cases abound of Harvey's generosity. He has, for example, bestowed annual Christmas gifts on every administrator, faculty, and staff of the Hampton family and he has provided funds and release time for faculty development—to assist over fifty administrators and professors to obtain their terminal degrees. His benevolence is further exhibited in the case of Hampton family members who experience an illness, a misfortune, or a family death. He is known to send flowers or to call the person. The late Margaret Simmons, an English professor, and one of his closest confidantes, attested to his empathy. "He is a very compassionate person. When my daughter died, he and Mrs. Harvey were so supportive. And I hardly knew him. At every point, when I have something to go wrong personally, if he was aware of it, he has been there offering his assistance and support." He was there during Simmons' late husband's lengthy illness. In fact, on one occasion, Harvey was so concerned about his welfare that, unbeknown to Simmons, he tracked him down where he finally located him in the hospital. Likewise, during her own lengthy illness and her demise in 2002, he exhibited the same compassion. Simmons once remarked: "Dr. Harvey knows how to be a friend."

Often his philanthropy and caring for others extend beyond the campus, even sometimes into retirement. Martha Dawson, who retired in 1991, gave this account of his concern. "When I wanted to retire, [Harvey's] question was "What are you going to do?" "I think I want to write," she responded. "And that's how I got the book done. I stayed right there on the same salary for that year. When I told him it was time for me not to stay on campus housing because I was retiring, I decided to pick out a house, and he left his office and came right in this house to help me look at it. And that's the stuff people don't know that I just appreciate, because I was a single person." In another example, she cited his assistance, after her retirement, in aiding her twin grandchildren. Their mother died while they were young, and the twins were reared solely by their father, Dawson's son. When they dropped out of college, the President assisted them in getting into Hampton University with financial aid. Both graduated with honors. "When my youngest daughter was in school, and there was something that [Harvey] thought I should know, he would tell me. He is just a gem, a beautiful human being," Dawson proclaimed. His wife, Norma, asserted, too, that, "He is a generous man,"

But for Harvey, serving is a passion, duty, and joy to help others. He said, in accepting the Role Model of the Year Award by the 100 Black Men of Virginia Peninsula, Inc. on April 17, 1999, that, "Perhaps the greatest love that I have outside of my immediate family is serving others. I have been fortunate in my life because I have been given the power to serve. Think about it. Think of the joy, thrill, and exhilaration of providing leadership in combating ignorance, poverty, disease and misery. Think of the joy of taking raw coal and making it into a polished diamond as thousands of Hampton graduates have become in the twenty-one years that I have been president. Think of the thrill of providing a setting where faculty members can do important research on such things as breast cancer, hypertension and diabetes as faculty members of Hampton are doing as I speak. Think of the exhilaration of bringing in atmospheric scientists and saying to them 'reach for the stars' as scientists at Hampton are doing by launching a weather satellite in collaboration with NASA and the French government. Think of the joy, thrill, and exhilaration there is in assisting those whom the system has taken advantage of, such as two of our coaches who were improperly jailed down in Lubbock, Texas. Think of the joy, thrill, and exhilaration of hiring a former mayor—who had years of practical experience of running a city—as a political science professor after her defeat in a bitter, divisive, racist-tinged election. And the list goes on."

It does continue. The late Jessie Rattley, who had deep respect for Harvey, was that former mayor of Newport News, Virginia and the first black woman to head the National League of Cities. She vouched eagerly for Harvey's personal and collective service. "When I was not reelected mayor in 1990 after serving the City [of Newport News, Virginia] for twenty years, he called and asked if I would be interested in coming to Hampton to share with students in the political science department my experience. He wanted me to devote time in doing that and work with development in bringing resources to the campus. I have enjoyed it and am very grateful to him for that opportunity to share twenty years of experience of politics in the real world with students. I would like to think that I have something to offer that would benefit those students."

Similar stories can be repeated on an individual and collective level of Harvey's philanthropic feats and his desire to "right wrongs, ease human suffering, provide guidance and direction, uplift the downtrodden, and ultimately change the course of the universe." Rattley cited the Hampton Harbor as an example of Harvey's collective uplift. She said while many African Americans gripe about their poor treatment and their lack of respect by white businesses, too few pool resources to own them. "I see Dr. Harvey as one who tried to change that. It would have been easy for him to rent housing space from some white owners, but instead, he had the vision to build [Hampton Harbors] and the mall through federal grants. So we have the complex where we can rent to our own students and where we can receive funds from the rental from apartments and the businesses to help provide scholarships and opportunities for students at Hampton

University. And if there were more like him, we could do much more than we have done to keep resources within our own community." Harvey strongly believes, as did Rattley, that uplift through philanthropy, along with economic development and education, is central to group racial progress.

Installing a Service Door

"In our long and arduous struggle for liberation, I have remained a staunch advocate of education, economic empowerment, and self-sufficiency as the ultimate salvation of African American people."[1]

—William R. Harvey

Uplifting Through Education and Economics

Harvey maintains that:

> Our progress as a people can be no swifter than our progress in education. Our requirements for leadership, our hopes for economic growth, and the demands of citizenship itself in an era such as this all require the maximum development of all of us. . . . Education is the keystone in the arch of freedom and progress. Nothing has contributed more to the enlargement of this nation's strength and opportunities than our traditional educational system. For the individual, the doors to the schoolhouse, to the library, and to the college lead to the richest treasures of our open society; to the power of knowledge—to the training and skills necessary for productive employment—to the wisdom, the ideas, and the culture which enrich life—and to the creative, self-disciplined understanding of society needed for good citizenship in today's changing and challenging world.[2]

But he also believes, "Neither education nor scholarship can be of much value unless it is combined with social awareness and action. For anyone to become comfortable without thinking about the many social problems which affect our lives daily would certainly amount to dereliction."

Harvey has fused social awareness and social action with education in his years at Hampton University, because this academician thinks higher education should play an active role in uplifting the community—one that extends beyond the boundaries of the ivory towers. He contended: "My personal philosophy is that institutions of higher education should be involved with their communities in a number of diverse and important ways. To gather, transmit and absorb knowledge is not good enough. Knowledge must be shared. Institutions of higher education should try to uplift their communities through educational, economic, cultural and political ways. Institutions and individuals ought not to shy away from this kind of community service. Throughout its history, Hampton University has not."[3] For Harvey noted that, "Central to the Hampton University mission is a tradition of meaningful service for the purpose of improving the quality of individual lives and advancing the total society."[4]

Like Hampton's founder, General Samuel Chapman Armstrong, who commanded the Hampton students "To Lead and To Serve," President Harvey has, too, rekindled his spirit of leadership and has sheltered Hampton's tradition of service, like the mighty Emancipation Oak, for the generations of the twenty-first century. In looking back, Harvey reminded us, "The Emancipation Oak . . . provided the shelter for what was among the first, if not the actual first, organized education for African American people in Virginia. Traditionally, the Oak has symbolically sheltered the University's dream of an 'Education for Life' and its commitment to service. Many of Hampton's programs are designed to perpetuate this tradition and, like the outstretched branches of the magnificent Oak, these programs extend beyond the walls of this institution, enriching in a most profound way individual lives, the immediate community, the nation, and the world."[5]

As the portal to Hampton's traditions and values—"to lead and to serve"—commencing with the Freshman Studies program, students are required to complete five hours of community service, either on campus or in the community, which include such activities as: tutoring children; volunteering at the homeless shelters; ushering at concerts, plays, or the museum; and working on various university committees. This service requisite extends to the Honors College program, where participants must perform at least 150 hours of community service on a local, national, or global level. The Honors College, in partnership with the school system in Hampton, Virginia, also provides student mentors for low income students to increase reading, mathematics, language and social skills. Moreover, the Honors College's Intra-Campus Service Team serves as an extra resource in assisting faculty and staff in any capacity needed. This spirit of community service also reaches into almost all student organizations on campus, where they volunteer their time, energies, and talents in such activities as tutoring community youths, registering voters, and assisting the elderly in a variety of activities. In fact, the requirement to serve in a variety of community service projects is included in the constitution of every student organization. Furthermore, a service learning component is found in many departments on campus.

Clearly in line with Harvey's philosophy of viewing service as a means of uplifting the community culturally, politically, educationally, economically, socially, and spiritually has been the institution's tradition of developing cooperative-oriented leaders—educators, entrepreneurs, health care providers, scientists, ministers—in a holistic approach to education and community empowerment. As Harvey reiterated, "For Hampton University, the notion of the 'Ivory Tower' has never been applicable. On the contrary, it has throughout its existence extended its services and resources to the larger community."[6] Accordingly, this holistic approach to service includes the spiritual leaders of the black community who have assembled annually since 1914 at Hampton University for the Ministers' Conference. Under Harvey's presidency, the Hampton University Ministers's Conference, with a current membership of over 8,000 ministers, choir directors, and organists, increased significantly from the 900 members in 1978. The conference, headed by Michael A. Battle, Hampton University's chaplain from 1976 to 1996, and currently directed by Timothy Tee Boddie, is the largest and fastest growing interdenominational movement in the black church. Speaking before the Ministers' Conference in 1999, Harvey proclaimed that these leaders "examine and devise solutions for social issues that plague our churches, our families, our nation, and our world." He pointed out that:

> Two things have not changed since the start of the Ministers' Conference in 1914 and will not change in 2000. The black church and the black college are the backbone of our race and our only hope for survival in the twenty-first century, the twenty-second century, and every century thereafter. The world that awaits us, our children, and our children's children has previewed for us its feature presentations: immoral leadership, disillusioned youth, abandonment of values, absence of spirituality, resurgence of ignorance and hatred, and intolerance of fellow human beings. In such a world, there are but two shields strong enough to protect us: God's magnificent grace and mercy, and education's potential to enlighten and refine. I submit that these are not only options for African Americans, they are vital necessities! And that is why the work of this Ministers' Conference is of vital importance. Through exposure to knowledge, ideas, and concepts—and with continual emphasis on honesty, decency, dignity, integrity, self-respect, and respect for - others—Hampton offers nourishment for the head and the heart. Through the teaching of our Savior Jesus Christ, you and your churches offer nourishment for the heart and soul. Together, we provide them an "Education for Life," a life that is worth something, that amounts to something, and a life that is pleasing in the eyes of God.[7]

The Annual Black Family Conference, which Harvey initiated upon the recommendation of the Hampton alumni in 1979, stands as a shining beacon in addressing critical social and economic issues facing the black family and in proposing solutions to them. Through the institutions of education, church, and family, important values can be communicated and nourished. As Harvey noted in a speech, "The Christian Man in These Times," "Until we can strengthen the family as a unit, it is going to be exceedingly difficult to achieve any accomplishments in any other area."[8]

The President is a strong advocate of economic empowerment and self-sufficiency as a way to strengthen black families and communities. He asserted, in a speech before the Economic Empowerment Trade Fair Exposition, April 9, 1992 in New Brunswick, New Jersey, that, "I hold to the conviction, with greater tenacity than ever before, that unless we achieve economic empowerment, we will never truly be free. . . If African Americans are to achieve economic empowerment and, therefore, freedom in the most meaningful sense, then we must shift our focus from mere consumership to ownership. We must embrace the idea of entrepreneurship as the most viable solution to the problem of black unemployment, black poverty, political disenfranchisement, and other social and political ills."[9] His firm belief in economic empowerment as the source of African American salvation, the precept that has guided his personal and professional life was instilled by his father.

In an address delivered to Omega Psi Phi Fraternity in Hampton, Virginia on November 24, 1985, he contended:

> We've dealt with and mastered many frontiers in America, such as freedom, voting, education, networking in our black churches, in black colleges, in the courts and in fraternities and sororities. But, until we develop a class of entrepreneurs who own businesses that produce products—not just for black America, but all America—we will not move forward! Yes, our new frontier must be entrepreneurship, ownership of buildings, small businesses and big businesses. The road to riches is waiting for those who can build a better

mousetrap. It is not easy; there are many problems. These include increased federal, state and local regulatory burdens; continuing economic uncertainties; inflationary pressures, high cost and limited availability of capital; defective management counseling; tax advantages and inequities and rapidly advanced technology.[10]

Harvey's commitment to economic empowerment is more than lip service. Through several outreach programs, such as the HUBAC program, the HU-Care Program, and the Nursing Center, the University has enhanced the socioeconomic status and health of black families through its educational services, as well as contributed to the economic vitality of the surrounding communities through job creation and other ventures. The Hampton University Business Assistance Center, which has been in existence since 1982, assists in the start-up of small businesses. According to its director, Charles Wooding, the center's staff, along with the School of Business faculty, provides management counseling and assistance in all phases of business formation, stabilization, and expansion. These services, which offer free counseling, are available to any small business or those with minority owners, including women. Since its inception in 1982, the Center has assisted approximately twenty-three hundred clients in establishing a variety of retail and service businesses in the greater Peninsula, including convenience stores, clothing and shoe stores, janitorial services, beauty establishments, day care centers, printing shops, fitness centers, and restaurant construction, research and development, service stations, building services, dry cleaning, and landscaping. Formally established through a grant from the Economic Development Administration of the U. S. Department of Commerce, the Center is funded, in part, by Hampton University.

Funded by the Department of Agriculture, the Hampton University Rural Business Assistance Center Program (HURBAC), a nonprofit organization under HUBAC, is designed to improve the quality of life in the traditionally agricultural/natural resources dependent communities of Surry, Southhampton, and Isle of Wight counties in Virginia and to create jobs and lower unemployment. This technical assistance center for rural, small and emerging businesses offers assistance to new and existing businesses; assists in business plans and loan application preparations; offers business seminars; and helps identify sources of financing.

The *Hampton Community Development Corporation* (HCDC), organized September 1992, was initiated by Hampton University through its Hampton University Business Assistance Center and has served over 363 persons. HCDC, with its own tax exemption and 501(c)3 status, is designed to enhance the quality of life in the City of Hampton and the Peninsula by creating housing and housing opportunity, and by initiating economic development opportunity for the purpose of creating jobs for low and moderate income persons. In addition to spearheading the formation of the HCDC, Hampton University committed a loan of $100,000 to the HCDC, which is matched by a loan in the same amount by HCDC's funding source. This fund is allocated for low interest loans for home purchases to Hampton University employees whose incomes fall within the "low to moderate" criteria established by the U. S. Department of Housing and Urban Development.

Other projects implemented by HCDC have included the Project Youth Bill, a one-million-dollar project for a job training program initiated by HCDC in partnership with Hampton University, the Hampton University School of Business, the City of Hampton, and the Hampton Redevelopment and Housing Authority; a certified Nurses Aide Training Project implemented in partnership with the Hampton University School of Nursing; a project from which loans were, and will be made to businesses which have committed to hiring low income persons; and the establishment of a small-business incubator which provides a venue and core services for new businesses to start-up at a substantially reduced rate. The incubator, in partnership with the Hampton Community Development Corporation, includes office space and furniture, computers, clerical help, utilities, janitorial services, telephone answering services, and security, as well as conference space for training employees or meeting with clients. The incubator, a

4,000-square-foot building with ten separate offices, also presents free business seminars by attorneys, CPAs, and other professionals. Additionally, with its Hampton University connection, the incubator can use the resources of the University's School of Business to assist these small businesses in developing marketing plans, budgets, and long-term business plans. The incubator was the brainchild of Charles Wooding, director of HUBAC, and William Thomas, the incubator's executive director.

To further fortify families and communities, the University has addressed the issue of improving the health, economic welfare, and self sufficiency of the poor. The Hampton University Nursing Center, established in 1986, provides a program of health care services which emphasizes the implementation of health promotion and health protection activities for client groups in urban and rural communities. The Nursing Center programs encompass multiphasic health screening, family-centered health education, and health counseling. The Center's Health Mobile provides primary health-care services to medically unserved and underserved homeless, infants, children, men, and women in Newport News and Hampton, Virginia. In addition to the Hampton University Nursing Center, the institution sponsors the HU-Care program, funded in 1998 for $4.8 million by the Department of Labor. HU-Care, which stands for Hampton University Career Advancement and Resiliency Empowerment, is a Welfare-to-Work program offered at the University. It provides free career and job skills training for teacher assistants, child care, pharmacy technology, information technology, manufacturing technology, food service, and office management. While participants are in training, they receive child care costs and bus fare to and from work and school.

Under Harvey's presidency, the University has not only reached out to partner with the government, but the corporate sector and foundations, in an effort to further strengthen the African American family unit and its institutions by increasing opportunities for minority youth. Invariably, he emphasizes the crucial role of HBCUs in the lives of youths; thus, to support them is "an investment in the future of higher education, in the salvation of the young." In speaking before the Olin Foundation on April 24, 1989, Harvey pointed out that, "Hampton, by the very nature of its history and mission, needs no demographics to identify its mission for the '90s and beyond. Its mission shall remain what it has always been—the solid preparation of youth for the edification of themselves and for the enhancement of the marketplace. What the demographics have done is to underscore the urgency of that mission, and Hampton has responded and shall continue to respond to that urgency." And "the exigency of that mission is the expansion of opportunities to include more minorities and related issues, which include increased literacy, increased enrollment in schools of education, in math, science, engineering, computer literacy, and in the implementation of academic programs and support services geared to the specific needs of minority constituency." But "laying history and mission aside," he continued:

> It remains for us to begin now to commit to a series of strategies to assure our survival and success. These strategies ought to include the following: the targeting of minority students in junior high school before they begin their college preparatory tracks; the use of resources and expertise in helping to reverse the high school drop-out rate; the implementation of measures aimed at increased parental involvement in the education and recruitment of minority students; increased resources from both private and public sectors for scholarships and financial aid for minority students; the early identification of gifted minorities and the implementation of increased incentives to attract and retain minorities in higher education; the incorporation of counseling and remediation programs into curricula; the development of curricula which respond to minority cultures and minority needs; increased efforts to attract and retain more minorities in the fields of math, science, and engineering; the establishment of mentoring programs for minorities, particularly at majority institutions where the problem of retaining minority stu-

dents is becoming more critical; the removal of all vestiges of
racism in the university environment and in society at large;
the implementation of programs to eradicate illiteracy at all
levels of society. . . .

In conclusion, he declared, "With the help of foundations, corporations, individuals and themselves, many colleges and universities have
already begun to implement these strategies." Of course, Hampton
was among them. But its outreach programs, too vast to discuss here,
augment the academic, professional and personal growth of the University community and diverse constituents beyond the halls of ivy.
Only a smattering sample of outreach educational, recreational, and
work-oriented programs for youths, from the gifted to the academically and economically marginal, is profiled.

Given the University's commitment to help put students in
the pipeline in the science and technical fields, and thereby
increase the representation of minorities, many of these outreach programs target public school students for instruction and
support in the sciences and engineering. Other outreach programs are designed to improve student performance in particular
disciplines. The Hampton University Center for Fusion Research
& Training (HUCFRT) has, for instance, a high school to postdoc-
toral pipeline for minority and female students in fusion science.
This center is engaged in world-class, cutting-edge interdisciplinary research in fusion science with the departments of physics,
mathematics, computer science, and engineering.

Additionally, outreach programs sponsored by the Department of Mathematics, through its partnership with the Hampton
Public School System, target both students and teachers. It helps
prepare ninth-grade students for the challenges of high school
mathematics courses, while it conducts in-service courses for elementary teachers. Such courses are designed to develop further
their problem-solving skills; to enhance teachers' understanding of
basic concepts and skills in mathematics; and to encourage the
theoretical linking of various topics in mathematics and other
components of the elementary school curriculum. Moreover, in

conjunction with the Department of Engineering, the Department contributes significantly to the Cooperating Hampton Roads Organizations for Minorities in Engineering Program (CHROME). Selected high school students typically visit the mathematics laboratory where they are tutored primarily in algebra II and geometry.

The Hampton University Center for Excellence in Research, Teaching and Learning, in partnership with the Newport News City Schools and Hampton University's School of Science, gives selected high school students the opportunity to participate in science enrichment projects. The students work with mentors in the disciplines of botany, marine science, and physics. In addition to the laboratory experience, they learn how to use the Internet for research and retrieval of information. The grant is funded by the National Science Foundation.

The University's Aviation Career Education Program (ACE), sponsored by the Department of Airway Science and funded by the Eastern Region of the Federal Aviation Administration, provides for highly motivated students, ages twelve through seventeen, an opportunity to experience the field of aviation first-hand and to develop an interest in the field that could result in enrollment in collegiate aviation programs, thereby helping to reverse the dearth of minorities in aviation-related careers.

The Kiddie Kollege/Kiddie Kamp, sponsored by the University since 1982, offers specially designed academic and recreational enrichment activities for more than 100 seven- to twelve-year-old children from throughout the country. It provides youth with an interdisciplinary approach to the study of mathematics, science, and computer technology and emphasizes problem-solving, critical thinking, and creativity. Moreover, it provides a variety of recreational and cultural activities beyond the classroom, including field trips, swimming, tumbling, tennis instruction, basketball, soccer, volleyball, track and field, and gymnastics. Other programs like the Summer Science Camp for middle school students, a "Hands-On" classroom enrichment experience, which covers major science areas of biology, chemistry, mathematics, computer science, and physics, and the National Youth Sports Program, which combines science and recreational activities, and the Young Doctors Program, are designed to encourage youth to enter the field of science.

In addition to reaching out to K-12 youth, the University has also forged partnerships with the community college. Hampton University Community College Bridge Grant, funded by the National Institutes of Health, is designed to bridge the community college with a four-year baccalaureate degree granting institution. Students are able to gain work/study positions on the campus of a community college, so they can earn enough to be full-time students during the two-year associate degree programs. Students are assigned mentors at the University in biology, and special workshops are held for the community college students during the academic year. These students must also attend Hampton University each summer for research participation and study.

Beyond specific programs for gifted students, for students in specific scientific and technical disciplines, and for teachers, Hampton University is engaged in more comprehensive outreach programs related to educational and public policy issues. For example, annually since 1982, the Hampton University Center for Marine and Coastal Environmental Studies has collaborated with the Virginia Marine Resources Commission in hosting the Virginia Wetlands Management Symposium, where the University has been involved in establishing federal and state environmental policies related to the mitigation of wetlands damage, problems inherent in regulating nontidal wetlands, and periodic revisions of wetlands legislation. The program advances the aim of Marine Science outreach objectives to promote environmental conservation.

While addressing promising students, the University has not neglected the problems facing many urban youths. Adhering to the notion that the problems of youth and the general populace at large can be solved with education, training, and a job, Harvey conceived his brainchild, Jet Corps, a program designed to meet the critical needs of urban youth, while simultaneously helping to repair and replace the infrastructure in the nation's cities. Believing that the solution to problems of today's urban youth can be found in the 1930s, Harvey modeled the program after the New Deal-era Civilian Conservation Corps that puts participants to work at jobs that benefit the community. This University program, formed in cooperation with the City of Hampton, Hampton City School System and local businesses in 1992, and later extended to other surrounding cities, places particular emphasis on education, character building, training, and work. Since its inception, over 700 youths, ages 14–17, from the Hampton Roads area have participated in an intense twelve-month curriculum that places great emphasis on the enhancement of strong work ethic, education, discipline, spirituality, goalsetting, and character. Moreover, Jet Corps provides paid experiences that prepare the students for the workforce; improves behavior and provides leadership and discipline for students; provides practical skills for mathematics, communication, health, and life issues; incorporates spiritual, family, school, business, and community support; provides counseling, college mentor programs, and conflict resolution techniques; creates a forum for open discussion on drugs, alcohol, violence, relationships; develops character and produces productive citizens. It also helps students to prepare for test-taking and technological skills.

While the Jet Corps program focuses on both male and female youth, the President pointed out that he was particularly "troubled by the endangered species cloud which hangs ominously over the heads of young black males," so in 1989, he established Hampton's Opportunity for Program Enhancement Program (HOPE) to address the crisis of black males in post-secondary education. This program provides an opportunity for black males who lack the academic preparations needed to matriculate at the University. Students are placed in courses at the level of their preparation. Their activities at the University are strictly monitored by the coordinator. Students remain in this program for one year and are provided special study and tutorial sessions. At the conclusion, the student must be able to continue in a regular course of study or withdraw from the University. This program has an eighty percent retention rate, with some students continuing on as graduate or law students or entering the workforce as teachers, professional athletes, or business people working for Fortune 500 companies.

Another University outreach program targeting urban youth is the Connection Between Hampton University and Public Schools (C-UPS) Program. This outreach program provides continuing education for a specified population of high school students who are on long-term suspension/expulsion from Hampton City Schools, as well as students who are returning from various placements in the Department of Juvenile Justice. Students are chosen for the project on the basis of behavior which suggests a positive outcome from rehabilitative processes. Each student admitted to the program works from an Individual Alternative Education Plan (IAEP) developed by the program director in consultation with other staff. Each plan has an educational component and a personal development component related directly to each student's needs. The C-UPS Program is held on the Hampton University campus, and has served over 500 students since its inception in 1991. The University provides space and undergraduate student tutors from various disciplines.

Speaking before the New Jersey School Boards Association Convention in Atlantic City, New Jersey on October 23, 1997, President Harvey pointed out that, "In many of our urban and inner-city settings, the public schools are killing our children, and when our children are killed, then our communities are killed. And when our communities are killed, then there is no future for any of us." Thus for students who are failing in the public school system, Harvey has proposed a charter school as one of the alternative educational options. Charter schools are part of the public school system but are freed from many state and local regulations to encourage more innovative teaching strategies. "There really seems to be momentum all over the country for educational reform in the form of alternative educational options. If it is not obvious already, you should know that I am wholeheartedly behind this movement. As a strong advocate of public school education, I am behind this movement because it will, in my judgment, improve the education that our children receive, thereby improve public schools. I also endorse choice, because in all too many instances our current school efforts are failing our youngsters," he told the convention participants.

Three years later, on March 15, 2000, Harvey requested the Hampton School Board to consider a charter school on the University campus that would specialize in mathematics, science, and technology. He told the board that the Hampton University Charter School would use the University's superb resources to educate between 400 and 800 public school students in grades six through twelve. He was quoted in a March 16, 2000 article by reporter Dave Schleck in the *Daily Press* as saying, "Clearly, this is an idea whose time has come." He pledged that his proposed charter school would raise student's standardized test scores and alleviate overcrowding in the district's high schools. Moreover, he proclaimed, "If I don't do that, I want you to take the charter away." The charter school is a "win-win situation for everyone," he said.[11]

Apparently, the Hampton City Board of Education did not eventually see it this way, even though the two had worked in close partnership for two years. The Board voted not to include Hampton University's charter school in the 2002 budget. There were accusations from both sides. Judith Brooks-Buck, who was hired to head the charter school and who worked along with Wanda Mitchell, former chair of the Department of Education, claimed that, "The paper did not give much of our side of the story," until Mary T. Christian, a member of the Virginia House of Delegates, who proposed the idea of a charter school to President

Harvey and Billy K. Cannaday, the former Superintendent of Schools, set the record straight. In an op-ed article in *The Daily Press* (Newport News), Sunday, June 9, 2002, Delegate Christian wrote:

> As a concerned and personally involved party, I felt the responsibility to research the issues and present the facts as I found them to be. Therefore, the following information is offered in response to the allegations made by the Hampton city schools.
>
> One of the first allegations stated that if a charter were granted, Hampton University would then provide all the funding necessary to run te school. Such an assertion is clearly illogical. If Hampton University intended to raise all the money, it would have been operated as a private school, and there would have been no reason to seek a charter from the School Board. Charter schools are, by definition, public schools.
>
> A second allegation stated that the budget was not submitted by the required deadline. The reality is, copies of the budget were submitted as required by the application, on Sept. 1, 2000. On Jan. 19, 2001, a revised budget was submitted as requested. On Feb. 21, 2002, still another budget was presented to the Hampton city schools budget committee. Each reflected expected allocations from Hampton city schools as well as the needs for staffing.
>
> Another distortion of the facts was that after a "sharpen the pencils" request to both sides, Hampton University had reduced its request by $5 per pupil and that the Hampton city schools had proposed an increase of $359. The budget director claimed that with this formula, Hampton University had reduced its request by a total of $600 and the Hampton city schools had increased its proposed allocation by $43,080. The document reflects that in reality, what the Hampton city schools had proposed was only in-kind contributions, with no cash being proposed for the budget. This means that the purported increase by the Hampton city schools had actually been a reduction from the $2,000 per pupil that had been previously proposed, to zero per pupil.
>
> Contrary to allegations that the selection process was not conducted properly, a computerized lottery, like the one used by Hampton city schools to select students for Jones Magnet School, was used. Applications were received from

182 families representing a diverse group of citizens that crossed all income levels.

The most egregious assertion came when teachers and other Hampton school employees were sent an electronic message from the superintendent claiming that the Hampton University charter school threatened their percent salary increases. Such a tactic caused unnecessary animosity in the community by using two issues that were clearly not related. . .

It was generally understood that we entered this project in the spirit of partnership. In fact, leaders in Hampton have been working for some time to promote a regional concept of working together and pooling resources for the Hampton Roads area. It is most disheartening that the school system and the city government now find themselves unable to even meet and discuss, within our own city, issues of such importance to all of our citizens, especially our children.

As one who was involved in this project from the beginning, my assessment is that a disservice has been done to the Hampton community. However too late to right a wrong.

Therefore, it is of utmost importance that all parties involved communicate openly about working together in the best interest of our children.

The Hampton City Board of Education denied Hampton University the right to present its case, even though the institution spent over $465,000 in preparation for opening the charter school in 2002. According to Judith Brooks-Buck, "We do not have plans for the charter school at this juncture, until the school board comes forth with an agreement." Though the charter school had not materialized in 2002, each student selected for the program was given a laptop computer by the President.

Translating Dreams into Reality

"You can't passively teach active participation in society."
—Ben Barber

On Hampton University's 125th birthday, April 1, 1993, President Harvey proposed the idea of the Leadership Institute, the architect's keystone for the institutionalization of service and the development of leadership. At that time, he stated:

In order to translate this vision into reality, it would mean building a leadership program into the entire University structure. Whether they were going to pursue physics, math, history, engineering, architecture, education, nursing, or any of the other 50-odd majors that we offer, every student that came to Hampton would be a part of this mandatory leadership program.

The four-year leadership program would teach that wise and courageous leadership and service must be dedications for life. We would honor and teach values, decency, dignity, honesty, respect for one self, respect for others, integrity. Before graduation, every student would be required to work one year in a school, community center, or some other community uplift program. There will be no restrictions on size or type of community to be served. It could be an affluent neighborhood or it could be a ghetto.

It is my feeling that it would take approximately $50 million to support this kind of program, because I would want every student admitted to Hampton to receive a full tuition scholarship. Room and board would be paid by their parents, guardians or student entitlements such as the Tuition Assistance Grant in Virginia or the Federal PELL Grant. Financing for the $50 million would come from individuals, corporations and foundations who share my vision of an academy for the training of outstanding leaders. To some such a concept may seem expensive, but it is not nearly so expensive as the continuing cost of welfare and the construction of more prisons. More importantly, an investment in the training of America's leaders is an investment in the nation.

The dream of having a Leadership Institute has been transformed into reality. It began, as previously noted, in the fall semester of 2000. In Harvey's vision and long-range plans, he wants Hampton University to play a pivotal and galvanizing role in the support of nationwide efforts to rejuvenate the spirit of service to others. His entreaty harmonizes with the vista of an increasingly outspoken cadre of leaders in higher education and in government who see in the spirit of community service a valuable and powerful social force for national renewal. In an address delivered at the 55th Anniversary dinner of the College Fund/ United Negro College Fund, in Columbus, Ohio on October 14, 1999, President Harvey called for a national service program. He stated:

> I would like to focus our attention on, revive our individual and collective commitment to, and hopefully initiate a national debate on something I consider to be one of the most basic and important of human responsibilities—service to others.
>
> While I am certain there is none among us who would deny either the importance or necessity of fulfilling a commitment of service to others, I am equally certain that there is none who could deny the frightening decline this commitment has suffered during the latter half of the twentieth century.
>
> There exists an unfortunate irony among our nation's most affluent citizens, those whose collective contributions hold the potential to shift the course of society. Only a small percentage of our leaders actually lead and, therefore, help those that are less fortunate than themselves. Relatively few share their resources in proportion to their capability.
>
> This does not apply only to the affluent, because, mind you, none of us is without this responsibility. Consider, if you will, that even the most disadvantaged members of our society are members, nonetheless, of the richest population on the face of the earth. They too have something—if only their personal time—that might be used in service to another. All of us must have a collective commitment to service, and this requirement is more imperative today than it has ever been before. . . .
>
> I propose that this country initiate a program of mandatory national service for all young people between the ages of 18 and 28. Included in the list as options for national service would be military service. . . .
>
> For those who do not want to exercise their national service obligations by being part of the military, another option could be the establishment of a National Service Corps. After receiving the appropriate training I can envision thousands of young men and women working all over this country in boys and girls clubs, recreational centers, wildlife parks, elementary school systems and many other venues.

Suppose they wanted to go to college first. That could be accomplished because every teacher, businessman or woman, TV personality, newspaper reporter, social worker, scientist, artist or what have you might be assigned to an underserved area of the country in order to fulfill their national service obligation.

Think about it. A teacher, social worker or doctor who had not completed his national service obligation could do so by serving others in some organized capacity. Still another option could be foreign service in the Peace Corps.

So you see, the options could be many. . . .

What would not be an option would be to get out of mandatory national service.

The length of service that I propose is fourteen months. This would include two months of discipline, rigor and training and twelve months of actual service. Just fourteen months. In that amount of time and through continual rotation, nearly every ill that plagues our society might well be eradicated or at least greatly diminished. While serving, those providing the service would likely reap all the inherent benefits associated with giving of themselves and benefit personally from the training and interaction with others. My proposal is not at all complicated, but it does require the sincere interest and efforts of us all.

An imperative component of this proposal is that it must have fair and equal application for every American, notwithstanding income levels, geographical location, educational backgrounds, financial status or political clout of the family. It will not work unless it is equal and fair across the board. Every American, unless mentally impaired, would be required to complete fourteen months of national service.

If that were to happen, I firmly believe that our young people would not only provide a service, but they also would become better citizens and subsequently adults.

You would see more humanity and less hate. You would see more civility and less cynicism. You would see more discipline and less destruction. You would see more compassion and less conflict. You would see more responsibility and less rage. You would see more ownership in society and less of the feeling that society owes something to someone.

In short, you would see more of a desire to make this great nation of ours a better place in which to live.

Until such initiatives are once again woven into the fabric of American culture, there are immediate ways in which we might commit our service to others. You could give of your resources. You could find the time to serve on boards. You could tutor and/or lecture in a variety of settings. You could make time to serve as a Big Brother or Big Sister. You could ask your own companies to establish major grants for student scholarships and professorships. You can provide meaningful internships and employment opportunities.

For me, service is truly an exhilarating experience. To realize how one's own efforts might influence the less fortunate is exciting, inspirational and gratifying. Lack of this realization may well be the obstacle that prohibits our commitment to service. And, if indeed it is, I believe I have offered to you at least some alternatives to revive this wavering commitment and enliven our responsibility to one another.

The Hampton University alma mater contains the lyrics, "O Hampton, we never can make thee a song, except as our lives do the singing. In service that will thy great spirit prolong, and send it through centuries ringing." If the world at large would allow their lives to do the singing through service, I am convinced that the song of life would be the sweetest refrain imaginable.[12]

Building a Stairwell for Student Living, Learning, Leadership, and Service

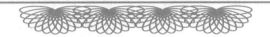

O Hampton, we never can make thee a song
Except as our lives do the singing,
In service that will thy great spirit prolong,
And send it through centuries ringing!
—Sarah Collins Fernandis, 1882
(Excerpted from the Hampton University *Alma Mater*)

"So if there are any among you who considers him or herself to be a baller, shot caller, or brawler, Hampton University is not the place for you!" exhorted President William R. Harvey at the Freshmen Orientation Assembly on August 21, 1999. And he forewarned prospective high school students, too, that "you need to make up your mind now that those traits will be left behind you. Otherwise, there is no need for you even to apply, because here, you will embrace the same values that everyone else does." In sketching the contours of Hampton values and imparting what it means to be a Hamptonian, Harvey tells freshmen or future students that "Hampton was founded with the philosophy of providing an Education for Life." And that philosophy is "timeless and still very appropriate." Although vast changes have transpired since its founding father, General Samuel Chapman Armstrong's time, "his principles of strong values remain at the center of the spirit of Hampton University," says Harvey. "First, we strive for honesty, decency, dignity, integrity, respect for others and self-respect. We strive for high academic achievement and excellence in all our pursuits." Second, "We do not

245

condone those who use foul language; our attitudes are not resentful or belligerent." And third, "We believe it is important to serve the needs of others. We know that it is right to help and share with people who are less fortunate than we are."[1]

Erika Turner, a member of the first class to graduate in the new century of the third millennium, exemplified these Hamptonian values. The mass media arts major and aspirant lawyer, interviewed prior to her graduation, was the editor-in-chief of the *Hampton Script* for the 1999–2000 academic year. She was also a presidential scholar and a member of the Honors College, where she tutored students at a middle school. As one of ten student leaders, she met monthly with President Harvey. So swayed by Hampton and Harvey's leadership, she pronounced:

> I have definitely told Dr. Harvey that I plan to send my kids to Hampton and a lot of my friends, seniors, who are graduating and thinking about the future a little bit, have expressed the same sentiments. I believe he is a great role model and he would be a great role model for my children. I have friends who attend other HBCUs, but I believe the Hampton experience is better. Hampton is at the forefront academically and technologically, and Dr. Harvey is moving us full speed ahead in the new century, so I want my children to experience what I have experienced. I think Dr. Harvey is such a great person and a wonderful leader for Hampton. . . . What is unique about him is his interest in the school, the students' welfare, our progress, which is so evident to me during these four years. I was interviewing Dr. Harvey for a story on the capital campaign and after the interview, he took time and talked to me about my future plans and what law schools I was applying to and wished me luck, and every time I see him he asks me if I heard from a school, and he makes an effort to see how I am doing. He is a busy person and I appreciate that. Dr. Harvey and the rest of the Hampton University family promote service and giving back. I am part of the Honors College and we are encouraged to give back to others, to serve, and to bring up those who are coming behind us. For example, as part of the Student Initiatives for the $200 Million Capital Campaign, students are encouraged to donate two dollars to the capital campaign and they receive a

button. They are taking an interest in our school, and I think they want to contribute to the campaign. There is a genuine sense of family here. They care about what happens to Hampton after they leave. I definitely plan to donate money after law school. I really care about Hampton and believe so many positive things are happening here that other students can benefit from. I think students here appreciate his leadership and he has our best interest at heart. I believe so many things are going on here that do not happen at other HBCUs. I think Dr. Harvey has set a wonderful example as an African American who is proactive and productive. Dr. Harvey has been a role model for me. If I see something is wrong, I don't sit around and complain.

When I asked what would she want the world to know about President Harvey's legacy and its impact on Hampton's students, she responded: "I would want the world to know Dr. Harvey sets such a wonderful example for us to follow. He encourages us to give back, to serve others, to challenge ourselves, to be professional at all times, to attend graduate school, and to further ourselves in terms of education. I want the world to know that we are well-prepared, and the best students in terms of academics and our commitment to serving others, and in giving back, and that we like to be challenged. We are the leaders of tomorrow."

Turner, an emerging twenty-first century leader who, like her role model, President Harvey, and in the words of her alma mater, plans to let her life do the singing in the tradition of countless other Hamptonians. Even though Turner graduated in the class of 2000, she would no doubt be excited to know that for the mass media arts majors following her, the Scripps Howard Foundation donated more than $6.3 million to the University to construct The Scripps Howard School of Journalism and Communication, the first multi-million dollar gift given to an HBCU. In addition to the money for the building, the contribution includes $1 million to establish a Scripps Howard Foundation Professorship of Journalism endowment, $200,000 for new media equipment, money for 15 student scholarships, and a visiting journalist program. Attracting students of cut polished stones, such as Turner, in the twenty-first century, is the fuel that powers Harvey's engine in the $200 Million Capital Campaign. Since Harvey is interested in the process of making them shine as brightly as he can, the campaign will allow the University "to obtain and retain the best professors" and to provide greater opportunities for curricular offerings, such as those in pharmacy, physical therapy, computer engineering, biomedicine, and physics. It will help develop the endowment of faculty professorships and chairs and establish endowed student scholarships, renovate or build new residential and classroom facilities, and provide support for the museum." Unarguably, at the dawn of this millennium where technology is the defining force of our lives, having a totally wired campus, which was completed in 1999, means there is a hook-up in every dormitory room and an increase in electronic classrooms to help students successfully compete in the computer-age marketplace. Undoubtedly, they will be well-prepared for it. According to America's Most Wired Colleges 2000 list, compiled by Yahoo Internet Life, Hampton University ranked number 72. In such an age of technological change, the $200 Million Capital Campaign will also allow the University to stand firm on the timeless value of service to others. As Harvey spoke in his Inaugural Address in 1978, "It is my firm belief that decency is as important as degrees, and I want them [students] to be good moral leaders who have a sense of commitment to community and service as well." One component of the $200 Million Capital Campaign is to develop The Leadership Institute, which is designed to take promising leaders, like Turner, and prepare them in their chosen fields of study to serve the community.

As the Leadership Institute prepares to train an army of servant leaders for the twenty-first century, likewise, the President has personally taken many students under his wings and mentored them, so, they, too, might soar like an eagle in the art of leadership. Clayton Bond, a 1998 alumnus of Hampton University and its 1997–1998 Student Government Association president, is a beneficiary of this special mentoring. On the cover of the spring 1998 *Hampton Alumni Magazine*, Bond and Charles Wilson, the 1997–

1998 senior class president, in a futuristic stance, posed with President Harvey on the lawn of the Mansion House. The headline caption reads "21st-Century Leadership."

Seemingly, Bond, a member of the Hampton Student Leadership Program and a presidential scholar during his matriculation at Hampton, is on that inner path toward leadership. He graduated from the Kennedy School of Government at Harvard University, with a Master of Public Policy degree in Political Advocacy and Leadership in June 2000. After graduation, Bond spent the summer as a political/economic affairs intern in the U.S. Embassy, Gaborone, Botswana in Africa. In September 2000, he was awarded a Fulbright Fellowship, where he began pursuing another master's degree in environmental change and management at Oxford University in England. Upon graduating from Hampton University, he was accepted to both Oxford and Harvard; however, neither would allow him to defer, so he reapplied to Oxford and was admitted. When he completes his studies at Oxford, he plans to enter the foreign service for at least three years and eventually become an elected or appointed public servant. But as a freshmen at Hampton, according to Rodney Smith, President of Ramapo College and former vice president for student affairs, he was not so sure of his footpath until he came under the influence of President Harvey. Smith recalled:

> I can tell you several examples of success stories, that I have seen in students who have taken advantage of the opportunity to be mentored by Dr. Harvey. One person, in particular, I am thinking about is Clayton Bond. Clayton came here as a freshman, wide-eyed, bushy-tailed, curious to learn; his major at that time was marine science. And there was a quiet quality about him that said there is more to this young man than meets the eye. And he was very assertive, and he went over and introduced himself to Dr. Harvey at the first reception [for freshmen students]. I was watching him. They started talking, and over the years he has been able to work himself into leadership positions and has taken advantage of

every opportunity to talk to Dr. Harvey. Going back to that first year, I remember that we talked to him about Harvard and whether or not he would be interested in Harvard. And his response was, "Gee, me, little old me, I could never get into a school like Harvard." And that was his response in the freshman year. But over the years, in working with Dr. Harvey and understanding the possibilities and in appreciating his own potential, the young man went on to change his major to political science, went to the Kennedy School of Government, also studied at Oxford [for a summer] and also served as an intern with the Prime Minister of Great Britain. And that's an example of the kind of tutoring, mentoring, and encouraging that I have seen from Dr. Harvey. He's done it with several students on how to be successful. He keeps his eye on them. He doesn't forget people, particularly students.

While Bond does not recall this specific occurrence in his freshmen year of being encouraged to attend Harvard by the President and Smith, he graciously acknowledged, "That might have happened because I'm that kind of person. Well, yes, I mean that would be typically me, I suppose. But I don't fully recall the quote." But he can explicitly recall President Harvey's influence on him.

One of the big ways was his leadership style. It was important for me to see. I think Dr. Harvey is an excellent leader, and I think he is an excellent leader because he thinks for himself. He is strong enough and bold enough to make decisions that he feels or knows is in the best interest of Hampton University, which sometimes might not be popular, might not go over well with faculty and students, but which need to be made. I think that certainly is admirable and worthy of acclaim. That's where he had an influence on me, especially as a freshman or sophomore; his style is one of more empowerment. I want to digress for a moment. The thesis I wrote for this degree I am working on, "Neighborhood Redevelopment in Detroit," the models, the ways of thinking about neighborhood redevelopment just in general, are asset-based and one of empowering communities building upon their plea of "I am weak, give me money." I think Dr. Harvey was really helpful to me in showing me that there is a lot one can do for oneself and a lot that one should do for oneself, so that you have pride in yourself and in your work.

> That was very important to me. Like kind of knowing how dif-
> ferent departments at Hampton are funded, how many have
> to raise their own funds, in some ways can be viewed as more
> of a challenge than an opportunity, but I kind of like to view it
> as both and more an opportunity than certainly a setback or
> anything like that. I don't expect anyone to just give me any-
> thing and I don't think people should expect that.

When I inquired whether his view of leadership and self-empower-
ment had changed under Harvey's mentorship, he said, "It was
something that might have been there within me, but I didn't really
think about it a lot, and so seeing Dr. Harvey's example and talking
with him about his leadership and leadership style, in general, was
very helpful to me to make that an important thing in my view of
leadership and in my view of life."

As a student at Hampton University, Bond noted that he
interacted with the President many times, either through the
office hours he would set aside for students, or, as he stated, "I
would take advantage of opportunities after different programs
in Ogden Hall, or when seeing him on campus and knowing how
busy he was, he still took time out to talk with me. I valued that a
lot and learned a lot from it and from him. . . . I know the influence Hampton had on me in terms of just seeking out opportunities and not being so passive about things. I certainly was not
passive when I got to Hampton, but I wasn't necessarily as driven.
I was driven, but Hampton definitely helped me to be more so in
terms of locating opportunities and doing what I can to take
advantage of them."

In exploiting opportunities, he found a friend in President
Harvey. "Dr. Harvey took an interest in and supported my pursuit
of various opportunities, including a study trip to Oxford in the
summer after my junior year, which played a major role in my
desire to pursue a master's program there; an internship in the
British Parliament in the summer after my senior year; my Fulbright application to the U.K.; and the master's program in public
policy. Indeed, Dr. Harvey definitely encouraged me throughout

my years at Hampton and in my post-Hampton years to 'dream no small dreams,'" said Bond.

Although Harvey believes, "It is important to provide opportunities for the best and brightest," likewise one must afford "some opportunities for those who may not be the best and brightest. Hampton does that inasmuch as we allow 10 percent of our current class to come to Hampton who may not have the requisites," he contended. These students "may have the scores but not the grades, or the grades but not the scores." In his opinion, he argued: "I don't think colleges ought to acquiesce because the student hasn't reached a certain level of development. Colleges and universities should not gear themselves to their clientele, but vice versa."

Harvey believes in giving people an opportunity to succeed, like Nefertari Kirkman-Bey, the sophomore class president for 1999–2000, and the senior class president for 2001–2002. Upon graduation from high school, the precocious Kirkman-Bey exemplified those students who do not meet all of the prerequisites for entry into Hampton. When she graduated from a highly ranked charter high school in Detroit, Michigan, emphasizing mathematics, science and technology, her GPA was only 2.5. Kirkman-Bey, a mass media major, with an interest in music engineering technology, wanted to increase her chances of entering Hampton, one of the three schools of her choice, so she entered the Precollege Summer Bridge Program at Hampton University. "What happens is if you do get straight As in the summer [program], you are able to come to Hampton as an enrolled freshman. If not, you are not accepted into Hampton, so for me this was my opportunity and my last chance to be accepted into the University of my choice." This is what Kirkman-Bey, who was a member of the Student Leadership Program, the dean's list, the University choir, and the NAACP, said about Hampton University while matriculating there during her sophomore year.

My experience has definitely been a positive experience. I think I came with a lot of determination that a lot of other people didn't, because I did not want to experience what I had in high school of having a low GPA and not being involved. So I came into the school my first year, I ran for office and I won freshman vice president and I got 3.3, and from there my GPA continued to go up, and I continued to get more and more opportunities to be at more and more programs at this institution. It has been nothing but positive. I have learned so many things, met so many people and had so many experiences that I think that this is something that I can carry with me forever. Just from the Student Leadership Program, I have learned small things in terms of communication, small things in terms of etiquette, small things in terms of professionalism, to be well-spoken and simple things that get you a step ahead of someone else—things I did not know prior to coming to Hampton and things I did not know prior to joining the Student Leadership Program.

When the Academy of the Arts and Sciences was seeking music engineering technology majors as interns, the President, who initiated this program at the University, took time to write her letters of recommendations. As a student leader who met with Harvey on a monthly basis, Kirkman-Bey, whose initial major was music engineering technology, offered these insights.

When I think of Dr. Harvey, I think of a man who is very personally in touch with the students. When I first met Dr. Harvey it was in precollege, and during my tenure here for only a month at precollege, I saw President Harvey walk back and forth across the campus, and he would always speak to me. And there are a lot of campuses that you go to and people have never seen the president before. You can always go to his office if you are a student and schedule an appointment with him. I think that is phenomenal, because on a lot of campuses, people are unable to get in contact with their presidents, vice presidents, provosts. When I see him in meetings where [other students] are not able to see him, I think that he is very cognitive and willing to listen to what we have to say at all times. He will try his best to make sure that if we bring something to the table that is of good value, he will try his best to support us in all aspects. One example would be the

student initiative in the $200 Million Campaign. Campus Life
Board [composed of student leaders] came up with the idea
of the student initiative.

Like Kirkman-Bey, Clayton Bond noted the President's willingness to listen to students. "As an advocate for students,
through my job as SGA President, I can say that Dr. Harvey was
always supportive of resolving students' concerns that I brought
to the table, especially at our monthly meetings with student
leaders, Dr. Harvey, and top administration—be they residential
hall concerns, general campus concerns, or concerns regarding
University policy."

As one of the student leaders who attended the monthly
meetings with Harvey and the monthly meetings of the administrative council, Erika Turner would agree with Bond and
Kirkman-Bey.

> We update Dr. Harvey and other members of the admin-
> istrative council on activities of whatever group we are repre-
> senting. I will normally discuss on what upcoming issues are
> going into the Script and if we have any needs like computers
> then I will bring that to the attention of Mr. Scott [then vice
> president for business affairs and treasurer] or Dr. Harvey. Dr.
> Harvey will regularly ask for input on various projects that he
> is working on. He asked for our input about the student
> union center and what the student body would need. I men-
> tioned that the *Script* needed more room and additional com-
> puters, so we can publish a high quality publication. During
> the administrative council, the student leaders bring to the
> attention of Dr. Harvey concerns of the students. The presi-
> dent of the Student Government Association mentioned
> compensation for resident assistants in the dormitories, con-
> cern about parking fees, and the SGA president wanted a
> sidewalk in front of the new union, so students could access
> it easier and that was something that was taken care of right
> away. Most things that we bring to the attention of the coun-
> cil, Mr. [Leon] Scott [President of the Consolidated Bank in
> Richmond, Virginia] or Dr. [Rodney] Smith [now President of
> Ramapo College] will write it down and bring it back to the
> council and it is taken care of immediately. They don't have
> any problem taking care of things we care about or feel need

improvement. I have known him [Dr. Harvey] for the four years I've been here and he is a good listener. I will definitely send my children here. I served on a task force for administrative effectiveness. Dr. Harvey, who appointed me as a representative, is proactive. He wanted to look at various departments and assess how they function and come up with recommendations on improving them. My group looked at graduation and registration processes as things that students are concerned with. I thought it was appropriate that he, too, was concerned with those two areas and we basically looked at how they function and made recommendations for improving them. He is always trying to improve.

A similar view was also shared by Cicely Harris, then senior class president for 1999–2000, who met with the President for two consecutive years as a student leader and who felt that he was decisive and attentive to students' issues. "Being a good listener, he asks us questions so he can expound on our answers, so he will know what we are talking about. For example, if we want to get campus excitement up or if we are talking about entertainers to bring to the campus, he will ask, 'What kind of entertainment? Are you interested in gearing it toward the parents or the students?' Then he would have us to take an active part in deciding things."

For some students who have limited interaction with the President and minimal involvement in student activities, their perceptions of the President differs. Harris stated, "They are stand-offish about his image. What she has experienced, however, is at variance with their understanding. When asked if she ever offers another perspective, she responded this way. "I impart to students that President Harvey is trying to help us out. He looks into our concerns and get things rolling. We wanted a phone in the student union, and within a week and a half, we had the phone. We were noticing that with the $200 Million Campaign, we should have more technology, and we should have a student union comparable to other black colleges. It would attract more people if they see we are renovating the campus and trying to keep in time with other institutions. We spoke to him in 1999 about our concerns. Now we have a student union being built. Although I will be graduating before I see it, I am excited that it will attract other students and bring more of a campus interest, because it will have a movie theater and bowling alley, so people on campus and off campus will enjoy the student union."

Keisha Taylor, a 2000 graduate in Mass Media Arts, has a close-up perspective of Harvey and vehemently disagreed with the misperceptions of the President. Having served as Student Representative to the Board of Trustees during the academic year 1999–2000 and having worked closely with the President, whom she regards as a leader and a hard worker, Taylor has, too, heard comments about the President as being distant or aloof. "Probably it is not extremely widespread, not a majority—but I think that it is a pretty good amount. I think I attribute that to the fact that a lot of times President Harvey is not seen during day-to-day campus life. Usually, we see him during specific events that are University-related, and maybe we don't see him often just walking around campus during weekdays, because he is often away trying to get funds for the University. I think that a lot of people don't understand that he's out on business for the University to make our University the best that it possibly can be and that's the reason for his not being seen. But for people who don't know that, they may think that his not being there is a sign that he doesn't care about student life, which is very untrue."

Taylor, who was an honor student and a recipient of an award as one of twenty-five top communications students in the nation, took the time to present a different perception of the President to her fellow students. She said, "I let a lot of the students know that he is an excellent person to work with and that he really has our interests at heart. And I tell them that they should just look at the things he is doing, with the campaign, and the implications that will have for Hampton. We're getting a new student union, which we definitely need; he has rebuilt the stadium which is going to be great for the football team. These are all things that are done for the interest of the student body here, as well as academic changes. I know that he is doing a lot for academic changes, especially for the school of mass media."

Rebecca Sanders, editor-in-chief of the *Hampton Script* and a business major, has, as well, met monthly with President Harvey. When ideas are presented to him and the administrators in his council, she noted, "Everybody comments on them. And then Dr. Harvey gives us feedback on whether or not that concern or that situation can be amended or can be paid attention to. And he is pretty good about hearing the concerns of the students, especially at those meetings. And I have seen a lot of things for the past two years change." She, too, feels that he is a really good listener. But she said, "A lot of people, I think, they misunderstand Dr. Harvey, especially because they don't see him often. But to be perfectly honest, when things are not going the way students would like it, Dr. Harvey generally doesn't know that it's going on. Because when he does find out about it, I have seen a lot of changes happen. I used to be a resident assistant in Stone and so was our SGA president. And we brought to his attention just some small minor things that needed to be done cosmetically, like in the bathrooms. And the next day, it was done. Some things are feasible and some things are not as far as requests from students. But yes, he's an active listener and he's also very active in getting things done."

For his detractors, she conjectured that, "They just don't take the proper avenues to get things done. Or they just don't have the understanding that sometimes it takes a little longer to get the larger things completed. I think the main concerns of a lot of students are dormitories, cafeterias, and things like that. It's not that they are not aware of that, but it's that everything happens in stages. But I have to say that in my five years, I have watched so many dorms have cable, and Internet access, so it's not like concerns are not being heard. I think everyone is just in a hurry to get things done and they are not looking at the fact that it takes more than just one day to complete a project."

In meeting with President Harvey on a monthly basis as a student leader, she gained, along with other leaders, a different perspective that other students do not have.

> I guess the impression that we get is that he is definitely a powerful man and he makes things happen because Hampton is a pretty prestigious University. As far as a one-on-one person, we really don't know him, because we don't have access to him, but being in meetings with the administrative council once a month, I have an insight that others don't, so I do see how things actually get done. But as an outsider, I think you miss that.
>
> I think you try to listen and, as a student, you do understand where other students are coming from. You try to not necessarily correct them, but give them information so that they can come to their own specific conclusions. Because everybody is going to have an opinion whether or not they like somebody or dislike somebody. I can only give them the information that I have or the presumptions that I might have about someone else, but I guess it's all about their own experiences with him and how they associate what their positive and negative images are about Dr. Harvey.

President Harvey would say to these students who have concerns, as he did with the entering freshmen for the academic year of 1999–2000, that "Hampton, like all other institutions, has areas which must be strengthened. We work diligently to bolster those. Hampton, like all other institutions, is faced with external and internal challenges. But you may rest assured that we face each challenge with realism, with planning, and with confidence. In sum, our efforts to advance this great institution are impacted by the inevitable forces of an imperfect world. As such, we do not exempt ourselves from negative criticism, nor from reasoned and informed dissent. Indeed, these have—through the years—worked to increase our capacity for excellence."

As a strong champion of the President, Sanders opined:

> Dr. Harvey is a very hard-working man and I think that as a black man he is probably one of the greatest role models that I have seen and a lot of students won't say that and won't believe that and don't have that conviction, but if they ever

see Dr. Harvey speak or just look around and see how Hampton has come from the 1970s to the year 2000, its just phenomenal. That man has the ability to raise $200 million, which is completely mind-blowing. I don't think people really realize how great, how grandiose, that really is. You know, to do that all for education for African American students, I don't think people really look at that and see what an accomplishment that is. I think that people, unfortunately, misunderstand his raising money and not paying attention to the students, but what he is doing by raising all that money is ensuring that Hampton will be there for my grandchildren. He has ensured that this school will be here for a very long time and I think that sometimes people think in a very small box instead of outside the box. I think Dr. Harvey thinks outside of the box. Even outside of his being president, as an entrepreneur and as black man, he has done all of that for himself and his family and that is phenomenal because we don't see that in the black community. And I think people need to step outside of just seeing bugs in the dorm, and those things, and see the grander picture of what the entire spectrum of African American education is at Hampton and that it's going to be here for a very long time. And that both me, my children and my grandchildren will have the opportunity to attend Hampton.

Admittedly, she acknowledged, "I have to say that before I was a part of this council, I really didn't have too much of a feeling for Dr. Harvey at all."

Keisha Taylor admitted also, "Before actually working with Dr. Harvey, I knew that he was interested in student life, but I thought he was probably more interested in the University as a whole. Now I understand that his interest in making the University better is directly proportional to making students of the University better and I really got a very good understanding of that in working with him this year." Taylor, along with other student leaders, feels that the misperception is clearly related to the level of student participation and sense of integration into the University beyond the classroom. She argued, "Those people who feel that he is strictly out for financial reasons or that he doesn't care about students and their lives here at Hampton, are the people who choose not to involve themselves in campus activities."

When asked if these students understood the connection between his raising funds and his lack of visibility during the week, she answered, "They don't see it, because they don't care to see it. I honestly believe that's what it is. I can say that on campus I have seen Dr. Harvey, and he will stop and talk to you. Now when I lived in the dormitory, I never had that personal experience, but I have had the experience where you will see him walking on the street, maybe from his home to the office, and he will stop and talk and ask you how are you and things of that nature and I think that is an effort on his part to get the students to see that he is genuinely concerned about our welfare. But there are some people who are going to think that is just a front. People are funny that way. I wonder sometimes if the man would have to turn a trick or do cartwheels before people would actually believe that he is seriously, genuinely concerned about us."

Rodney Smith, then speaking as vice president for student affairs, has seen him "do cartwheels" during his tenure at the University from 1992–2001. He told this story about an incident with a young man that occurred in his first year as dean of students.

> I'll give you a story that most people don't know about. I got a call about three o'clock in the morning. I was told that there was a young man on the top floor of the Du Bois Building, and he was getting ready to jump. This was a young man who had been expelled from school for marijuana. And not many people know about this and I don't talk about this, because this was a private incident. But they got the fire department—this was after about two hours of President Harvey counseling and working with this student personally to get him to come down. So by the time I got to campus, Dr. Harvey had already counseled him down, escorted him over to the University Police to receive more counseling and guidance, and had serious heart-to-heart talks with him. I took over about five o'clock or so in the morning. The following day, Dr. Harvey had already told him to come to see him in his office. After talking with him, and hearing the young man

explain that his life was over and he had always wanted to have a college education from Hampton—Hampton had always been his dream—Dr. Harvey gave him another chance and said, "I am going to give you a chance but I want you to do something with this opportunity. I don't want you to throw it away." And that young man, even today, he's still fighting to finish his education. But he still checks in from time to time to let us know that he is doing well. That's not something that we talk about often, but that shows the depth of involvement of the President from the student who is gifted and talented and can go to high places to the student who just needs an opportunity and who needs that counseling. I don't know if any other counselor or director of a residential hall would have been able to counsel that student down that night. And Dr. Harvey took the time, got out of his bed, and came over. Not many presidents I know would have done that, because they have staff, and the police. But that's the level of his concern for every person, every student on this campus. He did it himself. And there was never any publicity about it; there was never any news in the newspapers; there was never any talk about it on campus.

Collectively, Smith provided additional support for the President's concern for students.

Now on a group basis, Dr. Harvey has gone from residential hall to residential hall to talk to freshmen. He's done this on occasion from year to year. I remember one year, when I was Dean of Students, actually it was two years in a row, Dr. Harvey accompanied me to speak to students in residential halls about policies, about issues, and to answer questions on a one-to-one basis, kind of like armchair chats. This is another thing that people never hear about him. This was a group of about 100 or so young men—freshmen—all with questions, all with concerns, all with some issues. And he sat down and spoke to them about an hour and a half, basically serving as a role model. I sat there and I learned. What I learned from him all these years, in all these different roles that he has played, which most of the public never hears about, is that leadership is at all levels. You have to lead anyone who is a part of that family, whether it be someone who is picking up papers around the campus to the incoming

freshmen, you belong to everyone and everyone deserves
some time and attention and the concern has to be across the
board. There is no concern for one group over another. And
that's what I have seen from him. His concern and his caring
reaches the groups at every level of this institution.

When Smith was asked whether Harvey has armchair chats with the
women students, he replied, "He does it as often as he can. Sometimes he may not do it all during the year. Sometimes what he does
on a group basis is walk to the residential halls and chat with groups
of students. On a more organized level, the residential hall director
would call a meeting, say at 7:30 PM, and he would attend that meeting to talk to students and answer questions, and this goes on sometimes two or three times a year. On a more informal basis, he walks
around more than most administrators, actually more than all the
administrators do. Even when there is nothing going on, he walks
around and he talks with students about different things happening
on campus, how things are going with them, or he may visit a dorm
or residential hall unannounced. And he would walk through or he
would get into conversations with groups of four or five students
and then that normally attracts more students to stand around and
talk with him. That happens repeatedly."

The conversation might center around "the University, scholarships, different programs, access to computers, global issues,
political issues. And they enjoy that. Particularly, political science
students like to sit around and chat with Dr. Harvey about those
issues. I should also tell you that once or twice a year when we
have severe weather conditions, he gets out and personally gets in
his car or puts on his raincoat and he walks the campus to look at
safety and security issues for students and faculty. When I was
solely the student affairs officer, sometimes we would run into
each other and if he were walking, I would walk with him, or if he
were driving, I would jump into his car with him and we would ride
around and check the campus and stop certain places and run into
buildings. We've done that on several occasions. But people don't

know about those things. You know you have your staff to make you aware of these things, but you also need to check some things out for yourself. And that's what he does," said Smith.

Members of the Student Leader Program echoed the perspective of Rodney Smith. Like Smith, Keisha Taylor, along with other student leaders, learned many lessons from the master teacher and gained an "education for life" as a participant in the Student Leadership Program. She avouched:

> My experience of being the student trustee to the board has been a phenomenal one. These are meetings that I attend with movers and shakers in the black community and in the community at large. Dr. Harvey's influence has been a great one on me. He has shown me leadership and I really feel that I have learned a lot about how to get things done in the order in which it should be taken, like who you should go to when you have a problem. Now I understand more about the hierarchy of getting things done. I think that is very important that I can take to the business world, because there is a definite chain of command and that is something that everyone should know before getting into the real working world. You cannot always go straight to the top when you need to get problems solved. I've learned that.
>
> Things can get done without having to talk directly with Dr. Harvey. Like you can get a lot of things done by talking to other [people] who are here specifically to help students. But he has always made himself readily available to me and to other students with his open door policy. I have never gone to him during his open door policy. Usually I see him at meetings, or I might be able to slip in maybe a little bit better than other students would be able to.

Taylor has also absorbed another valuable lesson from the President.

> One thing that I admire about him the most and that I have learned from him is that although he is a leader and a man who is sought after very much, when talking to him, he talked to me almost as if I were one of his children. I remember having a conversation on a ride back from a Board of

Trustees meeting and I was just sitting with him shooting the breeze and talking to him about my career opportunities and things of that nature and he was just giving me his honest opinion and was talking to me more like a father figure than the President of the University. And that was mind-blowing to me because for him to have the position that he has, he really didn't have to take the time to talk to me one-on-one about my life decisions. He really made me feel that what I did was important to him. And I think that's something that he taught me. That no matter how far you have gone in life, it's always good to speak to everyone and to acknowledge everyone's feelings and to make everyone feel that they have something to offer. And that's exactly what he did. And I think that this is one of the reasons that he is as successful as he is today.

Participants in the Student Leadership Program, like the aforementioned ones, act as a liaison between the administration, the student body, and also the Hampton community. Moreover, they serve as role models and as leaders by promoting the values and expectations of the University through cultural awareness, and educational and social activities for the student body.

Unquestionably, this program, designed to facilitate development and to enhance the leadership learning experiences for selected Hampton University's students, serves as a nurturing ground for some of Hampton's most successful alumni. The Student Leadership Program, initiated in 1976 and expanded under Harvey's presidency, has become, according to Rodney Smith, "a model student leadership program for other institutions around the country. The University of Virginia and the University of Richmond use it as a model, and Tuskegee, Chicago State, and most of the presidents who have gone out of here have carried the model with them to their other institutions." These student leaders are selected to enter an intensive training program that provides experiences in interpersonal skills, development, leadership theory, personal style assessment, and personal growth. Each student leader is required to review and sign a written contract, which states his /her roles and responsibilities to the Student Leadership

Program. If the student leader fails to keep his/her agreement or performs below standards, he/she is warned and/or dismissed from the Student Leadership Program. The program places immense value on developing the total student who devotes his or her time and service to the Hampton community.

The Student Leadership Program attracts approximately 400 applicants; however, it is a highly selective program and only about 125 students are selected. Kirkman-Bey pointed out that there is a high demand for the program. Because the process is so rigorous, she said: "A lot of times people self-eliminate because they become discouraged. And once people make it through the first steps, then we [committee members] have to do a process of elimination on our own." Student leaders are a part of the selection process. According to Kirkman-Bey, "We look at the activities that they have been in, but we look at the consistency. We look at people who have been members of organizations for two and three years, not someone who just joined last week because they knew the information was coming up. We also look at the GPA. If you have a 3.0 or a 2.5, we look to see if you have kept it steady. We don't like to see people who have shot from 2.3 to 3.0 and then back down to 2.3. That's very inconsistent. We look to see the kind of community service people have done. What is it that you are doing for the community that you have not been asked to do."

For Kirkman-Bey and other student leaders, "The rewards of being a part of the Student Leadership Program are many. "You don't get any money; you don't get any scholarships. But the Student Leadership Program is so competitive and people want to be a part of it so much because there are other things that are rewarding that you get from it. For example, we ushered for the $200 Million Campaign banquet. We ushered for Founder's Day and for Convocation. We put on programs like the Black-Jewish Forums, Miss Hampton Pageant, Homecoming, and the Orientation for Freshmen. We are also in charge of Parents' Weekend. We plan everything from who is coming to making sure the packages are sent out to the Parents. Student leaders are in charge of the elections. Student leaders are phenomenal on this campus."

As part of becoming a student leader, students participate in a retreat and orientation in leadership training. Kirkman-Bey asserted: "One thing about this program that I think I would have to basically let the people of Hampton University and the world know is that you have a large number of minority students who are simply phenomenal in all aspects—academics, social life, knowing how to network and be positive in our actions. I have seen nothing like it since I have had the opportunity to live on this earth, and I think it is a very, very rare thing that you do see."

Educating for Living

The Student Leadership Program is an exemplary model for understanding Hampton University's mission, which is geared toward "the promotion of learning, building character, and preparation of promising students for positions of leadership and service." With the opening of the newly initiated Leadership Institute, it is Harvey's dream to eventually mandate that every student, whatever discipline, be a part of its leadership program. Preparing its nearly six thousand students, who represent nearly every state in the nation and more than thirty-five foreign countries, for an "Education for Life" means the development of the whole person, which includes his or her intellectual academic education, his or her career, his or her social, spiritual, physical, psychological, emotional, and personal self. To equip them with such an education, there must be a system of governance and accountability for ensuring the product of a productive citizen. That system of governance and accountability starts at the top and ends with all constituents, including administrators, faculty, staff, and students, being responsible for themselves and for others.

President Harvey sets the tone, for example, when he welcomes each new freshmen class member into their new family and new home: "The Hampton family and our Home by the Sea!"

He might say to students, as he did to the entering freshmen class of the 1999–2000 academic year, that, "In choosing Hampton University as your institution of higher education, you have chosen the opportunity to mark your place in a history and tradition that are unmatched by any other college or university—anywhere. And, I might add—you have chosen wisely. For Hampton University's legacy parallels the legacy of a dynamic people, country, and world." In pointing out the traditional mission of the institution, to train young, newly- freed slaves to teach and lead their people to build an industrial system—a work ethic for the sake of self-support, intelligent labor, and the shaping of personal character, he asserted that this mission was grounded in the principles of service to others, learning by doing, and the attainment of an education for life.

"In 1999, on the cusp of the twenty-first century and 131 years after Hampton's founding, certainly many things have changed," he said. "However, many have remained the same. For example, even today at Hampton, we are still deeply committed to our founding principles. Woven throughout every thread of our culture are the timeless values of leadership, lifelong education, service to others, and exemplary character. These values are the compass that directs our course through the turbulent and ever-changing waves of society and they have led Hampton University to many great successes." He mentioned the technological advancement and preparedness as one of the most recent successes. "Beginning this year, every on-campus dormitory room and administrative office at Hampton University is wired for a computer. This means that the campus community is connected to the world via the Internet and World Wide Web. We are also connected to our immediate environment via HUNet, our Intranet system. HUNet will provide each student and faculty member continual contact and communication through assigned e-mail addresses and accounts—free of charge. This communication will enable faculty to offer items such as course talking points through e-mail for various class sessions. It will allow students the opportunity to ask questions and seek information outside of scheduled class time and faculty office hours."

Continuing, he contended:

> While Hampton's technological capabilities are impressive, I guarantee you that no aspect of our Home by the Sea outshines or is of greater importance than our academic offerings. Some examples include that for the third consecutive year, *Black Issues in Higher Education* has verified that among all American colleges and universities, Hampton University has the highest graduation rate for African American undergraduates with English degrees and the third highest graduation rate for African American undergraduates with communication degrees.
>
> I take immense pride in sharing with you that our newly established doctoral Physical Therapy program is the first to be established in the State of Virginia and the only to be established at an HBCU. And our School of Pharmacy is the first to have been established at an HBCU in the last forty-six years. Hampton's Ph.D. in Nursing is the first at any black school.

The President told students that a 1998 issue of *Change* magazine recognized Hampton University as one of the three most successful HBCUs in the areas of academic achievement and retention. Moreover, he professed to them, "For three consecutive years, Hampton University was named to the John Templeton Foundation's Honor Roll for Character Building Colleges. These positive recognitions, simply put, verify that Hampton's students are provided not only a relevant, but quality education in a caring and attentive environment. They come here and learn; they stay until they have finished; and we allow them to leave only when their work is done. Surely, no one could ask more than that!"

In choosing Hampton, these neophytes are expected to embrace its value system and are held accountable for upholding it. As noted in the introduction to this chapter, he emphasized three key ideals. Note when President Harvey underscores "*First, we strive for honesty, decency, integrity, respect for others and* self-respect" and "We strive for high achievement and academic excellence in all our pursuits," it is his way of emphasizing "Decency is as important as degrees." Thus, an institutional ethos undergirding an "Education for Life" does not separate academic excellence from character development of the student. Adhering to the precept that standards of behavior and values support academic achievement, in 1983, Harvey announced that he wanted an Honors Code at the Opening Convocation. By a mandate of the Board of Trustees, character building was a "must value—added to a Hampton University education." It is embodied in the Code of Conduct, which was adopted during the 1993–1994 academic year. The Code of Conduct, with its derivation in the nineteenth century at Hampton, has been transformed for the twenty-first century into an emphasis on character development, leadership, and service to society. As previously noted, it requires that all Hampton University constituents—administrators, faculty, staff, and students—abide by the principles of decency, honesty, responsibility, personal, professional and academic integrity, and respect for oneself and one's fellow man.

In a town hall meeting with the freshman class on October 24, 1994, President Harvey said, "Our emphasis on a code of conduct and character-building is at the leading edge of the move to inculcate civic values into the curriculum. Character- building is but one facet of the cultural environment we are determined to achieve, but ultimately, it is the most important one, for intellect without character is of little or no use to civilization. This initiative has implications for all of us—and most certainly for our students. As you spread the good word about Hampton, make certain that you emphasize our uniqueness as an institution which combines as its primary aims the promotion of academic excellence and the building of character in its students."

Besides graduating with an undergraduate degree in marketing, Rebecca Sanders can attest to receiving an "Education for Life" at Hampton in academics and character-building. Though

Sanders, who expects to enter graduate school in visual arts or communications, described herself as an average student, she was a student leader and editor-in-chief of the *Hamptonian* for the academic year of 1999–2000. She said of her experience at Hampton when she was only two months shy of graduation,

> Looking back, this has been the best five years that I have had in my short twenty-two years on this earth. It's an experience I just don't have the words to explain, but Hampton has been on both ends. There have been some positives and there have been some negatives. More positives than negatives. To see black people doing positive things every single day, especially when we are characterized as such negative people in the media all the time, is exciting to see. The environment is more of a learning environment—very competitive. It keeps you on your toes and prepares you for outside participation for when we leave here. I'm in the School of Business and it seems every year, they definitely have raised the bar on the type of students they allow at Hampton. The caliber of students at Hampton is phenomenal. Not only do they work hard, but they push themselves and they push their professors as well to teach them more. There are more teachers that are more qualified than there were when I began in the School of Business. There are MBAs and people that are coming from experience in the corporate world. They bring in people to speak with us and the program has really blossomed in the past five years.

Sanders has learned many lesson under the President's tutelage. She indicated that "one of the biggest things I have learned at Hampton is patience. I think I am a much more patient person than I have ever been. I've learned that it's really important to be thorough in all findings and research. I've learned the importance of being honest and really trying to improve upon myself and stay true to myself at all times and portray, I think, an outstanding person. Also, I think that Hampton teaches you a lot about leadership and how to come into your own self as a leader in whatever you do, regardless of whether it's in an organization or being a leader in your classroom."

Clayton Bond felt, too, that Hampton was instrumental in building his character by "helping me to stretch myself and surpass limits that I thought were there, that might not have been there, but I felt that I surpassed them anyway."

He does not think that he would have had this opportunity anywhere else—the kind of growth that took place in his undergraduate experience—if he had not matriculated at Hampton.

> I think Hampton had a huge influence on me in terms of the diversity of people. Most of the people I met, of course, were black. Yet, I met people from across the United States, people from varying social and economic backgrounds, with just lots of different interests—everything from physics to the visual arts. I thought it was great. I thought the professors were very helpful, experienced and accessible. I found that many of the administrators, especially Dr. Harvey and Dr. [Rodney] Smith very accessible and supportive, which I don't think I would have found anywhere else. I was one of the people who would take advantage of the Thursday office hours that Dr. Harvey would have and, in the matter of accessibility, I knew that was rare, so it meant a lot to me.
>
> I think the University through the faculty, through other students, through administrators, helped me be the best that I could be. I don't question that Hampton prepared me because I think it did in a lot of different ways, not just academically. I certainly found the classes I took challenging. I took a wide variety of classes because I started as a marine and environmental science major and then finished in political science the latter two years. I found the professors in the pure and applied sciences, the liberal arts, and political science faculty very helpful. People who were committed to making me work, making me learn, which was certainly important to me. That played a big role in not just helping me get to Harvard, but it made it possible for me to perform relatively well here at Harvard. But in addition, I learned to surround myself with people who were at least as driven as I was. They helped challenge me as well, and not just within the political science department.

Indubitably, for both Sanders and Bond, their mettle was tested at Hampton, like Booker T. Washington. As President Harvey forewarned the entering the freshman class members of 1999–2000 that they would, too, be tried, he said, "When Booker T. Washington, Hampton's most famous graduate, sought admission to the school more than a century ago, his character was tested through his sweeping of the floor in one of the school's buildings. When he completed this test, the principal examined the floor with his handkerchief and was unable to find a speck of dust. This was the admissions test in 1875 and though you will not be tested in the same way, there are other things that will be expected of you as a member of the Hampton University family."

He reiterated, to this freshman class with an average SAT score of 1011, that, "You will be expected to be serious in your commitment to your academic studies. This means that you will attend your classes, prepare your assignments, and complete all assigned work in a timely fashion. It means that for your enjoyment and for the enrichment of your cultural and academic exposure, you will attend various cultural events that are presented at the University. It means that you will learn to manage your time to provide an appropriate balance between studying, participating in extra-curricular activities, and socializing. We want you to have fun, and the fact that you have been admitted to Hampton means that you have the potential to succeed academically. However, Hampton has rigid policies regarding requirements for academic good standing. Therefore, I implore you to please work hard so that you will stay in good standing. More simply stated, your presence in this audience today does not guarantee your place in the graduation line of 2003."

While students are accountable for upholding academic standards of excellence, the Hampton experience is itself a family experience. Therefore, it is one which involves close collaboration among all University constituents beginning with the administrative leadership. It is typical of most faculty and administrators to have the interests of students at the center of learning. It is part of a larger culture that takes responsibility for monitoring and intervening on behalf of student's educational achievement. They go beyond the classroom and prepare students for the skills, values, and behaviors required for success. Though all constituents bear responsibility for the learning process, Harvey has ultimately assumed institutional responsibility for student's intellectual, personal, and moral development since 1978. Yet he believes, "The day-to-day responsibility for safeguarding the integrity of our academic program—which is at the heart of this institution—rests primarily with our faculty." While acknowledging that they do a commendable job in the areas of teaching, research, and scholarly productivity, he holds that faculty, along with administrators and staff, who do not make students "adhere to the highest standards of scholarship and behavior are clearly obstructing the efficiency of operations." While the President is interested in providing equality of opportunity for all students, he does not want to lower standards of scholarship and behavior under the guise of "nurturing." "When people are given the opportunity and allow it to slip away, they must suffer the consequences," he said. Harvey can cite a litany of rationales parents or students have used to explain not living up to Hampton's academic standards. "The first thing the students' parents say is that we are a predominantly black school and, therefore, we should be sympathetic to them despite their lack of achievements. One said he did not do well because there was not enough to do on campus. He said 'You know, I am from New York and we have a lot to do up there. See what I'm saying?' Another said that our dorms were not as nice as his house and that prevented him from studying."[2]

The accountability for students begins with their enrollment in the Freshman Studies Program, an innovative academic program initiated by the President and adopted in 1989–90. Harvey said that it is "designed to facilitate a smooth transition into the University experience; to provide an immersion in the Hampton heritage and tradition; to provide basic, practical instruction and exchange of ideas on practical and current issues, and to instill and reinforce a system of sound values, provide a comprehensive core of academic support programs to facilitate the delivery of services that significantly influence academic achievement." In remarks that he made before Phi Delta Kappa at Harvard University in September 1992, he asserted that, "Many students entering college have little concept of the potential it offers for their development and how to make wise use of their college years. Hampton University wanted to address the unrealistic expectations through offering University 101, which introduces students to the 'Hampton Experience' and facilitates their transition into the college environment." Moreover, it is important for students to know about their history and heritage. Since about 87 percent of Hampton's students are African Americans, it is important to make their experience "meaningful, coherent and fulfilling," noted Harvey. While the units of the course vary, they include: Learning as Innovation; Hampton University: Its History, Legacy and Future; African American Art, and the Art of Living in the Twenty-First Century. The program has faculty mentor advisors, as well as students.

It is the responsibility of student leaders matriculating at Hampton University, like Kirkman-Bey, to be accountable to entering freshman and to assist them in making the transition into their new milieu. She asserted: "There are lot of things that we do for that week, such as having to check freshmen into dorms. This is probably one of the hardest working weeks for student leaders."

Like other student leaders, Erika Turner expressed a strong sense of family feelings, since she, too, was embraced as a freshman by the warmth of her peers. "The University is so wonderful and unique from the minute you set foot on this campus. There is the Student Leadership Program. Once I set foot on campus, I was embraced by the Student Leadership Program who made me feel at home. The group leader I was in took us to her home and cooked for us and told us if there is ever anything we needed, let her know. The upperclassmen were very welcoming and giving, and told me if I needed to go to Wal-Mart or the bank to let them know and they would take me. Coming all the way from Michigan, I was hesitant about that, but the minute I came here I was put at ease. There is such a sense of family here at Hampton. Every since I stepped foot on this campus, I felt embraced by the rest of the students. I felt at home."

In addition to assisting freshmen, along with other duties, the student leaders are required to perform community service within and outside the campus. In fact, when Rodney Smith was vice president for student affairs, he indicated, "Most of our student organizations have a community service component written into their constitution, as well as, we now have a community service component attached to our freshman class and to our Honors College Program." Keisha Taylor stated, "I believe that Dr. Harvey is very concerned about us giving back and us doing community service. The University participates in a lot of community service opportunities throughout the Hampton community, and I think that he is a big believer in service because you have to serve the community that you are part of if you want to make that community the best it can possibly be. I think that he sees that and he holds each of the campus organizations responsible for some community service, so that the community can see that Hampton University is giving back to the community to make Hampton the best that it can be." Through the Student Leadership Program, the Student Government Association, the Peer Counselors, and some eighty-odd additional student organizations, many opportunities are provided for service, leadership development, cultural enrichment, and sports activities. In these organizations, students can also find just plain merriment. As the President noted to the entering freshmen, "Hampton is not always hard work; we also know how to relax."

Still for Harvey, "No matter the setting—on or off the campus—you will be expected to conduct yourself with dignity and as mature young men and women. Hampton does not tolerate disregard for policies governing room visitation and other policies related to residential life," he tells the freshmen class. Moreover, he also imparts these warning to freshmen, "You will be expected to abide by the policies regarding student conduct. This means that you will be expected to demonstrate self-respect and respect for others. You must demonstrate respect for University property—including the furnishings and facilities of all buildings, the grounds, and library materials. As well, you will be expected to respect the property of other students and of everyone with whom you interact." He also reminds them that "Hampton is not a sanctuary for the use of drugs or weapons. My advice to you is to stay away from drugs and drug dealers. Association with drugs and drug dealers has ruined more careers, destroyed more friendships, and may eventually cause you to go to jail or die. You may rest assured that any person violating our drug and weapon policy will not be at Hampton University for long. Therefore, I encourage you to study your Student Handbook and pay close attention to the information you shall receive regarding these matters because Hampton does not tolerate disrespectful, rude, coarse, unrefined or illegal behavior or speech. We never have and we never will! We do not honor the values of the ghetto."

Erika Turner stated, "My mother was impressed that students had to abide by this Code of Conduct. It has a great impact on how we present ourselves and how we interact with others. It encourages us to be professional and businesslike at all times. One student can leave a great impression on a company, and the type of institution it is." She offered this personal testimony on her summer internship. "During the summer, I participated in an internship program sponsored by the Freedom Forum. I worked at a newspaper in Tennessee and that newspaper never had a

Hamptonian as an intern, and they were impressed by my work and my professionalism. My editor made a comment to me one day, 'Goodness, I didn't know Hampton students were so bright,' and he wanted to hire Hampton students in the future. One person can make such an impression. I think [Dr. Harvey] is committed to being the best at all times." When she told peers who attended other HBCUs or predominantly white universities about the Hampton Honor Code, they were surprised or felt the University was too "strict or ridiculous or extreme." "I told them that is what separates Hampton students from other students. There is a correct way to present yourself, a correct way to speak. The world is changing. You cannot compete with others if you are not professionally dressed, don't know how to communicate with others, so the Honor Code definitely has a positive impact on HU students," argued Turner.

Turner is not only referring to the Code of Conduct, but the Hampton Dress Code. According to the Student Handbook, "The code is based on the theory that learning to use socially acceptable manners and to select attire appropriate to specific occasions and activities are critical factors in the total educational process. Understanding and employing these behaviors, not only improve the quality of one's life, contribute to optimum morale, and embellish the overall campus image, they also play a major role in instilling a sense of integrity and an appreciation for values and ethics. The continuous demonstration of appropriate manners and dress insures that Hampton University students meet the very minimum standards of quality achievement in the social, physical, moral, and educational aspects of their lives—essential areas of development necessary for propelling students toward successful careers."

On this premise students at Hampton University are expected to dress neatly at all times, and will be apprised of appropriate dress for various occasions which include the following: 1.

classroom, cafeteria and University offices; 2. programs in Ogden Hall, the Convocation Center and the Little Theater; 3. job interviews, both on and off campus; 4. traveling by public transportation; 5. church services; 6. residence hall lounges.

"Students will be denied admission to various functions if their manner of dress is inappropriate. Examples of inappropriate dress and/or appearance include, but are not limited to: (1) Caps or hoods for men and women at indoor activities. This policy item does not apply to headgear considered a part of religious or cultural dress; (2) Midriffs or halters, mesh, netted shirts or cutoff tee shirts in classrooms and offices; (3) Bare feet; (4) Short shorts (5) Shorts, blue or other type jeans at major programs such as Musical Arts, Fall Convocation, Commencement, or other programs dictating professional, dressy, or formal attire; (6) Clothing with derogatory offensive and/or lewd messages either in words or pictures. All administrative, faculty and support staff members will be expected to monitor student behavior applicable to this dress code, and report any such disregard or violations to the Offices of the Dean of Men or Dean of Women for the attention of the Vice President for Student Affairs."

Clearly, Rodney Smith, currently President of Ramapo College in New Jersey, was simultaneously impressed, when he was Hampton's vice president for student affairs, with the merging of President Harvey's visionary futuristic outlook and his traditional ethos and moral compass that propel him to stand firm on these timeless values of decency, dignity, and respect for others. So affected, he declared:

> When I stop to think about the things that he sees and the things that he talks about and the things that he encourages his administrative staff to think about are so ten and fifteen years advanced, but at the same time, so present-day and, yet, hinged so heavily on values of yesterday. If you notice, he does not lose sight of what it takes to make a young man or a young woman a value to themselves and to a broader society or world. He doesn't lose sight of that by

getting caught up in fads or fashion and things that young people, or the wider society, think that is the direction things should go. He has a very clear appreciation for the kinds of outlook, the kinds of attitudes, the kinds of values, that any successful individual should have, the kind of work ethic that any successful person, whether it be student, whether it be staff, or faculty should have in order to strive to a more complete full potential. He doesn't lose sight of that. Even though students may say, "This is what we want," he is able to communicate with students or with anyone and help them to appreciate the significance of values, the significance of a certain attitude, even expressing an aptitude. And so many hundreds and hundreds of people have, even if they don't get it right then, they come back later on and say, "thank you." He combines those values with present-day realities in terms of the existing resources, existing exposures, existing programs, and he combines both in a way whereby he is able to say this is what will happen ten years from now, or this is what we expect to happen fifteen years from now or twenty years from now. And that's what we're aiming to. He's one of those people when you talk about visionary, I think he's more than that. I think he goes beyond. I think he has a very solid grasp of the holistic reality for the past, the present, and the future.

While Harvey would appreciate Smith's kind expression, he simply would respond, "We groom our students to aim for the stars in whatever their area of expertise or interest might be. After all, we must continue to answer the question, "What do you call a Hampton graduate? As we have always answered it—BOSS!" He would say to friends and foes alike, "All of our initiatives are designed to help us provide for our students an 'Education for Life,' one that prepares them for the realities of the day and the demands of the twenty-first Century—one that teaches them not only how to make a living, but also how to live with dignity and in service to humankind. To this end, Hampton continues to promote today what it has promoted since its founding; academic excellence and the shaping of character through emphasis of the human values of honesty, decency, integrity, courage, respect for oneself, and respect for others."

Absorbing the virtues of the Hampton value system help prepare students to live with dignity in a race-conscious society.
Keisha Taylor would like for

> people to lose the preconceived notion that if you graduated
> from a HBCU that you are not as well prepared to be a posi-
> tive contributor to society as you would have been had you
> gone to a predominantly white university. I really think that
> you are looked down upon, or maybe you have to be looked
> at twice, before people realize the greatness of what we have
> learned here at Hampton. And it's not just that it's a black uni-
> versity, this is an outstanding one, whether black or not. It's
> not about where I went to school. It's about am I qualified to
> do the work. And I am. And I think that based upon the stu-
> dents that I have met here, the people who are competing
> against us for top jobs better be on their toes, because we are
> quite prepared to take on responsibilities of jobs in every
> facet of life. And I really think that is something people ought
> to know. Honestly, I get concerned when I have to compete
> for jobs on campus against other Hampton University stu-
> dents because I know just how qualified they are. To be
> accepted here among your own means everything and then
> you can go out into the world and face everything else.
>
> My experience at Hampton University has really pre-
> pared me for the life that I hope to lead, and I really think that
> Dr. Harvey is a person that should be honored. And I under-
> stand that no person was ever honored for what he received,
> but that honor has been rewarded for what he gave.

Taylor, as others before her, will "let her life do the singing." With
Taylor's testimony of her "Education for Life," seemingly, "The ultimate test of an educational institution lies in the quality of the students whom it prepares," as President Harvey pointed out, in an
address on March 2, 1997 at Virginia State University. "Administrators and faculty will come and go; curricula will be revised; technology, as we all can attest, will change overnight. But in the absolute
and utter scheme of things, many of these events will not matter
very much anyway. For the ultimate test of any institution lies not in
its staff or curricula, nor in its buildings and facilities. Rather, the
ultimate test of any educational institution lies in the quality of the
student whom it prepares—in the quality of their academic achieve-

ment, in the quality of the lives as professional citizens, and in the quality of their service and contributions to their communities and their world. Ultimately, students are perhaps the one constant in the educational enterprise, as generations of them continue to pass through our door."[3]

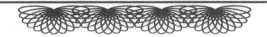

Bracing for Storms and Weatherstripping for Critics

"Criticism, as it was first instituted by
Aristotle, was meant as a standard of judging well."
—Samuel Johnson

"To avoid criticisms do nothing, say nothing,
be nothing."
—Elbert Hubbard

"A wise man gets more from his enemies than a
fool from his friends."
—Baltasar Gracian

Standing Tall on Principles

From the moment that the 37-year-old President William R. Harvey set foot on the campus of Hampton Institute in July 1978, his critics have been snipping and sniffing at his garment like bloodhounds set forth upon the mud tracks of Sojourner Truth along a dusty southern road on a stormy, windy night. In the teeth of the wind, as a giant oak tree, he sometimes bends but never breaks on the flight to freedom. Like the courageous Sojourner Truth, he stands up for what is right as he journeys towards the North Star of liberation, helping to emancipate a people through education and economic empowerment. As he moves forward, with eyes fixed upon the Star, he also looks backward, not to burn bridges behind him, but to build bridges of hope and reconciliation with friends and foes alike. "You must look back in order to learn and forward in order to teach."

When visionary, strong, effective leaders, like Harvey, speak and act with the courage of their convictions, they are lauded, damned with faint praise, and oftentimes persecuted. Their strengths or foibles, grit or cowardice, triumphs or defeats are identified as a symbol of people's hopes, fears, frustrations, envy, and aspirations—fulfilled and unfulfilled. Consequently, when Harvey is venerated by allies and vilified by adversaries, it is because he stands firmly on his principles. His collective and individual detractors, waving a red flag, speak of him in double-edged superlatives, noting that he is (1) "too autocratic," (2) "too imperial," (3) "too ambitious," (4) "too hands-on," (5) "too dedicated to perfection," (6) "too tight-fisted," and (7) "too [fill in the blank]." Charles Wilson, Board of Trustees member, reminds us that people are going to "demean and take shots at anything successful. Anyone who gets through life without critics has missed all the rungs in the ladder of life." "Even Jesus Christ was crucified," Martha Dawson added, "and He came to save us." In the glow of Harvey's starry crown as a liberator of the oppressed, critics have camped around him to dim the glimmer for twenty-five years of his tenure at Hampton.

But naysayers have not kept him from exercising the courage of his convictions, and promoting "what is right and what is fair, without regard for popular acclaim." Whether sounding a clarion call at the Annual National Black Family Conference in 1994 for the banning of handguns in the larger society or in instituting an African American/Jewish Community Relations Symposium to reestablish broken ties that occurred after the Civil Rights movement, he is not afraid to speak out against injustices or take a stand in the interest of "decency, dignity, and fair play." At the first African American/Jewish Symposium on March 23, 1998, for example, he stated:

Need I remind you that each time a colloquium of this nature takes place, or another group is formed, there is a spark of hope for the future of Black-Jewish relationships. It is only through open communication and understanding, however, that we can rebuild our alliance. There is no doubt that we will find more common ground once the gates of understanding are unlocked. And I say to you, as President of Hampton University—African Americans and Jews must be about the business of action! We must attempt to rekindle the wholesome relationship shared during the '50s and '60s. Based on the engaging and illuminating sessions held today, it appears that we are posturing for the challenge. Let us vow to keep the dream alive as we endeavor to generate dialogue and progress for leaders of tomorrow.

Likewise, at a National Symposium on "Stopping Hazing in African American Fraternities and Sororities," which was held at Hampton University on February 9, 1990, the President, in exposing an emerging abusive culture of Greek organizations, was not afraid to call a spade a spade.

For some years now our sororities and fraternities have woven a new history. And this new history speaks not of scholarship, service, or brotherhood. Alas, this new history speaks of moral degradation and human defilement. This new history speaks of the spectacle of hazing. Hazing, on far too many of our campuses, involves emotional, psychological, verbal and physical abuse where potential inductees are forced into submissive behavior and demeaning acts; are made to suffer sexism, elitism and brutality; are spat upon and brutalized with cattle prods, layered with paddles and branding irons; are sexually exploited; are forced to wear dog chains around their necks for prolonged periods of time; are cajoled into buying expensive gifts for their would-be sisters and brothers as a condition of their admission into the quote-unquote "Sanctity" of the Greek Kingdom.

And yes, on far too many of our campuses, potential inductees have paid the ultimate price for possible entry into the Greek Kingdom—the price of their very lives—from alcohol poisoning, from cruel beatings, from extreme exertion, from outright brutality.

He likened the atrocities to slavery, noting,

> These abuses, of course, sound all too familiar. Indeed, they hearken back to another time and another place, to a moment in history that is all too painful for most of our recollections—to a time when we, as a race, were forced to suffer the ultimate in human degradation; uprooted and chained and transported through that dark passage into an alien land; worked alongside the mule in the fields until the two of us were all but indistinguishable; violated sexually and otherwise; beaten and chained and lynched for the slightest offense or omission; made to pay the price for the transgressions of a less benevolent race. That we, as a race, have come to internalize such behaviors, to perpetuate human atrocities against which we rebelled so vehemently, is anathema to our founders, to our race, to me, personally, as it ought to be to you. One question which comes to mind is who, in the name of God, would want to enter such a demented kingdom.?

Harvey then made a plea for Greek organizations to return to their original purpose.

> Given the enormous dilemmas which face us in the world, in the nation, and among our race in the 1990s and beyond, I would challenge our Afro-American Greek sororities and fraternities to remember the legacy of their founders, to reject that which demeans, and to address seriously the more compelling issues of our day: the poor, the hungry and the dying; the homeless, the injured, the displaced and the disenchanted; the illiterate, the underrepresented among our scholars, our scientists, our mathematicians; the drug addicted, the incarcerated; the underprepared for the workplace; the aged and the infirmed; teenage mothers and potential suicidals; the millions of young black people who, but for our support, our example, our guidance and our love, will join the ranks of the already lost generation.

"You must remember that you cannot deny another man his humanity without stripping yourself of your own; that unless used for the unification of mankind, our actions are futile. Hazing, very clearly, is not intended for man's edification; rather, it is intended for his dehumanization," he said.

In concluding his talk, he stated:

> From my vantage point as a husband, a father, a leader, a president, and a Greek, the senseless, manic hazing which we have witnessed over the last several years must cease and will cease. And it will do so, not by the edict of a national inter-fraternal council, not a pan-hellenic council, nor by the edict of a national Greek organization or a University President. Rather it will cease by the grace of God, and in the name of all that is good and holy and right. Despite all of our good intentions and our achievements, if we do not conquer our perverse and inhumane tendencies, we shall ensure a demise which we ourselves have carelessly wrought.

As Mark Antony observed in his famous funeral oration for Julius Caesar, "The evil that men do lives after them; the good is often interred with their bones. So let it be with Caesar."

And so let it be with Harvey, who was doing some good and trying to right a wrong in taking a stand against racial injustice when he hired Johnnie Cochran, the celebrated lawyer, to defend two Hampton University women's basketball coaches and one of their husbands after they were falsely arrested, harassed, and accused of a scam incident in November 1998 at a Wal-Mart store in Lubbock, Texas. The three were handcuffed and held for several hours and only released after the store's security tapes showed none of the three had any contact with the victim, a white woman. During the detention, the pregnant assistant coach became ill and was threatened with having a towel placed down her throat. Though the Mayor of Lubbock, Texas came to Hampton University to publicly apologize for the incident, the Chief of Police did not. Harvey knew he must rail against such unconscionable acts and rail against racial profiling by the criminal justice system on behalf of people of color. A federal suit filed on April 19, 1999 alleged "clear racial overtones" in the incident, and further noted, "This treatment of a pregnant African American female is mindful of the events of the Civil Rights movement of the 1960s where police would strike pregnant African American females in the stomach, causing them to abort their babies on the street."

So let it also be with Harvey, who, in the split between "town and gown," knew that he was doing some good when he demanded an apology from James Eason, the mayor of Hampton, who mocked the competency of Hampton's ability to plan its physical plant adequately. On October 24, 1986, the Hampton University Board of Trustees had announced its intention to develop the Hampton Harbor Project, and requested the City of Hampton to rezone the University's land. James Eason made a public comment that he hoped the school's residential and commercial project would be compatible with the downtown redevelopment. The Mayor further indicated that a poorly planned and executed development could be detrimental to the City of Hampton's renewal efforts. Harvey demanded an apology from him, and along with the Hampton University Alumni Association, charged the city with insulting them. "I assume he thinks he can make those kinds of negative statements without having to apologize. However, my position is very, very clear. I will call his or anyone else's hand who, in any unfounded way, make negative statements about Hampton University," said Harvey. The President further added, "It was the height of presumptuousness for you to, or anyone to, assume that an institution which has the high quality reputation of Hampton [University] would enter into a construction project without appropriate planning. The undisputed beauty of our buildings and grounds is a testimony to good planning."[1]

To add fuel to the fire, the Mayor had also mentioned, in a press conference, the incorporation of Hampton University's undeveloped acreage as part of the city's downtown future renewal plans. In a *Times-Herald* article of November 8, 1986, Harvey responded that Eason had demonstrated "the height of presumptuousness" by suggesting that personnel in the city knew how to plan HU's property better than the University did.

Harvey stated that ". . . by building two parking garages on the water showed that city planners left a lot to be desired as it relates to their expertise, because land on the waterfront was prime property all over the world." Harvey also said that by thinking of the property off Settlers Landing Road as anything but HU's domain to use to its best advantage was ridiculous. As the verbal war escalated, Harvey was quoted as saying in a November 20, 1986 article in the *Daily Press*, that "one only need to look at the Booker T. Washington Memorial Bridge (which crosses Settlers Landing Road) to see an example of how the city and state worked their will and took HU land. 'Yes, we [were] paid for it. But it was part of a prime development site that the University did not wish to give up.'" Lucius Wyatt said, "When Dr. Harvey arrived, the crossing of Hampton's land for the building of Settlers Landing Road had just been settled. And the road was to come closer to campus, but Dr. Harvey objected to it because, at that time, it would have come right straight through where Hampton Harbor is now. We would have had less land on our side, and more land on the other side of the river, so he objected. He was the only one. The previous President had agreed to it and [Harvey] got the Board to reverse that decision. Settlers Landing Road was changed to come farther north of the campus with a smaller piece of land on that side. Dr. Harvey was the main force in having the crossing of Settlers Landing Road changed from its original location, making it possible for the apartment complex and commercial complex for Hampton Harbor. In fact, it was his firm stand that brought about that change."

Wyatt, who served on the Industrial Development Authority, noted that external to the contiguous area of the campus, Hampton University owns approximately twenty acres of valuable land in Hampton Roads North near Langley Air Force Base. He said, "The city would like to have that land so they can develop it as commercial property. When they first approached

Hampton, we refused to sell for the price that they were offering us. . . . But after Dr. Harvey came, we said we wouldn't sell the land, period. . . . And, as of today, we are still holding that land."

Acutely aware that many African Americans were routinely losing their valuable land daily across the country, Harvey did not intend for that to happen under his watch. Yet, while standing against negative racist statements and other unfair practices, he worked to extend an olive branch, building on past relations he had established with the City of Hampton and the Mayor. Eason had, for example, spoken only a year earlier, in 1985, on campus as the Founder's Day speaker. He had called for a spirit of cooperation and noted that the University and the City of Hampton may eventually develop a model approach in assisting small and minority-owned businesses. The two leaders met and confronted their differences, so Harvey invited him and the other city council members to the campus for a tour. Eventually, the City and Hampton University, which is one of the city's largest employers, cooperated in a partnership to build the Hampton Harbor Project. As always, Harvey's ultimate interest is the progress of the University. Though there have been frays with the City of Hampton, with the election of the first African American woman mayor in 2000, relations between town and gown should continue to improve.

Once again, so let it be with Harvey to know that he was doing some good when he challenged the media for unfair and negative coverage and portrayal of the University. Despite its successes, Hampton University was constantly picked on and poked at like vultures hovering over dead bodies. Take, for example, the incident that involved the alleged transcript altering charges brought by the local newspaper. According to the minutes of the Hampton University Board of Trustees, the President informed the Board that following a preliminary hearing on February 28, 1989, for the head football coach, who was charged with seven counts of criminally altering records and forgery, he was found not guilty. The judge concluded that there was no criminality involved. Several Board members opined that it seemed as if it was a political ploy by the Commonwealth's Attorney, Chris Hutton. Lawyers on the Board said that since it was clear that there was no pecuniary gain on the part of the coach and his alleged tampering, it was just as clear that there was no criminality. Chairman LeFlore said that "a first year law student would have used better judgment than the Commonwealth Attorney in this instance. Therefore, the elected Commonwealth's Attorney must have been politically motivated."

> The President pointed out that in spite of the judge's dismissal of all charges, the local newspapers, dissatisfied with the verdict, exploited the judge's decision. The newspaper reported negative comments made during the trial in six of seven newspaper articles or editorials and attempted to cast the University and him in a very negative light.
>
> The President shared with the Board some of the Letters to the Editor that were printed in the local newspaper regarding this situation.
>
> Chairman LeFlore commented that the Executive Committee had been kept informed about this matter and that he and the President were regularly in contact. He also noted that the members of the press had made use of devices to trap or set up Trustees to respond to them about the development of events related to this matter.
>
> The Chair pointed out that he thought the President exercised extraordinary restraints and discretion regarding this situation.

When Hampton alumni, faculty, and staff, as well as others, cautioned him not to openly extend a dialogue with the local media, and, in particular, with the *Daily Press*, said Martha Jallim-Hall, he eschewed that notion. Harvey's experience with the press as a young boy and man growing up in the South was very positive. He often says that if it had not been for the press, the civil rights message of blacks would not have been told, and therefore, gains would not have been made. Harvey often talks about his healthy respect for a fair and objective press. When colleagues point out that there are certain columnists at the *Daily Press* who have never written anything positive about him, despite all of the good that he has done for the University and the community, Harvey dismisses these comments with a simple, "that's their problem." When members of the Hampton University and wider community complain that they think that some at the Daily Press are jealous, resentful or racist in their actions toward him and Hampton, he tries to explain the psychology of the situation to them. "Yes," he says, "there are some who do not like a strong, independent Black man or organization. Others are jealous. Still others are resentful of personal or professional success. Do not worry about them. Change them if you can. Remember, however, our work speaks for itself and those at the Daily Press or anywhere else cannot change that fact. Whatever their problem, he refuses to stoop to their level. So, in spite of the cautions of others, he extended invitations for the leadership and editors of the *Daily Press* to visit the campus and talk with administrators. As a result of his peace offerings, relations have improved significantly and the University receives more positive coverage for its achievements. In 1998, the *Daily Press'* publisher was the co-chair of the $200 Million Kick-Off Campaign event.

So let it be with Harvey, that he was doing some good, as well, when he instituted a strict drug enforcement policy and a sexual harassment and sexual misconduct policy on campus. Similarly, in 1998, when the President developed a plan for a totally wired campus in order to integrate technology into the living and learning campus environment, some disgruntled faculty and staff wanted to maintain business as usual. Likewise, during his early tenure, when the young President wanted to change the model for operating the University, constituents thought that he was moving too fast for the venerable institution. But all these changes improved the campus milieu.

Even when leaders like the President do not initiate changes, they become the symbolic scapegoat for them. Take, for example, the name change from Hampton Institute to Hampton University. It was Ben Head, Board of Trustees member, who recommended the change, and a committee headed by Mary Christian, then Dean of the School of Education, and later a member of the Virginia House of Delegates, was named to study the feasibility for the change and to make a recommendation. But as the leader, he received the flack, and was charged with being "behind the plan." Many local alumni opposed the change, feeling that they should have had a say in the decision, while others felt their longstanding traditions would be annihilated. Initially, the late Jessie Rattley, the former mayor of Newport News, Virginia, was one of those alumni who was hesitant about the name change. She said:

> Because so many people do not like change, they opposed it. Change brings pain. And people are skeptical. But he was able to present his case and it was accepted; he went forth, and gradually, we saw the changes that he was bringing. He wanted to put blacks in a different light. It was good to talk about working with the hands and the head, with the emphasis on the trades, but I think he wanted to bring a new vision. And that was to get into other areas that we had been barred from before, to institute curriculum changes, to institute the image from an institute to a full university, and to offer more degree programs and broaden the curriculum to meet the changes of the world. This was good. And I think we are beginning to reap the benefits of it now. He broadened the opportunities that our students would have in the world today, and I think he should be given a lot of credit for that. But many people, of course, felt that we should remain the same and just train tailors.

Lucius Wyatt, an alumnus, supported the change from its inception. He noted:

> Yes, there was great resistance to that and I never understood why. I am an alumnus and I was always for changing the name. It began back in the sixties, really. We tried to change the name and for one reason or another, the alumni didn't like it, as well as, I believe, the faculty. But at the time

Dr. Harvey, or whoever brought it to his attention, he began to work on it and there was a change made. By and large, most of the alumni accepted the change. But there was a group of alumni who objected to it and they were concerned about the fact that they could no longer have anything with Hampton Institute on it, although with university status, Hampton Institute was the undergraduate college. But when it comes down to paraphenalia, like caps and sweaters, and T-shirts, etc., the University said that we would no longer have these things because we were not Hampton Institute; we were Hampton University and some of the alumni became very upset about that, and that was another one of those things he finally was able to bring about some reconciliation. Dr. Harvey has a way of working very cooperatively with the upper leaders.

The alumni controversy was another matter that preceded Harvey's arrival, but it became a full-blown controversy during his early tenure, said O. G. Taylor, a Board of Trustee member from 1972– 2000, who looks upon the President as an aggressive first-class visionary. "Before President Harvey arrived, there were some problems. They felt they were not being recognized." Some alumni were concerned about incorporation and representation on the Board of Trustees. Taylor said that after the national leadership changed, the problem was solved. "The national organization gave him high marks because of the things he was able to achieve. Dr. Harvey works to bring in these difficult personalities as they can be useful to the University and have some things to offer."

Lucius Wyatt agreed with Taylor that the problem with the alumni existed prior to the President, but Harvey, the bridge builder, worked to smooth out relations.

> When Dr. Harvey first came to the college, even with [former presidents] Dr. Hill and Dr. Hudson, and Dr. Holland, too, there was this movement on the part of the alumni, the national alumni, to separate itself from the college and to become a separate corporate body. Naturally, the University was resisting that all through the years. Now the University provides an alumni office, with a director, with staff, and with support for the national officers to travel to and from the

college for meetings. See, the alumni was an unincorporated body, and they were coordinated somewhat by the director of alumni affairs, although they had their own president and officers. But they were considered as a part of the University and they were supported financially by the University. Some in the alumni felt that they wanted to be on their own, and have their own federal ID numbers and they could put on whatever affairs they wished to raise money for the University, or for the alumni group. So, the alumni was up in arms at that time, and there was resistance by the college, and so the relationship became very strained—I mean extremely strained—with the Board of Trustees and the President. And it was just almost unbelievable the way the relationship had fallen apart. Alumni chapters were withholding their funds. The groups were meeting with the Board of Trustees, and at times, were most discourteous, not to the extent of any kind of altercations, but they were just discourteous, period, and wouldn't listen to anything. They had a lawyer and we had gone to court for several things. And so things had become fairly disorganized with the alumni in terms of any cooperation between the college and the alumni. And Dr. Harvey came in and there was great resistance against him because Dr. Hill had just left and, of course, Dr. Hill was an alumnus and here came Dr. Harvey, and he was very aggressive. And that group, a small core of the alumni, really disliked the idea of working with Dr. Harvey and resisted him tremendously. And Dr. Harvey worked hard, along with the leadership of the alumni, to bring about some reconciliation of those differences, whereby they could incorporate and yet work with the college. And they did incorporate. With his leadership and with the assistance of board members who were alumni and the overall Board of Trustees, they brought about reconciliation and things have been uphill ever since. I mean really moving up ever since that time.

In 1999, the National Alumni Association gave over $1 million to the University.

President George Herbert Walker Bush's
Visit to Hampton University

When President George Bush (1988-1992) visited the campus in 1991 to deliver the Commencement address and to receive the honorary Doctor of Laws degree, President Harvey praised him for his "personal and professional commitment to historically black colleges and universities." He noted the following Bush initiatives: (1) his appointing a Presidential Advisory Board to advise him on ways of strengthening HBCUs; (2) his directing the Office of Personnel Management in conjunction with the Secretaries of Labor and Education, to develop a program to recruit more HBCU students for part-time and summer federal positions; (3) his inviting Hampton University to nominate a student for a semester's White House internship; (4) his encouraging the development of the Historically Black College and University/Minority Institutions Consortium, which was awarded $54.3 million; (5) his directing the White House Initiative Office to pair fourteen HBCUs with seven Midwestern majority universities to improve the research capabilities of HBCUs; (6) his signing Executive Order 12667, which directed twenty-seven agencies to increase opportunities for the participation of HBCUs in federal programs. As a result, increases in total funding over fiscal year 1989 were reported by most agencies. HBCUs received $776 million in FY 1989 and $894 million in FY 1990, an increase of $118 million.

In conclusion, he said of President Bush, "You supported historically black colleges and universities before it was fashionable to do so, and you stayed with us after some thought us anachronisms."[2]

In President Bush's address, he spoke of "the economic, social, and educational implications of the new world order." Then he challenged the graduates to ". . . assume responsibility for shaping an international commonwealth of freedom. Believe in yourselves. . . . Don't abandon your passion for ideas or causes.

Work hard, but serve your community. Be a point of light. Build a truly great society."

"It is an honor to have a President to visit the campus," Harvey said, "whether it was President George Bush or President William Jefferson Clinton." Supporters, like Lucius Wyatt, agreed that it was an honor as well.

> Being a Hamptonian, and a member of the administration of Hampton University, to have the President of the United States to come and speak at Hampton's Commencement, to me was a great honor and achievement, although there may have been some who objected to it. But even if there was a president who was controversial, it would have still been excellent for the University to be of such stature that they would attract a President of the United States, because very few colleges get to that level. Of course, there were many students who said that Bush did not sign the Civil Rights Bill, but to have him there was a great achievement for Hampton University, and the community felt the same way.

Wyatt continued by saying that, "In an indirect way," it [Bush's visit] generated more funds for the University, "because Hampton University was known to more people as a result of having the President of the United States speak at its Commencement. No doubt about it. Because it was carried on national TV and in national newspapers. Some people may not have ever heard of Hampton University had it not been for that, and for it to have been of sufficient importance for the President of the United States to come here to do that also meant something in terms of projecting the image of the University.

But many student dissenters at Hampton and other critics disagreed, believing it was an insult to invite President Bush, who vetoed the Civil Rights Act of 1990, a bill which would have made it easier for men and women of color and white women to sue against unintentional employment discrimination, to this HBCU campus. On the day of graduation, some students politely protested by remaining silent or by raising their clenched fists after Bush's speech.

Prior to Commencement, Martha Jallim-Hall, then the director of student activities, remembered how she handled the student protest:

> Of course, I had to call Dr. Harvey a number of times to let him know that I had all of these student groups who wanted to protest. And he said to me, "What is in the Handbook and how do you normally approve student activities?" And I told him what the procedure was and he said, "Just follow the procedures. This is no different from any other student activity." And Dr. Harvey wanted me to "make sure that, once we approved the petitions for the students to protest, to make sure that the students were safe. And while those students are protesting, there may be others who have different views, and they, too, have the right to protest. So make sure that they are safe and make sure we have security to protect the people that are protesting." So you can see his vision and his concerns for our students and their safety and, even though they were protesting, it was a learning experience for them.

Harvey believes an "education should teach one *how* to think, not *what* to think." So he met with students and encouraged them to express themselves. But he did not back down or apologize for the President's invitation when some students protested his visit. He was not afraid of the students, not afraid of being unpopular with them, not afraid of being called "not black enough," and not afraid to assume leadership. He was interested in promoting lifelong living and learning. For Harvey has seen too many students who objected to an administrative decision as a student, but return only nine or ten years later to thank him. He understood the perennial and dualistic conflict of African Americans in negotiating culture and identity with the economic benefits and social visibility to the University, as Lucius Wyatt noted, that can accrue from a visit by the President of the United States.

He understood, too, the role of power and politics in the larger scheme of things on the journey towards the North Star of liberation. President Harvey did not shy away from the controversy that swirled around the student protest because he knew he was "right." The newspapers around the country captured the event differently. *The Washington Post*'s headline read "Bush Visit Bares Tensions at Hampton;" *The Atlanta Constitution*'s, "Speaking at Black School, Bush Vows to Fight Bias;" *The Hartford Courant*'s, "Bush Received Coolly by Black Graduates;" *The Detroit Free Press*'s, "Bush Tells Graduates He'll Fight Bias, Seek Free Trade;" *The Richmond Times*'s,"Bush Ignores Silent Protest, Vows to Fight Discrimination;" *The New York Daily News*'s, "Prez Visits School of Hard Knocks." Locally, the student objection prompted a flood of comments from the community, some favoring the dissent and others intimating that if Hampton students did not wish to hear the President, perhaps he should speak at another university where he would be more welcome. The students' protest was polite and the event was considered highly successful.

Whatever route Harvey takes on his journey toward the North Star for collective educational and economic empowerment, when the "chilly winds of adversity" are at his back in the darkest hour of the night, he wears his garment loosely and "soars on the wings of faith." He believes, "One can spend too much time fighting criticism and not get anything done. But if you are focused and have well-tried objectives and you are disciplined, and you pull everything from point A to point B, then I think that you've done that. We've got critics, but I don't really pay that much attention to critics because first of all I try to be fair. I try to do what's right. I try to do what's best. Practically everything I do is well thought out and I try to educate, I try to explain, and if there are those who don't agree, I try to bring them along. But I don't spend a lot of time on that. I try to bring Hampton forward and I think the record shows that we have been able to do that because we have been focused, we have been disciplined, and we don't allow ourselves to be distracted by those people who don't get the full view of the vision until later on."

He believes that "Many are called, but few are chosen" because among us, our ancestors, as well as our generations to come, there are countless individuals who "for lack of [courage] missed or will miss the call to leadership. The opportunities to serve humanity and, in so doing, to better the world will never be theirs."[3] So let it be with Harvey.

Standing Tough on Excellence

While Harvey stands tall on principles, the taskmaster stands even tougher on striving toward perfection. In constructing a culture of excellence at Hampton in the pursuit of all things, the Hampton family members are expected to share in its cultural ideals in all entities of the University. And for Harvey, this means "one must have a sense of purpose, one must have a good work ethic, one must be focused, one must have discipline, one must have compassion for others, one must have a sense of service, and one must not be dissuaded by people who don't understand your views, your mission, or your objectives."

Hence, members who lose focus of the aim-toward-excellence vision and the institutional means for achieving it might be taken to Harvey's proverbial woodshed. "I laughingly tell people that I will bring men and women in here and verbally throw them against the wall just to see how they respond," he said. It is an administrative style he sometimes employs to hone and test the mettle of Hampton family members, particularly those administrators in leadership roles. As he stated earlier, "I have to train people the way they need to be trained. And sometimes they go outside the lines and I have to bring them back. And sometimes that's a variable prompting me to try to let them understand what is the right way to do things and to educate at the same time that you are giving service. So that's an important part of my job, because I try to make people better by teaching them what is the right thing to do. And sometimes you have to go to that proverbial woodshed."

Charles Wilson, Board of Trustees member, a 1949 alumnus and a member of five generations of the Hamptonian family who regard Harvey as a no-nonsense taskmaster, has seen him take family members to the woodshed. He will tighten the rope until you 'squeeze Uncle' [give up]." Wilson stated, "If you can't or won't play the game of education and be the fiduciary of the people's children—that includes faculty and all on this campus—and you don't make the greatest contributions you can to the students and their development, I think he would say, let's cut the cord. You're not coming up to snuff." He said of Harvey, "We are lucky to have found him as a commander."

Likewise, Martha Dawson agreed with Wilson, noting Harvey's orientation is, "If you can't do the job, move out and let somebody else do it." Though the President is not hesitant about using the threat of "cutting the cord" and standing ready to severing it, Norma Harvey said that her husband is a "generous man and does not like to fire people. He is concerned about their jobs and families." The late Jessie Rattley, senior lecturer in political science at Hampton and former mayor of Newport News, Virginia, concurred that he is a compassionate man who "gives people an opportunity to fail and a graceful exit to leave their position" when they are not performing up to par.

Undergirding this facet of Harvey's no-nonsense and tough administrative style is the belief, he asserted, that "people are inherently good and that people are inherently smart, and that people inherently have a good work ethic. But you got to know how to pull it out of some people." As in any family, some members, from whom he had to "pull it out," grasp his vision and learn valuable lessons from the master teacher in the woodshed. For example, Martha Dawson, who was on the receiving end of both commendations and criticisms by Harvey, noted that:

> Many years ago, he used to write us a letter, and in that letter, he would tell us things that he dreamed about, the weaknesses of what we were doing. And he did not talk about the strengths all the time because he said, 'They're going to be there.' But what you did was work real hard, so

that when you got that letter you weren't going to see flaws that he had seen. And when he met with you, he would tell you, "Well, Dr. D., I see you're still going to have to do such and such a thing." Then you would sit down and he would give you ideas. "Let's see how we can do this together. Try so and so." And the other thing that would happen if he had an idea and you disagreed, you could say it to him, or he would say to you, "You know, maybe we should have done it the other way." And he would give you credit for it. You felt free. And that's why I say he's really been sensitive.

JoAnn Haysbert agreed with Dawson that in building a team in his aspiration for excellence, Harvey recognizes the need for participatory decision-making; therefore, she noted, "He will collect and pick the brains of those who sit around him to ensure the decision he makes is the product of the best thinkers. He will listen to everything that has to be said around the table, and I think that's a virtue that most people have not tuned in to. They're so busy focusing on his making the decisions." In listening to "what you have to say," Haysbert indicated that, "you have to be sure that what you say is sound. If not, he will question you down to the point that you realize it's not. So you can't say just anything."

Haysbert cited an example where an administrator "made some statements that were simply unfounded—indeed, were untrue." She said the administrator indicated in a report that Dr. Harvey had not been in his building in the last five years. "Now, Dr. Harvey lives on campus. Anybody who knows anything about him knows that he knows Hampton University frontwards, backwards, sideways, eyes open. That's a stupid statement to make. So to make a statement like that would upset a person who has given his life to the institution," said Haysbert. Normally, the President has an affable, kind, courtly manner. But in the "context of people being inefficient," Haysbert said, "his temper soars" when individuals "do not think about whatever has to be done. And they miss the ball when they should have caught it, because they knew it was coming directly into their hands, and their lack of catching it would affect what was going on at the University."

Administrative decision-making requires accurate information; therefore, it is incumbent upon the President to ask questions and to seek further clarification of a topic. So, sometimes when Harvey questions individuals, Haysbert contended, "They will feel what he is after." At other times, individuals may feel the pounding of the anvil in the woodshed. But she reassured us that when he asks "ten questions because of a point you have made, he is not trying to discredit you. He's trying to make sure what you are saying is sound, because he is going to factor that into a decision he needs to make."

Haysbert recalled presenting a report from a task force to the President, and one of the sentences stated, "We have few classrooms to accommodate large classes." The President told Haysbert, "I don't think this is correct." She responded, "Dr. Harvey, don't worry about that statement because I am going to take it in a different direction anyway." Still he wanted to check it out, so he called the registrar's office and asked, "How many classrooms do we have that can hold in excess of forty people?" When the registrar gave him the number, he turned to Haysbert and stated, "You see, that statement is not correct." "Nothing can get past him," said Haysbert. "The person who wrote the report was not definitive in his comments and he has to be attentive to details to make sound decisions."

Whether probing for decision-making clarity or jostling family members to aim for excellence in other organizational goals, Martha Jallim-Hall concurred that, "Dr. Harvey wants people to do well. And I think sometimes he pushes you, and doesn't know not to push you as much. He is the type that wants a lot for people that work around him and with him. He actually wants the best. And I think it might hurt when people don't do their best." The late Margaret Simmons was also aware that "Harvey does not ask any quarter, but he does not give any either." And she admitted that, "He can drive you into the ground, but I guess you can say he is trying to bring out the best in you, but you don't always see that. Sometimes you ask why doesn't he let up. He can drive, drive, and drive you. He can drive you to tears. It appears to be an attack, but it really isn't. He wants to show you can do it."

Having served on a round trip as faculty and as administrator for over twenty years under Harvey's leadership, Haysbert, who thinks of Harvey as a perfectionist, has a close-up perspective and offers these insights of his unrelenting "pressing, pressing, pressing" of people to do more.

> Dr. Harvey is a good teacher, which means he will spot talent early and put you in places that you are not ready to be trained. So maybe that is perceived as pushing, pushing, pushing. But I know that he will do that. He will put you in places to give you some experience and obviously, if you are not ready for that, these new experiences may come hard to you. Or they may come as a challenge because you want to rise to the call. In other cases, if you have a position, if you are a dean, you have to expect to be pushed. Why? Because you are a leader. So again, he is pushing people who are in a position where they must be results-oriented and they are not doing that.

Harvey explained his own motivation for pushing and pulling the Hampton family to a higher performance or taking them to the woodshed when they do not respond. "I have tried to make sure that they understood the responsibility that they carried to be a dean or vice president, and to give them the kind of exposure and experience that will make them better." Unquestionably, he, too, wants results. It is inherent in his entrepreneurial spirit. "I've heard him say," contended Haysbert, "'You academics just take weeks and weeks to do things. Business-oriented people are more results-oriented.' Academics are thinkers and sometimes have to go around the barn to get to the front door because we are so accustomed to teaching the process. We often feel that we have to go through the process rather than cut straight across the track and win the game. In the business world, you can cut across the track, so that you can be the one at the head of the production line. I think he is pushy. He wants results and if he has to push you to get them, that's what he has to do."

Robert Binswanger, then chair of the Board of Trustees, championed his entrepreneurial zest in the educational process and credited Harvey with understanding the importance of education, but he also said, "Higher education decision-making is much too slow for Bill Harvey. And that's where his business instincts move and he gets the decisions made, but sometimes, in education, that's not to be in the best interest of academe. Others like Jean Zeidler, former director of the museum, and Dennis Thomas, former director of athletics, would see Harvey's entrepreneurial actions as those of a thoughtful visionary who seizes opportunities, plans his movements, and makes things happen in the best interest of Hampton University. Thomas, who praised Harvey as the consummate visionary, thinks he has a "uniqueness and versatility that is difficult to find in many successful leaders." Thomas and others find that Harvey has "these visions" many years, perhaps ten, fifteen, or even twenty years, before he embarks upon bringing them to fruition, but he is constantly building stepping stones along the way. Many Hampton family members, as well as the larger community, may not catch these visions of the master teacher or his sometimes block and tackle method for achieving results until later. Harvey said, "You know sometimes it's kind of like your children who, when thirteen, fourteen, or fifteen, think their parents are crazy. When they get to be twenty-one or twenty-two, they are amazed at how smart their parents have become. But what has happened is they now see what their parents were trying to tell them. And in many instances, that's the case here."

Like Harvey's analogy, sometimes some Hampton family members may not catch the grand scheme of his visions of excellence in building a first-class university, or may not comprehend or may misinterpret his method for bringing out the best in them or preparing them to become master builders and teachers. Rather, they sometimes see and interpret the actions of the head of the family as coercive. Harvey, who is aware of his "halos and warts," knows that sometimes he is looked upon as a "person with a fist in a velvet glove," although he says fear is not a motive for his leadership style. Whether it's myth or reality, the campus lore brims with individuals who spin yarns like Paul Bunyan, of the "Doc Stories"—tales of Harvey's warts that grow and grow until a legacy of fear, blended with envy and respect, permeates the University. "There may be one person or several individuals who have had an unpleasant interaction with Dr. Harvey, and they will repeat their experience to one or two or three people, and those three people will repeat it to three more. And as the story is told and retold and as people hear little pieces of it, it becomes legendary, kind of 'folktale-ish' even," contended Margaret Dismond, the former executive assistant to Harvey.

The "Doc Stories" seem never-ending with the "street committee." The ensuing themes, some previously noted, run through the mosaic folk narratives of the "street committee": his excessively strong work ethic; his autocratic style of leadership; his need to always be right; his unpredictability; his sternness as a taskmaster; and his temper. Whether real or imagined, people treat them as authentic and respond to that perception. "By the way," said Harvey, "have you noticed that most of the rumors that come from the 'street committee' are wrong?"

One lore abounds of an omnipotent, omniscient, and omnipresent penumbral force, permeating the campus, like the black folk character of High John de Conquer. Thus, individuals guard what they say or do. One rendering of his near-photographic memory is reported this way. "He has a magnetic tape brain and he will tape a conversation and remember it for years. So you better watch what you say when you are discussing things with him. Don't think he is going to forget." Some family members, who act as the "Doc watchers," check the vital signs of the President's body language—facial expression or body posture—for the disposition of his temperament before they enter his space. When he communicates verbally and nonverbally his displeasure with incompetence or with individuals going "outside the line," it is bolstered by an eclipsing height. One watcher described him this way:

> He is so tall that he can physically tower over people. He will look you square in the eye and not blink, and that alone will rip some people to shreds. From the height and the staring, he can sometimes win just from those two things. When he is happy, he'll smile and laugh. But sometimes when he smiles, his eyes do not. They are cold and straight, but there is a smile on his face. He will wrinkle his brow, and that is clear and apparent that something is wrong or going on. When he gets angry, that bolt of lightning pops out on his face. He has a wrinkle that comes down his brow and evidently when he gets angry, it kind of changes into a position that looks like a bolt of lightning. His face tells it. He doesn't hide it well, although he tries. He is passionate. When he is upset, he crosses his legs and taps his toe, or folds his arms and holds them close to his chest. You better watch out.

Prior to becoming Harvey's executive assistant, Margaret Dismond, who regards Harvey as a sharp visionary with brilliant ideas, taught in the Department of English. At that time she, too, feared Harvey. She had heard that he had a "quick temper, and that he can be very strong and very mean—unbending." She had also heard that "he was a tough taskmaster and that he wanted things done right. And if you didn't do them right, if you slacked off or if you weren't doing the work that you were getting paid to do, you were going to hear about it. And if it were definitely true, you were going to be reprimanded for them in some way. If you are not doing anything wrong, then you don't have anything to fear."

The late Margaret Simmons acknowledged that Harvey is a perfectionist and that his "temper is short sometimes." But she presented this interpretation of his style. "He might explode but he calms right back down." It is because "he is impatient and he doesn't suffer other people's mistakes too easily. He doesn't suffer fools at all." But she knew the compassionate Harvey that supported her when her daughter was killed, though, at the time, she barely knew him, who supported her husband during his illness, and who supported her during her own extended illness. Those who know him best and have worked closely with him, such as Simmons, Margaret Dismond, JoAnn Haysbert, Martha Dawson, Dennis Thomas, and Lucius Wyatt, understand that the dignified, results-oriented gentleman's temper might flare only in the context where an individual or a team does not fulfill obligations at work, where an individual provides filtered or inaccurate information, or where an individual refuses to be accountable for his or her action.

Not only does Harvey expect family members to be accountable for their actions or to fulfill their obligations at work, his strong work ethic dictates that they should go beyond the call of duty—to give more than 100 percent. Thus, when critics want more pats on the back for doing a good job for what they are paid to do, JoAnn Haysbert forcefully disagrees with them. She exclaimed:

> Doesn't reward you! That is simply not true. I think that a reward is something you're going to have to earn. If you get a reward from Dr. Harvey, you earned it. And when he rewards you, he rewards you well. But if you think that you are just going to do any kind of job and get a reward, if you are going to work to the clock and get a reward, that's not going to happen. If you think that you are going to get a reward for what you are getting paid to do, that's not going to happen. You have to go beyond the call of duty to get a reward. But if you do that, my experience has been you'll get it. I have gotten rewards. But I don't work to the clock. I've

> gotten rewards and I don't just do what I'm being paid to
> do. . . . I watch my people the same way. They come and clock
> in from 9 to 6. What are they going to get a reward for?
> Maybe I just learned too much from Dr. Harvey.

Being results-oriented and being a tough taskmaster can certainly be beneficial when managing the finances of the University. The President is definitely concerned about keeping an eye on the bottom line and running the school like a business, which some Hampton family members think can be at the expense of the well-being of people. Martha Dawson has seen his sensitive side, as well as his hard-nosed side, and would agree that Harvey is "budget conscious." But she has her personal account of the "Doc Stories." "Several times there were some things I wanted to do, and he would always use this expression: 'Where's the money coming from?' He was very budget conscious, so if you went in there with the budget, you knew he was going to cut some of it. He had this idea of not being Uncle Sugar. Don't come to him—Uncle Sugar, you know—like you're growing up and you have this uncle who would give you a little money for candy. Dr. Harvey would say, he is not Uncle Sugar. This is not welfare. If you want money, you'd better go get it.' If we got the money, that was fine and that's why you would have the deans to write proposals to get the money."

Similarly, Lucius Wyatt, Harvey's longtime financial leader and a member of his first team, would agree that the President held a tight rein over the University's budget and had the "final word" about it. But he acknowledged that "the team concept existed," and Harvey "got ideas from us and maybe some of us were strongly in favor of one idea versus another, but he always made the decision about which ideas were put into action." While they were in accord on most issues, he vividly remembered one incident where they were not. Wyatt, along with the building superintendent, contracted to replace exterior doors to the Administration Building. Wyatt said,

> When Harvey realized that the new doors had been installed, he became very upset, and said we were needlessly spending the University's money because, in his opinion, the old doors were adequate and were not in the condition we thought they were. And he had quite a lot to say to me about having done that without first getting his approval. Perhaps two weeks later, he and I were entering the building from the waterfront side and he remarked, "Mr. Wyatt, these new doors were a good idea. And I think they were needed." And I reminded him that he had really taken me to task, and had almost given me a reprimand about having installed the doors. And he said, yes, he knew that, but these doors were really needed. So he apologized.

The President's very close friend, Arthur Greene, stated that Harvey is a "complete person in relation to his fellowman, so in any circumstances where there are two sides of an issue, if he can be shown that he was wrong, he is strong enough to accept it, but he doesn't like to. He likes to be right. He is extremely competitive and hates to lose." Furthermore, said Greene:

> You know a leader has to be brave enough to take a position and believe in the position and believe in his ability to express that position. He also has to be someone who can convince someone who is not quite sure, or convince someone who is totally against it, that his way of looking at it is probably either better or a little more acceptable than their way of looking at it. Nobody wants to be wrong and nobody is ever always right. But absolutely nothing gets done unless you take a position. And I think that people can view his level of assuredness in a positive way—self-confident, leader, visionary, advocate—or they can view it in a negative way—arrogant, cocky, conceited. And I think a lot depends on where your mind wants to take you. If you have common goals, you need the input of everyone and the strength of everyone to achieve that goal. Or you believe you don't need anyone. You can do it by yourself. And one of the leader's jobs is to bring everyone to the same table. And I think he does a very good job of that, but he realizes that once you are at the table, you have to move on.

Harvey's transformational type of leadership inspires others to share in his vision of change. In contrast, the transactional model of leadership, the more dominant one in higher education, advocates a shared governance, but it is less effective for sweeping changes. Accordingly, JoAnn Haysbert, along with his wife, Norma Harvey, maintains that "Dr. Harvey is not a dictator." Haysbert said,

> He is a leader and president. A president of a university has to be one that makes the final decision, not because they just want to make it, but because the responsibility rests with the man or woman who has that final decision. There is no one else that you can pass the buck to and say its him or its her. It is you. Whether that decision is good or bad, it's your decision. So when some people may view his decision-making as a dictator type, I don't, because I understand administration. I understand leadership. I understand a president's role. And if he were not the kind of person to be able to make final decisions, last word decisions, and bear the consequences of those decisions, then what would they call him?

Timothy Tee Boddie, the chaplain of Hampton University, who also regards Harvey as the visionary, understands that as a practical-idealist, Harvey "sees what he wants to happen to the University, how he wants the University to move forward, and proceeds to make that happen." He provides a sociological explanation of what some family members interpret as an autocratic, hands-on method by Harvey as really "a style of leadership rooted in the African American community." Boddie thinks it is "a model that we had to take because of the necessity to ensure that things went well. It started with African American preachers who often headed these types of institutions, the most notable of whom was Dr. Benjamin Mayes, a preacher. And even though Dr. Harvey has this Harvard degree in educational management and educational administration, and he is very effective in his understanding of educational models, still I think in there is a need, out of necessity, to oversee and to be involved in almost every aspect of the University." Boddie is convinced that Harvey's style is "absolutely grounded in his Southern background. I don't see how you can get way from that. Here he is from Brewton, Alabama, grew up in the church, and understanding, too, that he went to Talladega, and understanding, too, that when things went well, the president or the pastor got the appreciation, but when they went badly, they got the blame. To avoid that, you were involved in every aspect of the church and in his regard, as far as I can tell, he is involved in everything."

Boddie theorized about its efficacy. He felt it works in some contexts, but as the institution grows, it becomes less effective as a model. However, Boddie said it can be argued that this model is necessary still, even at Hampton, given the success that Hampton has enjoyed over the last twenty five years.

Within most families, including one as large as Hampton University, undoubtedly there are members who see the lessons that are being taught by the head from a different perspective. As Joffre T. Whisenton, former president of Southern University and now a higher education consultant, noted, in a personal interview, anytime a president of a university says "No, you will have critics." But Harvey responds to the myriad of interpretations of family members with his usual characteristic self-assurance. "When you're doing what you know is right, it really doesn't bother you when they beat you up about it."

Whisenton knows also that Harvey is right. As a higher education consultant, he said, "Not only do we use Dr. Harvey and Mrs. Harvey as role models, we also use Hampton University. In reference to Hampton's excellence, Whisenton, the keynote speaker at the opening Fall 2001–2002 Faculty Institute, humorously made this claim: "If you would see other universities, you would not catch the next plane to Hampton University, you would catch the one that has already left." Clearly, for Whisenton, Dr. Harvey has brought the University from excellence to preeminence." He pointed out that:

> Dr. Harvey has a penchant for knowing how to work
> with people rather than work on people. And it's too bad we
> can't clone him, because it's a lot of work being a president.
> You have to make a lot of tough decisions. A lot of people

don't like those decisions. But he has been able to work with the entire community—students, faculty, staff, the Board of Trustees. But with all of those opportunities, I need not mention the excellent leadership he has developed. Some individuals coming from Hampton University are going out to head up similar institutions and that is totally remarkable. So he has been able to develop leadership over the years in terms of helping people to improve themselves. I know it makes it tough for him when he develops someone and then they leave to go take a presidency. But as he helps another institution, it provides an opportunity for another individual to move in and get an opportunity to improve himself or herself. And he does that across the board—not only with males, but with females also. So to me, he is just the most remarkable individual.

Perhaps Walter Lippman said it best when he remarked that "the final test of a leader is that he leaves behind him in other men [and women] the conviction and will to carry on."

Building Beams of Leadership for Women

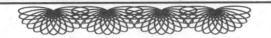

> "I sought to get the very best talent that I could and,
> as a result, what I did was open up the doors for a
> number of women."
> —William R. Harvey

Before it became fashionable to hire or promote women, irrespective of color, as executives and CEOs in the nation, in the state, and in the higher education academy, President William R. Harvey, the visionary, was ahead of the curve. When he assumed the mantle of leadership at Hampton University in 1978, with the exception of Mae Barbee Pleasant, his executive assistant, women were not seated at the table of his administrative council. The status quo was quickly reversed, however, when Martha Dawson, appointed by Harvey in 1979, became Hampton University's first vice president for academic affairs and the first woman to hold that position in the State of Virginia. More than two decades later, fifty percent of his administrative council members are women. These administrative council members are among the 210 women in leadership positions from chairs, to directors, to vice presidents, appointed by the President between 1978–2002. By the twenty-second year of his presidency, women's leadership had increased to almost 60 percent, up from 22 percent during his first year.

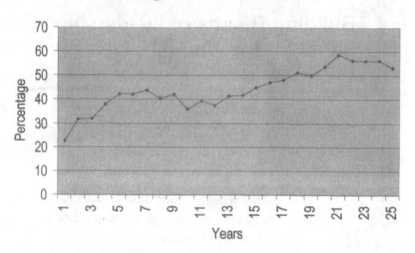

Percentage of Female Administrators

For Harvey:

It was the right thing to do, because I have always tried to get the very best talent that I could find. And if that were male, fine; if that were female, fine; if it were black, fine; if it were white, fine. So, for me, it was a very simple answer. I sought to get the very best talent that I could and, as a result, what I did was open up the doors for a number of women. There is no doubt about it, there is a glass ceiling both in corporate America and in higher education for blacks, for women, and people of other color and the like, even though that's eroding a bit now. Thank goodness! And to me, that's foolish, because if you are in corporate America, or in government, or in higher education, you ought to seek the best talent you can get. And that was my motivation. And as a result, what we have been able to do, I think, is really become a role model for other higher education institutions. When I came here, my council was all male. Now my administrative council is half female and half male, and my motivation, as I said, is simply to get the best available talent for this wonderful place called Hampton University. Now, my first chief academic officer, Dr. Martha Dawson, was a female. My current chief academic officer is a female, Dr. JoAnn Haysbert. And in between, I have had males and females. I have tried to seek and search for talent wherever I could get it, and, as a result, we have done that. We have given people opportunity; we have exposed them. I have tried to make sure that they understood the responsibility that they carried to be a dean or vice president, and to give them the kind of exposure and experience that will make them better.

Martha Dawson, a former vice president of academic affairs, agreed that the President "gives you an opportunity to grow" and does not treat women as mere figureheads. Making the distinction between a manager and the mark of a true leader, she posited that "a leader creates a milieu where you can allow other people to grow." If she had a creative idea, she indicated that she could always discuss it with him. "It might not have been an idea that he was ever interested in, or we may have gotten it done at a particular time, or he may have come up with another idea. But you were allowed to be a leader. A manager just tells you what to do, how to do it, and it's boring." Dawson, who had opportunities for college presidencies but chose to remain as an administrator in academic affairs, said that, "Even though I was older, he helped me to develop my leadership skills. You can have a lot of talents and you don't even know you have them, but someone has to give you that chance and encourage you to do it and recognize you can do it." She said, "I used to be timid, you know; people are not going to believe that. But I can be, but not anymore. So often women in these positions are just figureheads." But the President, whom she described as both "sensitive and extremely hard-nosed," treated her like a "strong person." And, "If I was going to be a leader, he helped me to be one." She stated:

> In my generation, women just didn't get many opportunities to lead. You could be a teacher, but not any place where you could be in the lead. But I think he was really quite ahead of his time to even think about bringing a woman in, especially a black woman, to be the chief academic leader. You know research tells you the perception of women in these roles is that we are soft and we cry and all that stuff. But one of the things that he did, he didn't treat you with any kid gloves. If you were to take the role, you were treated the same way as he would treat the men. And that's what I liked about it. In other words, you couldn't go in there and whine,

you couldn't do this and I can't do that. You've got to do it. That's your job. And I never felt that he was condescending in any way. I felt that he expected me to do things he wanted me to do, things that I didn't know that I could do.

Just his being with me and talking about plans made me feel comfortable that we were on the same team, and it wasn't going to be the case of your running up to the president and back to the vice president. I was in charge of academics and there was just no other way that it was going to be. And if there were some things that teachers wanted to do, they had to come through the system. Many times, women are just there to smile and grin and are just a fixture. I've been blessed to not have had that.

As the vice president of academic affairs, the President would stress to her the importance of being accountable and "don't upbuck it" [pass on decisions]. "He would say, 'Dr. D., is Dr. So and So reporting to you? You handle it. Don't come to me with that stuff.' Even though he was young, he was very supportive and helped me to grow tremendously." Describing her experiences of working with Harvey as exhilarating, she pointed out that he would always come up with some idea and would ask, "What do you think about so and so?" Clearly, "The leader develops and creates. In my opinion, if you are really a leader, you bring other people along and develop them. You are mentoring; you are building bridges for people. You're making your mark, but you're pulling other people along. A manager just keeps things intact. And the evidence of his leadership is where we [were] in 1999 to where we were in 1978. It was Hampton Institute. Now we are out there competing," said Dawson. She reminded us, as well, of the President's emphasis on team work, and how he changed the academic culture when he put deans on his team and made them and other administrators a part of his annual administrative retreat held in Nags Head, North Carolina or Hilton Head, South Carolina. "You know, all of this is just like traveling. It grows on you. It gives you hope," she said.

Dawson acknowledged that Harvey not only builds an atmosphere conducive to personal and professional growth, "he is

sensitive to putting people in positions with talent. It is no accident," she pointed out, "that so many individuals under Harvey's
administration have become presidents at other institutions. I
can tell you that the key to being successful in higher education
and administration comes from having good, warm experiences.
And at Hampton, they got it. That's why they look good in their
interviews. He has been a vendor of leaders."

Elnora Daniel, who was appointed President of Chicago
State University in 1998, is among those leaders the vendor produced. She graciously affirmed Harvey's assistance:

> I shall be eternally grateful to William Harvey for the les-
> sons learned. If I think back to my early interactions with him,
> the thing that sticks out most in my mind is that he promoted
> people and not gender. And that to me is so significant when
> you think about how chilly the climate is for women in the
> academy in the past, specifically, and even so today. The fact
> that he promoted me and other females to higher level
> administrative positions was a seminal event in my life. I am
> not so certain that without his awareness and attention to my
> attributes that I would be where I am today. I have to, in all
> honesty, give him credit for that because I think when I
> became vice president for academic affairs, there had been
> only one other female and that was Martha Dawson. And so,
> from the beginning of his tenure as President, he has always
> looked at the competence level of individuals rather than the
> gender. I think it is a sterling characteristic—a wonderful
> ability he has to look beyond the gender and to look at the
> competencies of the individuals. That has happened not only
> to me, but other females as well.

Dianne Boardley Suber, the second female vice president from
Hampton University to be selected for a college presidency, agreed
with Dawson and Daniel that Harvey assists both men and women.
She felt that he is especially supportive of women's more collaborative leadership style.

> I don't think he is at all intimidated by women leaders.
> He doesn't feel threatened or upstaged by us. In many in-
> stances, men tend to be very cautious about having women in

their professional circles that they think are going to upstage them. And that is not an issue here. I don't think he's uncomfortable or cautious about people upstaging him in any venue, whether it's male or female. I think he recognizes the strength that women bring to the table. I think it's a very positive thing for those of us who are women. He has been extraordinary in terms of the women he has promoted.

JoAnn Haysbert is another example of Harvey's ability to look beyond the myopic eye of gender and to promote based on talent. She concurred with other female administrators that regardless of race or gender, the "vendor of leaders" is a master at spotting new talent. The President identifies people across the campus who have great potential and encourages them to get the proper experience and training to assume leadership, whether at Hampton University or another venue. "I have certainly talked with him on occasions about people that I think have the potential and whom we ought to look at in the academy, particularly at Hampton, to assume certain positions. He, in turn, has always taken the leadership of identifying people to me and putting them in the pipeline for the next level." He is particularly sensitive to the development of young people.

Martha Jallim-Hall, then assistant to the provost and director of international programs, was one of those individuals mentored by Harvey and put in the pipeline for leadership training. Even as a student, Jallim-Hall, who is from the Virgin Islands, noted that, "Dr. Harvey has served as my mentor and he is almost like a father figure to me. Not only to me, but to my sisters as well. Dr. Harvey is available for students to talk to. Even now, I can talk to him about different things that may not necessarily be related to my profession, as well as about my career, like where I would like for it to go, the kinds of things I need to do in order to move on, and he's very helpful with that." When she graduated from Hampton University in 1986, he asked if she would be interested in working for the University as a residence hall director. She responded in the affirmative, and noted that such an opportunity would give her time to work on her master's degree.

"That's exactly what I want you to think about," he said to her. When she performed her duties well, he expanded them. After completing her master's degree, she served as the director of student activities. "I had not envisioned that for myself," she mused, "and I was tickled because he had such confidence in me and my abilities. And I must say that a lot of advice Dr. Harvey gave me through those years when I was director of student activities, I find true today." Barely a few months into her newly appointed position as director of student activities position, she recalled one of his wise counsels.

> When I was first appointed director of student activities, I had a student leader group call me into a room—a hundred and fifty students. And they told me that because they could not register early, they were going on strike and they would not work with the freshmen. Sometimes student leaders, athletes, and other special groups were allowed to do that, but because they were not allowed to register early that year, they assumed it was my fault. It was the day before the new students were to arrive, and student leaders were to assist them with the registration process and to acclimate them to the campus and to the University culture, and that's their responsibility for pretty much the first two weeks of school. So I was a little shocked because I wasn't expecting it. I didn't know quite what to do, but I knew I could not give in to their demands. So I listened and told them, "I will get back to you." So I called Dr. Harvey and told him what had happened. And he said to me, "You go back in that room, and you ask them who wants to remain a student leader, you come with me. And those who do not want to remain a student leader, you ask them to just leave the program because this University has to function and we cannot allow personalities to get in the way of people doing a good job. If you believe in this program, then this is what the program means, and this is what the program stands for. Those of you who do not like that and would like to do something else, you are free to go." So I went back and told them, "I understand your feelings and your concerns, but the program was designed to help new students, and some of you disagree with some things that have happened. However, if you don't like the program any

more, you are free to leave and we will not hold that against you. Those of you who want to continue, please feel free to stay and we will work together. If there are only three or four of you, we will work to make the program better. But we will not change what the University has deemed necessary for this year." And, of course, I didn't back down, because I remembered Dr. Harvey saying that you can't run a program based on personalities of people, because personalities change and you will never get the job done or the goal of the program will not be met. You have to stick with the policy. You have to stick with the goals and the objectives, and he basically told me if you stick with that, you will not go wrong.

Jallim-Hall reported that none of the students walked out of the room.

The apprentice has also learned the valuable lesson of being fiscally responsible from the master teacher. "Dr. Harvey has always told us that if you have a dollar, you cannot spend a dollar twenty-five. And the advice he always gives to seniors during the senior banquet is to save some money, buy some property, invest money, and not to overspend. When I would sometimes complain about needing more money for my student activities budget to do more things or different things, he advised me to explore other opportunities, other ways to try to get things done, simply because we are a private university and there may not be enough funding available."

Jallim-Hall is quick to point out, "He gives young people an opportunity to succeed and to do well, probably because he was so young when he became the President of Hampton University."

I have seen a number of young people whom Dr. Harvey has taken an interest in and I am one of those people, and I always tell people that I am a product of Hampton. And it's through Dr. Harvey's mentorship and his leadership that I am where I am today. He encouraged me to get my master's; he encouraged me to work on my doctorate; and that's all been his doing. I know there are several people on campus, and even upper-level administrators, whom he has really supported that way because he wants to push you to do the best that you can do. Dr. Harvey does not want you to produce at 100 percent; he wants you to produce at 110 percent. I remember when I was coaching the Honda All-Star Academic Team and we won second place. I was so proud to tell Dr. Harvey about our accomplishment. And he said, "Well, Martha, second place is good, but you have to win first place." And from that point on, I tried to push myself so that everything is good. As he says, "Everything we do at Hampton, we must do it well. We must do it beyond 100 percent, because it reflects on the entire institution." And I really appreciated that because it makes you do your best, whatever you have to do.

Even when you may not perform according to his expectations, in her leadership training with the master teacher, Jallim-Hall noted that he "never raises his voice" with her. Rather, "He will talk with you and he will listen to you and he will tell you, 'Okay, I understand what you did, but this is really the way you should have responded,' or, as a result of something you didn't do, that may reflect negatively on the University. For instance, I was trying to contact an organization to try and raise some money for the students. And I did that without consulting with the development office. So he told me that while you may contact an organization and they may give you $500 for your students, we could probably have contacted that organization and gotten $5000. Then he will let you see that there are procedures in place that would help a university or an organization to function as a whole. He's very much a teacher who guides."

For Jallim-Hall,

> Dr. Harvey is a leader, but he also knows how to follow. And that's very important, because sometimes he will allow younger people, or he will allow other people to assume the leadership role in certain projects and will allow them to grow. He puts people in places that will allow them to develop themselves. A lot of things he can do himself, but he wants to make sure that administrators get experiences that will prepare them for the future. So, in a sense, he could lead the group, but he allows others to lead and he follows because he is there and he is supportive. Dr. Harvey has allowed some administrators and staff to go to the [Virginia] General Assembly and talk with legislators about funding for

Hampton University. And I happen to have been one of those
people that actually went to the General Assembly, and we
talked with them about the funding that we would need to
support Hampton University, though it's a private institution.
As a result, we did get some funding for the museum.

Jallim-Hall asserted that, "Dr. Harvey has mentored a lot of students
and even professionals as well. I think there are quite a few people
on campus that can say that." For example, even though Elnora Daniel is no longer on Hampton's campus, she can say that, "During my
tenure at Hampton, numerous leadership roles were assumed and
Hampton's President, William R. Harvey, made most of these administrative appointments. His forward thinking and openness to the
appointment of females to leadership positions provided opportunities for all who desired to excel."

Debra White, the assistant provost of technology and a
member of his administrative council, would eagerly concede
that she is among those individuals mentored by the President
because of his obliviousness to the chilly climate in the academy
toward women. After a brief stint as a consultant for the University, in 1999, to assess the campus network infrastructure, the
President offered her a position as the CIO (Chief Information
Officer). Though White was employed officially in 1999, she had
previously had a long-standing affiliation with the University as
an IBM Marketing Representative with a specialty in the higher
education segment, and had cultivated relationships with a myriad of individuals on campus. But she felt it was essential "to
develop a relationship with Dr. Harvey." In 1991, she had such an
opportunity to meet him. "He and I had just had some frank dialogue about the University, about his partnership with IBM, but
from that dialogue, we started to talk about different issues, like
my professional desires and what I wanted to do long term. So I
began to look to him as a mentor."

In the role of counselor, the President was instrumental in
assisting White with developing her career path. "I shared with

him that I wanted to do more and my thoughts were that I
needed to leave IBM in order to really get back into higher education. I was an employee of IBM with a specialty in the higher education industry, but I felt that something was missing. So I had
several conversations with Dr. Harvey about my feelings and my
desire to do more, my desire to get far more involved. At that
time, in the early 1990s, he said to me, 'You really need to get a
doctorate—you need to invest more in your education if you are
going to really have an impact, play a role in higher education,'"
she said. White took his advice, and completed her MBA degree
in 1993. "In 1994, I left the Hampton Roads area and became
Chief Information Officer at a small private school in Rhode
Island. My husband was in the military, so we left Rhode Island
and we were in Memphis. I was still contemplating what I needed
to do when I got a call from Dr. Harvey saying I needed to consider this opportunity. And I was very flattered and a little bit surprised. But anyway, the long and the short of it was, I came back
to the Hampton Roads area and I started pursuing this dialogue.
Now in pursuit of the dialogue, he reminded me of what I needed
to do for my continued growth in the higher education field. And
he said, 'You've been thinking about this, but now you have definitely got to start to make some moves to do this.' So I went out
and now I am a part of the George Washington Program in Higher
Education Administration and I am a doctoral candidate in 2002."
As a member of the President's administrative council, White
concurred with other female administrators that regardless of
gender, "Dr. Harvey treats us all the same." At Council meetings,
she has observed that "he takes time to help everyone through an
issue or through a process. And maybe I don't know what makes
this unique, but I have experienced his wisdom being shared not
only with women but also with men. And maybe there are other
presidents who have the good old boy network and don't invite
women in, but I see Dr. Harvey nurturing all of us. . . . Dr. Harvey

is a risk taker, and in making decisions, he takes time with every-one to say here's why we should do that or should not do that and here's what it means for Hampton University." Moreover, for White, the President involves all constituents of the University, "making sure that all voices are heard, not just a particular group." And in the meantime, he forces you to ask yourself "What is it that we are trying to accomplish here?"

For White, his style of leadership is empowering. In develop-ing the infrastructure for the Hampton University Information Technology Strategic Plan, she noted that, "He has allowed me to be involved in some very key decisions. For instance, when we were talking about wiring the campus, he and I talked about the financial part of doing that, and about what it would mean for the campus. We went back and forth on that. Through the questions he asked me, he prepared me to see what kinds of issues would drive a president's decision. So I began to frame my discussion and my reports in such a way that he would have all the information he needed to make an informed decision. So he helped me under-stand the role that the President plays in the decision-making pro-cess and the role that the President plays with the Board of Trustees in the decision-making process, and then how the person at my level in the University interacts with the Board of Trustees."

She further acknowledged, "What Dr. Harvey particularly helped me to do was to take that plan from an operational view and truly make it a strategic plan and then present it and ask for support at the Board of Trustees level." He provided guidance in helping her to prepare for the Board meetings and the opportu-nity to interact with its members. White said:

> I understood and watched the whole impact of having the opportunity to talk to the Trustees on a one-to-one basis and to forge the agenda in that setting as well as in the fol-low-up meetings. I had the opportunity after those things to say [to the President] "Tell me what I can do to improve. What did you like? When this person said that, where was he really

headed?" I had discussions with him on the front end and the back end. When the strategic plan was presented to the Board of Trustees, it was a nonissue. They endorsed it and we got their approval to move aggressively forward. And as a result of all of that, Hampton University was named [by *Yahoo* in 2000] to the *100 Most Wired Colleges in the Nation*. And we were the only Hampton Roads university that was so honored. I thought it was a wonderful endorsement and recognition from the national organization that Hampton University is on the move in the technology arena and this was the first year that any of the HBCUs made that list and Hampton University was one of the two.

White has learned valuable lessons from Harvey even when he has taken her to his "proverbial woodshed." She cited an example.

We were doing a virtual tour and putting that on a CD and folding that into an e-commerce application as part of our capital campaign. What that really says is that we are going to do a mailing to our friends and to the alumni, and present them with this miniature sized CD with the suggestion that once you have taken the tour, you make a donation to Hampton via the Internet. We had worked up the tour, and it was time to decide how many CDs we were going to order. In my conversation with Dr. Harvey, he said, "Get me 1000." Well, I said, I was thinking more like 5000. Then he said, "Let's just start with 1000." Well, when I went back and looked at the pricing, I went out on a limb and made a decision counter to his and ordered 5000. The price for 1000 and the price for 5000 was essentially the same. And what I learned, in doing that, was that even though I may disagree, and even though I may be right, after the President has made a decision, I don't have the authority to unmake that decision. Even though I may be right.

In the woodshed, the master teacher employed his soft hammer to teach a lesson. She stated:

What he told me was, "Debbie, I don't like this," in a very calm voice. "I have a problem with this." That was one conversation. And then, I paused and hung up from that. It was a Friday afternoon. He was stern in what he said, but he didn't raise his voice and I think that was what really caught my attention—the fact that he did not raise his voice. And I knew that this was a very serious matter, so I gave it a lot of thought over the weekend. I had an opportunity to see him on that Monday, and I took the initiative to say to him that I had thought about what he said and I admit I did something that I should not have done. That I reflected on the example that he shared with me and I assured him that I had learned from that situation and I had grown.

She indicated that the President has taken time to share with her an example that he had gone through with the Board. "The rules say that if you are on tenure track and you are not tenured within a certain amount of time, then you are terminated. There were two teachers—one was a very good teacher, and the other was a good teacher, who fell into this bucket. And he went to the Academic Affairs Committee of the Board of Trustees to personally make a plea to them that even though our rules say this, here are two people who would be terminated, and it would help us if Hampton University would move to keep these two wonderful teachers. He made that case to the Board. He told me he felt he was absolutely right. However, the Board made another decision. And elevating it to that level helped me to understand that relationship."

She admitted,

> I felt very strongly I was making the correct decision for the University; however, I understand the context in which that happened. And that's when he shared with me the trustee story. I then called him back after I had left the office and I thanked him for sharing with me the trustee story and it had underscored in my mind the fact that you can't have anarchy. You can't have people in an organization, or a president can't condone people in an organization whose actions are counter to his, even if those actions are right. Things got a little bit lighter in that conversation. And again, I said to him, "I took the time and reflected on what I had learned." And he said, "Well, you know, I was going to send you a letter of reprimand, but I think you have learned from this and that's not needed in this particular case." So that's a good example of a how I felt I grew experientially, because sometimes you can't see the forest for the trees. And he helped me understand the

importance of following directions, even if I believe that it's not correct and if I felt so strongly about it, I owed both myself and him the opportunity of the information I had gathered, and that I should not have taken a step until I shared that additional information with him.

From corporate America, White has brought a bottom-line approach to higher education that melds with Harvey's philosophy of running the school like a business.

> In my opinion, the bottom line is what does it mean for the person carrying the backpack? Though I do not allow my people in information technology to think anything other than to ask that question of themselves in everything that they do. That everything must be framed to benefit that statement. That is why we are in business. And what I brought from corporate America is that philosophy. I also brought the whole issue of what I will term as customer service—how we talk to people, how we get involved in their projects, how we show a leadership role, and I always try to get my people to not get caught up in what I call the small stuff. Because if we get caught up in the small stuff, we can't get anything done. Dr. Harvey is results-driven, so I know that when I am going in there to talk to him, I frame most of my conversation from a bigger perspective with the customer being the student.

Yet, she is always mindful of how that can be done within the context of being fiscally responsible.

Like White, Jeanne Zeidler, who worked as the director of the Hampton University Museum for over twenty years, has learned many lessons from Harvey, her mentor. She noted that:

> The most important thing that I have learned from him is to keep your eye on the future and keep your eye on where you want the institution or the program to go and to be open to trying some different paths and some flexibility in ways to get there. Be open to opportunities as they come to you and not to make instant snap judgments. Something may come along that doesn't fit immediately into the plan or the direction that you thought you were going, but [one should] be creative about it and think about the opportunities that come before you.

She gave this example as a lesson she learned in being open to opportunities that come before you. When the President first considered restoring the Huntington Building to house the museum instead of reconstructing the Academy Building or erecting a new edifice, she thought to herself:

> Oh, my God, we'll just have leaky roofs. And how are you going to take that old building and put climate control in it? It'll never happen. It'll never be right. But I didn't say that to him. I just got kind of discouraged and I thought, what is he thinking about, just abandoning that [Academy] Building and it [Huntington] is no good for anything else and why am I looking at that old rundown building? It might have a nice dome in there, but it's a mess. And it's a library; it's not a museum, and you can't do anything with this building. This is a bad idea. But we did look at it, and it was exactly the right thing to do. I brought in a consultant and instead of seeing what was here, we saw the bones and the structure and what it could be. [This] is a real example of keeping your options open, keeping yourself flexible, not prejudging situations until you investigate them.

"Of course," she acknowledged, "some people would say, 'Oh, you can't make up your mind where you're going to be. You have a facility problem and you can't set a goal and meet and achieve it.' But different opportunities present themselves and this building presented one. And this ended up to be the best solution for us."

From the master teacher, she garnered the "idea that there is a larger goal at the end. And there is more than one way to get there. And some ways may be better than others."

Zeidler has much praise for Harvey's support of her leadership role on campus and in her past roles beyond its borders as a school board member for Williamsburg-James City County, Virginia, as a Williamsburg city council member, and in her position as the mayor of the City of Williamsburg, Virginia. As an elected official, she proclaimed:

> When I think about how I got there or where I got the confidence to do it, I think that's where Dr. Harvey has been

very critical and very influential. One of his really strong characteristics as an administrator, as the boss, if you will, as the
leader, is that he gives you the chance to perform to your
capability. He doesn't make prejudgments or assumptions
about what your limitations are or what you can do. And he
really does that in lots of different ways. He expresses a confidence in you, not necessarily by always patting you on the
back or verbally saying so, but by what he asks you to do and
the amount of responsibility that he gives to you and then
doesn't tell you how to accomplish the end result, but gives
you the flexibility to figure it out and do it. I have done things
in the last twenty years that I never thought I would do or
would be capable of doing. And I think that it's because of
this work environment. The environment that he created
really provided the atmosphere so that you felt free to try
things, you felt the confidence in yourself that you could do it
and there was nobody who was negative about it. There was
nobody saying you don't have the training or the skill or the
personality, or you are not articulate enough, or you don't
write well enough, or you've never done that kind of thing
before so don't try it. It was always encouragement. Here's
what we want to accomplish as a university and what part you
will play in it to help us accomplish the goal.

Zeidler's previous environment, in which she was employed, was
not only less empowering, but it also had a dearth of women in leadership positions. She found a different situation at Hampton University, and such contrast was noted at her first faculty institute.

I remember that we took a break, and it was astonishing
to me on that break to go to the ladies' room and have to
stand in line because there were so many women on the faculty and in leadership positions. It was a really silly thing to
say that you had to stand in line to get into the ladies' room,
but to me it was a real symbol of a much healthier environment. It is an environment that doesn't judge you by your
gender, or your race, or your age. I came into a situation
where my immediate supervisor was a woman. It was Dr.
Dawson. And Dr. Haysbert was her assistant, and there was a
really good mixture of men and women. It was just a very
interesting and refreshing environment and I think that's part
of what makes Hampton as good a place to work as it is.

With the University providing a nurturing milieu for women, Zeidler
was able to tap into her unexplored potential as a fund-raiser and as
a leader and program developer.

> When I came here, I never thought I was a grant writer
> and I never thought of myself as one who could be very effec-
> tive in bringing in corporate dollars. And in the last ten years,
> we've brought in a lot of foundation money—national foun-
> dations—into the museum to help us. I had been a supervisor
> and a manager before, but always with more constraints on
> being able to plan the program and the future of the institu-
> tion I was directing. Here, if you have a reasonable idea and a
> reasonable plan for achieving it, Dr. Harvey lets you try.

The renovation of Huntington Building as a facility to house the
museum served as an example of her involvement in planning the
future direction of the institution.

> When I came here, I knew the museum needed a new
> facility. At one point, in about 1988, a good friend of the
> museum, Barbara Forst, came to me and said, "I'm going to
> make a contribution," and she wrote the University a check
> for $25,000 and I went to Dr. Harvey and I said that I certainly
> could use that in lots of different ways, but I said this was the
> money for a feasibility study to see what we should do with
> this building. And he went for it and was very supportive. He
> had input into this feasibility study, but he basically trusted
> my professional judgment about what was needed in this
> building, what kinds of spaces, what sort of public access. Of
> course, I never renovated a building before and, of course,
> we had consultants, but I think the whole process of develop-
> ing this facility from a library into a museum is a really good
> example over a period of years of the amount of confidence
> and responsibility which he placed in me and which gave me
> more encouragement to know that I could reach further and
> try to achieve it. And I think in terms of a multimillion-dollar
> renovation project, this is a place where another president or
> another administrator might really have stepped in and put
> his hand in it. Now it isn't that he didn't know what was going
> on, or have ideas, or make suggestions, but he did not
> micromanage this process. He really did trust my judgment.
> And that was not only important to the real quality outcome

that we have, because I am the museum administrator and he is not, but it was also important to empower you, not just me personally, but the museum staff, to say we are in sync with what he wants for the University, and that he is trusting us to get from here to there and figure out professionally what, in our best judgment, is the way to do this.

For Zeidler, the real influence and strength of the President is "his ability to trust you with responsibility and allow you to take risks, to fail sometimes, and not to slap your hand, or make you feel like a loser, but just to say we tried that, now let's try another way. Let us pick up and move on as long as we're heading in the same direction."

Beyond the campus, the President supported her election campaigns financially, but more importantly, she thinks the support came in the form of encouragement. He was extremely supportive when she told him there was a strong possibility that she might become mayor, and he reminded her of the fact that although she worked a full-time job at Hampton University, and the office of mayor would make a lot of demands upon her time, he had full trust that she would do her job. Zeidler said:

> I think part of what enables a person on this campus to do public service is an ethos about Hampton University—which has been here since the beginning and which has certainly been reinforced by Dr. Harvey's administration—that's part of what you do. Part of what you use your knowledge and your training and your good sense for is to serve your community. That's part of what this University is. And so, in that way, you don't do it to neglect what you have to do specifically on your job at Hampton University, but public service is an extension of my work here. And I feel that this kind of thinking permeates the culture at Hampton University. Dr. Harvey encourages people like me by setting that atmosphere on this campus and carrying out the tradition of that here at Hampton.

Clearly, Zeidler views Harvey as a "role model for public service" and as leading by example. He encourages others to follow his lead, and like Zeidler, Mamie Locke, the dean of the School of

Liberal Arts and Education, heeded that call when she became the first black mayor of the City of Hampton, Virginia, in 2000. Locke, who characterized Harvey's leadership style as "bold and forward thinking," stated that "Dr. Harvey was one of the first individuals I approached when I was considering entering politics. He was encouraging and supporting of my efforts. He has continued to be a source of guidance and support as I have continued in my political development. I have always said to others that I am fortunate to have an employer that supports and encourages civic responsibility and involvement. Dr. Harvey is that kind of leader who is supportive of community involvement at all levels."

As others have noted, Locke said that he has helped women.

> Dr. Harvey is very encouraging and supportive of women. His interest is in finding and promoting the best leaders and managers, irrespective of gender. As such, he has never been reluctant to actively assist women in being the best that they can be. Specifically, he taps the resources early, assigning a variety of tasks to determine one's strengths. As an individual demonstrates competency, he provides more opportunities for the person to demonstrate leadership and management skills. He also offers constructive criticism as a means to help individuals grow and develop professionally. It is Dr. Harvey who suggested that I be named assistant dean in the newly formed School of Liberal Arts and Education. Ultimately, my performance in that role led to his appointing me as dean. I would say that prior to these positions, I was given opportunities to serve and lead various committees and task forces to demonstrate leadership skills as a prerequisite to assuming the administrative roles. Again, this is Dr. Harvey's way of determining one's skills as well as continuing to move forward.

Locke, who said that Harvey has served as a role model and mentor, proclaimed, "Dr. Harvey has had a great impact on my management style. I have clearly come to understand the difference between being an administrator and being a manager under his leadership and direction."

Taking Care of Its Own

Not only has the President provided a supportive environment for mentoring women as leaders, who, in general, have a more collaborative leadership style that synchronizes with his team approach, he provides the chance for diverse individuals with talent and skills, particularly alumni, to serve the University. Effie Barry, instructor in health education and an alumnae of the University, stated, "I am just very happy that Dr. Harvey seems to have an unwritten philosophy about the University taking care of its own in terms of providing the opportunity for alumni to give back to the University through service. . . . I would imagine, once they graduate, they have a desire to be able to give back in some way to their alma mater—teaching, serving on the Board, being active in fund-raising, or whatever the situation might be—and my dream had always been to teach at the University. And I am very grateful to him for letting me become aware of the teaching vacancy and allowing me to apply for the position."

Barry initially offered her assistance to the University when she was introduced to the Harveys in the 1980s.

> I first became acquainted with Dr. Harvey and Mrs. Harvey in the middle 1980s. My first meeting with them was at a reception held at the White House and we started chatting. And, of course, when he found out that I was a Hamptonian and I discovered he was President of Hampton University, then it was a quick and fast friendship. And so, over the course of the evening, we just talked, and at departure, I made the statement that if there was ever any way I could help my University for him to just give me a call. Several years went past, but there was never really any kind of personal interaction. In 1990, I had a very unfortunate incident occur in my personal life which led to my divorce from my husband. And during that period of time, Dr. Harvey reached out to me. He invited me to come down to the University to speak at the Student Leaders Assembly, which was held at the beginning of the school year, and I indicated to him again,

that if there was anything I could ever do for the University, just call on me. And, as fate would have it, at the end of that particular year, he gave me a call and indicated that if I was interested in teaching at the University, there was a possibility that I might be able to acquire a position since there was a vacancy in my area of health education that had opened up as a result of [a] retirement. So I came down and I interviewed for the position, and was considered to be the best candidate for the position, so I started my teaching experience at Hampton the fall semester. And, my experience at Hampton as a faculty member was basically a dream come true.

While teaching at Hampton, Barry lauded Harvey for encouraging her and others to pursue their terminal degree. "I think Dr. Harvey has been instrumental in encouraging a lot of us who did not have our doctorate degrees to begin our study, complete our study, and acquire our doctorate degrees."

"Hampton University is always number one in my heart and had it not been for the training that I received at Hampton University, I would not have been able to make some of the accomplishments I have made in my life, Barry noted of her alma mater. "I think that Hampton prepared me in terms of molding me into a well-rounded person. I think the legacy of Hampton encourages development of character and concern for others and a sense of comfort and security and confidence. All of this I attribute to my experience and my association with Hampton University."

The late Jessie Rattley, former mayor of Newport News, Virginia, and senior lecturer at Hampton University, who was always interested in supporting her institution, shared sentiments of her alma mater that paralleled Barry's. Such an opportunity presented itself, when by chance, Rattley, then an elected public official, came upon some information concerning the application to HUD for the completion of the McGrew Towers. The application had already been turned down because of some omissions. Since the final decision was imminent the following day, it was crucial to make the necessary corrections by that time. Rattley tracked down President Harvey and made him aware of the problem, and he was able to do what was necessary to get the application approved, and the funding for McGrew Towers was approved. According to Rattley:

> We always had a good relationship. But when I was not reelected mayor in 1990, after serving the city for twenty years, he did call and ask if I would be interested in coming to Hampton to share with students in the political science department my experiences over the last twenty years in politics. He wanted me to devote time in doing that and working with development on bringing resources to the campus. And I was very pleased and I said I would love to try that. In the meantime, I had a call from Harvard. They asked if I would come and serve as a fellow in their program and teach a course on politics at the Kennedy School. And, of course, I was very impressed with that also. So what I did was call Dr. Harvey and discuss it, and it was his recommendation that I go on and take the Harvard assignment first, and then I could come to Hampton after I finished that. He deferred a semester so I could fulfill that experience at Harvard. And that shows, I think, greatness. And I have enjoyed [Hampton University] and am very grateful to him for that opportunity to share twenty years of experience in politics in the real world with students. And I would like to think that I have offered something that would benefit those students. From the feedback, I think that has occurred. So if you talk in terms of my association with him, I think it is just one of mutual respect. He's in the political area and he's wise to be there because everything is controlled by politics, but in addition to that, he is a businessman and I think Hampton is very fortunate to have a business person at the helm because to run an institution, to be president of a university, you must have some business acumen to be successful. There are things that are needed, there are buildings and programs, and unless you are involved in politics and business, you stand a poor chance of getting very much for the institution.

Preparing Women for New Vistas

The astute businessman is, in addition to his political *savoir faire*, prime promoter of women's leadership and a mammoth marketer of their talents. He promotes women not only from within the ranks of the University and encourages them to use their abilities to serve the institution, he is also interested in creating leaders to serve the higher education academy. He said, "I view as part of my role, that of teaching, that of grooming, that of making people better, because I feel that higher education is a very important venue and I don't think it just runs itself. I think that leadership is the key and what I want to do is to produce other leaders to not only help Hampton University, but also to go out to other institutions." Out of the eight persons from 1990 to 2001 to become presidents of other institutions, two have been women, who, according to the American Council on Education In the March 28, 2002 edition of *Black Issues in Higher Education,* are included in the Fifty African American Women College and University Chief Executive Officers, in 2000. Another woman, Johnnye Jones, the former dean of the School of Science and professor of biology, was appointed to the position of provost at Jarvis Christian College in Texas.

As previously noted, Elnora Daniel, President of Chicago State University since 1998, and Hampton's former executive vice president and provost, was one of the two women appointed as president of a higher education institution. "I've worked with Dr. Harvey for twenty years," said Daniel. "And he is not only a mentor but a friend. I have studied at the feet of a master. Two traits, development of diplomacy and political acumen," she said, "I learned at the feet of the master." Daniel, knows that "imitation is the sincerest form of flattery," and she readily admitted to emulating President Harvey in her own role as President of Chicago State University. For example, like him, she had a library and student union constructed. In addition, she said, "Now that I am the President of Chicago State University, I have really extrapolated those elements of his model that work for me. You can't ever completely take on anyone else's leadership style, but what you do is extrapolate part of those administrative style models that resonate best with you." Those characteristics within his leadership model that are amenable to her style, such as his "high energy level work ethic that allows one to complete a goal and the constant journey towards academic excellence in all that you do," have been extrapolated from Dr. Harvey and his model.

To imitate Harvey is to follow a successful path. As Daniel knows, "He has always been involved in things that will keep Hampton on the forefront of major trends in higher education. He knows what's best for the University and he goes after it. He's a risk-taker and is intuitive. He knows when to take risks and when not to, when it's appropriate to fold the cards. His intuitive sense is something I really admire. It's not something you get from a book."[1]

Daniel is clear that the training she received at Hampton set her on the right course in her presidency at Chicago State.

> Three decades in Hampton's environment provided myriad and valuable life lessons on every dimension of administration from physical plant, fiscal management, pedagogy, to human resources management in a private institution. There are mentors, who advise and model behavior that I humbly attempted to replicate, who played a necessary and critical role in my professional development. They also enabled me to undergo a wonderful collage of academic and professional experiences, thus providing me the opportunity, as well as others, to benefit from the multiplicity of experiences that led to my current post.

Specifically, she made this point: "So many things I learned at Hampton that had to do with the uplift of people—the idea of promoting people to acquire some ownership and commitment to the mission. [Harvey] has a persuasive and charismatic personality and he wants to make people do their very best. I try to take those aspects of his leadership and get people in my setting to aspire to those ideas in a unionized setting, which is different from a private institution in a right-to-work state."

"I thank God every day for that preparation," Daniel was quoted in the *Daily Press* (Newport News) as saying. After taking over the presidency of Chicago State, a campus of eight thousand, Daniel stated she was happy to discover that there was nothing in the realm of her University in which she did not already have experience—except for dealing with unions, and that can't easily be blamed on Harvey since Virginia is a right-to-work state.[2] Dawson would agree with Daniel, who also served as the dean of the School of Nursing, that, indeed, she received her leadership training at the "feet of the master." When Dawson was appointed as vice president of academic affairs, she recalled that the failure rate for the nursing school graduates was in the nineties. "[Dr. Harvey] was tough on her. He said, 'It has got to change if we're going to have nursing. We can't have a failing program.' And Dr. Daniel went up there and she got on the nursing board. And he was so tough on nursing. She had to raise 100 per cent over her budget before she could get funds [from the University budget]. And I would say, 'You know you give other people their budget, maybe you ought to give her a little.' 'The money is not there, Dr. D. Don't ask me to give them anything!'" Under Daniel's leadership, Dawson said, "We got the health center, and then we got the van, and all that." But he made her a leader. Now she's a president because she had to go out there and raise money.

Daniel, then the new dean of nursing, in her first appearance before the Board recalled that pivotal event:

> At one particular Board of Trustees meeting, President Harvey asked me to present. As I presented and finished, one of the Board of Trustee members asked me why the scores of our baccalaureate graduates are less than students who received associate degrees and why can't they pass the board. Well, I wasn't planning to respond to that. But then, the

President said, "Dr. Daniel, if you don't take care of that, we will just eliminate that program." So that was a motivating factor. The scores came up to 90 to 100 percent. That particular accomplishment brought me to the attention of those who can make things happen.

Daniel, as quoted in the *Daily Press*, said of her mentor, "You know, when you first meet Dr. Harvey, he's tall, handsome, and little bit foreboding. But if you know him, you know he has a heart of gold, and I shall always love him." As the first female administrator from Hampton to be named as a college or university president, she credits much of her success at Chicago State University to her thirty-one years as a Hampton University administrator.

Likewise, Dianne Boardley Suber, the second woman administrator from Hampton University to be selected for a college presidency, was in accord with Daniel that Harvey's mentorship and model of leadership paved the way, in September 1999, for her to become the first woman president of Saint Augustine's College, a historic, 1,600-student college in Raleigh, North Carolina. Suber, whose career experience had been in public school education prior to her appointment at Hampton University, stated:

Dr. Harvey appointed me as dean of Administrative Services to bear the responsibility of three units that are really the lifeline of an institution—admissions, financial aid, and the registrar. With my coming out of public education and not being of the academy, he recognized that there was a difference between the academicians and the administrative side of the house. When he was looking for some expertise, and some guidance, and some management for the administrative side of the house, he actually hired me based on what he perceived as the credentials and the experience I brought to the table as opposed to academic credentials. When I started at Hampton, I didn't have a terminal degree and he actually stepped out and made me a dean, which, in higher education, caused some people to have some real concerns. But his objective was to bring a level of administrative management to those units. From the very beginning, he began to train me to be an administrator, not an academician. But

he also realized that to have any credibility in the academy, I
had to have the academician side of it, and I had the degree in
Curriculum Development, and I had certainly been a principal
with the responsibility of overseeing instruction, but the
hands-on curriculum and the academician piece of it, I didn't
have. So he moved me into the assistant provost role, where
he then assigned to me the Center for Teaching Excellence,
which clearly was a role designed for me to take that clinical
supervision piece I had and apply it to the academy and to get
the experience of the provost's office. [Harvey] further expanded my role as assistant provost for academic affairs,
which then got me involved in tenure committees, and instructional committees, to give me an overall opportunity to
understand how those pieces fit.

In that position, she wore additional hats. "I had the opportunity to serve as legislative aide and legislative liaison between
the institution and the General Assembly. [Harvey] sent me to
represent him at organizational meetings where presidents
were the participants. So there was a systematic planning, I
think, of my training. I didn't realize it at the time, but it was
deliberate in terms of one piece on top of another. He has a way
of saying he throws people up against the wall and makes them
see how they respond. I was being pushed to see whether I
would be pushed off the scale, whether I would have enough
strength to come back and say I don't agree with you. There was
a deliberateness in what he did. And I see it now in reflection,"
she asserted.

Of course in the throes of her training under Harvey, Suber
admitted:

Sometimes I would be overloaded, and it looked like at
one point that everything that came down the pike it was,
"Dr. Suber, you do it." And we would sit at council meetings
and [Harvey] would appoint a committee and he would say,
"Dr. Suber, I want you to serve on the committee, too." And I
began to think is this just some plot to just beat me to death
until I would get tired and say, "OK, you can have it all." So
there were times when I thought, "I'm being dumped on."

But in reflection, now that I am in that role, I realize that even being dumped on is part of the training, because the president's role is neverending. But [Harvey] also would say, "Well, let me hear your thinking." He would entertain the discussion, give you his side of it, and then give you the rationale for his thinking. Most of the time, as president, you didn't have a lot of choices of whether you did or didn't do it, but you did have the benefit of his thinking and what the rationale was. So you could consciously process the information and say well, I don't agree with it, or I do agree with it. So that when you get to a point where you are making your own decisions, you have the benefit of your thinking and the benefit of a person's who is a successful model. That's the piece that is so important to understand—that the model is successful. And so whether or not you choose to buy into it, or replicate it, or emulate the behavior, it is a model that is successful. It is financially successful, has credibility in higher education, and so you have to say to yourself, if I don't do this, what is my alternative? Does it have the same kind of presence that the model has?

Like Elnora Daniel, Suber readily admitted to the *Daily Press* that "There's no question that the experience at Hampton is the reason that has provided me the opportunity to serve as President of Saint Augustine's College." Harvey, the promoter of women, knows that "people look to Hampton for leadership." And he regards developing good leaders, regardless of gender, and placing them throughout the ranks of other higher education institutions as his duty. Like Goethe, the German poet and dramatist, Harvey, too, believes, "Whatever you can do, or dream you can, begin it. Boldness has genius, power, and magic in it."

Building Beams of Leadership
The Making of Presidents

"He who obtains has little; he who scatters has much."
—Chinese Proverb

"**H**ow does leadership help us to get where we want to go?" is a question President William R. Harvey often asks of himself and of others. One plumb line for Harvey is to build a lighthouse for leaders at the "Home by the Sea," incorporating the Harvey Model, to steer other higher education academies on a successful course toward "excellence, equity, diversity, and civility."

"And that's what has happened," he said. From 1990 to 2001, for example, his administration has served as journeywork for eight administrators who have stepped into the waters of the higher educational sea and are now navigating the terrains of other institutions in the states of Georgia, Maryland, North Carolina, Illinois, Washington, and New Jersey. Like a proud papa, the master builder beams with jubilation when he recounts this feat.

> I have had two of my women vice presidents to become presidents of other colleges. I have had six of my vice presidents who are men to become presidents, one of whom is a president of a bank. I had others to go on to become vice presidents for academic affairs and other kinds of positions. I view as part of my role, that of teaching, that of grooming, that of making people better, because I feel that higher education is a very important venue, and I don't think it just runs itself. I think that leadership is the key and what I want to do

> is to produce other leaders to not only help Hampton Univer-
> sity but, also, to go out to other institutions.

The President's dreams to produce other leaders have come to fruition. In 1990, he passed on his first torch of leadership to Oscar
Prater, Hampton University's vice president for administrative services, who was named president of Fort Valley State University in
Georgia. In 1994, Harold Wade, Hampton University's executive vice
president, became president of the two-year Atlanta Metropolitan
College in Georgia. Again in 1997, Carlton Brown, Hampton University's vice president of planning and development and dean of the
Graduate College, was appointed president of Savannah State Uni-
versity in Georgia. In 1998, Elnora Daniel, Hampton University's
executive vice president and provost, was selected as president of
Chicago State University in Illinois. In 1999, Warren Buck, Hampton
University's physics professor and its director of Nuclear/High
Energy Physics Research Center for Excellence, was named chancel-
lor of the University of Washington at Bothell. Once again, in 1999,
Dianne Boardley Suber, Hampton University's vice president for
administrative services, was selected president of St. Augustine's
College in North Carolina, a position she assumed on January 1,
2000. In 2000, Calvin Lowe, Hampton University's vice president for
research and dean of the Graduate College, was named president of
Bowie State College in Maryland. One year later, in 2001, Rodney
Smith, vice president of administrative services, took the helm of
Ramapo College in New Jersey. According to the American Council
on Education, in 2000, African American college and university chief
executive officers numbered 186, about 6.6 percent of the total
CEOs. Harvey has produced eight CEOs. In addition to developing
academic leaders, Leon Scott, vice president for business affairs and
treasurer, also left the University in 2000 to assume a post as the
President of Consolidated Bank and Trust Company in Richmond,
Virginia. Harvey believes that, "One of the reasons they were
selected chief executive officers is the fact that they were able to
convince the Boards of Trustees that the Hampton brand of leadership would work at their respective campuses."

At Hampton, Harvey has created a model, as well as a milieu, that launches leaders to journey into a vast ocean of personal and institutional potential, enabling them to break free of limits, to release their full human possibilities, and to hone and test their mettle for servant leadership. Under Harvey's ten-step model, which includes vision, a good work ethic, academic excellence, team building, innovation, courage, good management, fairness, fiscal conservatism, and results, mentees began their voyage into his ocean of leadership. As they are put out to sea, in Captain Harvey's vessel, they learned to sail against the winds and to tread turbulent waters to right its course.

For each of his administrators, he tests their mettle for leadership, sometimes, as previously noted, by verbally "throwing them against the wall and taking them to the proverbial woodshed." He said:

> That's part of my training, because the true mark of any man or woman is how they act in an adverse situation. I want to see how you act when you are pressed against the wall; I want to see how you act when things aren't going so well. Anybody can be with you when things are going well, but I want to see what your reactions are when you're getting thrown against the wall, when things aren't going well. You may not feel as comfortable as you want to because, you see, in life as well as in administration, there is not always sweetness and light. You are dealing with a lot of different kinds of people and a lot of different kinds of constituent groups, so I want our people to be prepared. That's why I do it and then I see how they respond. Those that respond well, I give additional assignments. Those that respond the way that I feel is inappropriate, then I make it more difficult, just to see how they respond and to see how through my help they can respond even better. And the ones who are willing to go that extra mile are the ones that I promote and push on out to get other responsibilities.

Each administrator who is willing to go the extra mile and whom Harvey promotes and pushes to take on additional responsibilities has his/her own war stories of being taken to the proverbial woodshed. But each learns invaluable lessons there, as he/she sails the high seas towards the presidency. Each bears an indelible imprint of the man's markings and his leadership Model. Consequently, each administrator extrapolates components of the Harvey Model, and puts his/her own footprints on it.

With full knowledge that each component of the Model works in tandem, eight of Harvey's proteges shared lessons of promises and perils learned under Harvey and the Harvey Model with participants aspiring to become CEO. This occurred at his first Executive Leadership Summit, "On the Road to the Presidency: Passing the Executive Leadership Torch," which was held at Hampton University on November 2–3, 2001. Sixty participants came from all over the country and as far away as Alaska to imbibe of the Harvey Model.

Oscar Prater, who was Harvey's first president, told the aspirants that he absorbed from the Harvey Model the preeminence of vision in "moving an institution forward," which he regarded as Harvey's greatest strength. The past president of Fort Valley State University and college classmate of Harvey's came to Hampton University in 1979. He and Harvey accidentally met at an airport, and Harvey invited him to come to the University as the vice president of administrative services. Upon arriving at Hampton, he believed vision was about predicting or broadcasting the future. The Harvey Model presented an alternative view. Vision was not predicting the future, but shaping it. "Vision describes an ideal future; it provides meaning and direction; and it forces one to break through barriers perceived to be limitations," Prater stated. From the moment of Harvey's arrival at Hampton University, Prater indicated that the President "had a vision of where he wanted the University to go and how the University was to arrive at the destination. Vision was the major guide that transformed Hampton University to where it is today," but the constituents of the University had to undergo a myriad of behavioral changes. "The vision put forth by the Harvey Model was for Hampton to become a world-class university. Dr. Harvey was willing to take the necessary risks. No persons or events scared him. He saw no limitations. He was of the demeanor to pursue whatever it took." For Prater, "The vision establishes direction for which the mission and goals are developed to move a university forward." So, in 1990, when Prater disembarked from Harvey's ship to steer his own course as President of Fort Valley State University, vision was the key element that guided his journey. From the Harvey model, Prater developed an enlarged view of vision; here, his focus changed, while serving as vice president of administrative services under Harvey, to a new paradigm of leadership. He shifted his thinking "to ends from means, to purpose from procedures, to results from resources, to outcome from processes, to goals from roles, to efficiency from equality, to revenues from expenditures, and to achievements from programs." He carried these visionary principles of the Harvey Model to his institution. He believes "Vision separates great presidents from the rest."

Likewise, Carlton Brown, who took the helm as President of Savannah State University in Georgia, in 1997, brought the Harvey Model to his campus. After studying with his mentor for a decade, he stated, upon leaving Hampton University, that, "Under Dr. Harvey's leadership, I have been afforded unprecedented opportunities to grow, develop and contribute strongly within the institution, the local and regional community, and on the national stage. To have had the opportunity to contribute to the history and development of this grand institution with the support of perhaps its greatest president has been a singular honor, one that I feel fits me uniquely for higher education leadership into the next century."[1]

Though Brown's voyage as an administrator at Hampton ended as vice president of planning and dean of the Graduate College, he began it as the dean of the School of Education from 1987 to 1990, and as dean of the School of Liberal Arts and Education from 1990 to 1996. In the latter capacity, Brown was charged, in

1992, with the duties of spearheading the University's Strategic Planning Steering Committee, which set the direction of the University for the year 2000. Moreover, under Harvey's mentorship, he worked closely with him, and sometimes represented the University at other institutions and governmental agencies across the nation. These experiences helped him to prepare for his presidency. So, Brown feels that Harvey "has always been the most insightful, driven, yet caring leader I've worked for."[2]

Speaking at Hampton University's 107th Annual Founder's Day Celebration in 2000, Brown, as President of Savannah State University, proclaimed that "Hampton is the unqualified leadership of historically black colleges in America," adding, "It is able to do so many things others can't do." As a leadership institution, "We [other historically black colleges and universities] can only do things after you go and do them." He noted that, "The difference for Hampton has been its vision."[3]

Brown has used the visionary principles he gleaned from Harvey and Hampton to steer his ship. Along with vision, Brown stressed the importance of good management at the Executive Leadership Summit. It is crucial, he stated, to have "risk-taking in the management process; otherwise, you will have slowdown in your management growth." At Hampton, he learned important management lessons, such as, "Any serious problem that arises should be addressed immediately. Otherwise, it grows." In addition, he grasped the importance of "management by challenge and support; management by inspiration; management by walking around; management by clarity of expectations; management by policy; management by open communication." He discerned quickly from the Harvey Model for management that "Last year's season of accomplishment must become next year's flow of expectations," and, moreover, "The job of the president is twenty-four hours a day."

Elnora Daniel knows that being a president is a twenty-four-hour haul. Before assuming the post of President at Chicago

State University, she spent thirty-one years at Hampton University; two decades were under Harvey's tutelage. As previously mentioned, she held positions at Hampton University from professor to chair, and from dean to vice president of academic affairs to executive vice president and provost. So Daniel would describe herself an academic president, "one whose career trajectory has taken an academic route." "If I consider the academic excellence element of the Harvey Model and its juxtaposition to academic presidency, I remember the importance of humanism, the urgency of education . . ." she said at the Executive Leadership Summit. She sees academic excellence as "the hallmark of any successful institution of higher education," so it is, for her, a paramount piece in the Harvey Model. For Daniel declared, "The constant journey toward academic excellence and high quality in all that you do has been extrapolated from his model as well as Dr. Harvey himself because of the early things he talked about in his vision for the University when he was being inaugurated. So the standard of excellence resonates so well with me. It reverberates in my mind as I try to transform a university that languished for some time in a state of anarchy to a very productive and vibrant university that is poised to accommodate shifts in paradigms and future perspectives in the realm of education."

Academic excellence is couched within one or more of the functions of a university, such as curricula development, teaching/learning, and fiscal management. Therefore, Daniel forewarned prospective presidents at the Leadership Summit not to ignore the multifaceted aspects of the functions of a university. "Those who dare to lead and to serve as president do not have the liberty of focusing on any one operation of the university. Rather, the role of president requires knowledge and attention to all of the many factors of the university. Specifically, the academic excellence in a university environment involves the establishment and maintenance of quality in, but not limited to, the five categories and they govern any conceptualization of leadership: creative and flexible administrative style, evaluation and planning expertise, human relations and decision-making skills, community development capabilities, and resource development and acquisition tools."

Certainly, for Daniel, a key ingredient of academic excellence that she learned under the Harvey Model, is "vision, which guides you to a world-class university." In addition, she emulates her mentor's policy of fiscal solvency. "The financial process at HU is lean and mean, and I try to emulate that at Chicago State University."

The successful President of Chicago State University attributes her personal and professional development at Hampton to three factors: her longevity; diversity of administrative opportunities; and her exposure to "the acumen and administrative genius of William R. Harvey."

Like Daniel, Calvin Lowe had many opportunities to hone his leadership skills at Hampton as first mate of Captain Harvey's ship. In 1987, he came to Hampton University as an associate professor in the physics department and rose from that position to become its chair in 1990. Later, he became the vice president of research and dean of the Graduate College. The University credits him with securing a $10 million grant from NASA to establish Hampton University's Research Center for Optical Physics. The University also acknowledged him for developing an international and national reputation at Hampton University in research, particularly in physics and atmospheric sciences. In addition, he helped to develop the Hampton University physics doctoral program, the University's first doctoral program, and also spearheaded efforts to enhance technology on campus.

The portentous lessons that Lowe garnered at Hampton under Harvey's administration are employed at his university in Maryland. Upon departing from Hampton, the Bowie State leader emphasized that teamwork would be one such lesson that he would especially stress. As reported in one newspaper account, when Lowe informed Harvey of his presidency at Bowie State

University, which serves about 3,000 undergraduate students and 2,000 graduate students, Harvey teased him about continuing to prove that Hampton University is a training ground for college presidents. "You have to do a good job so I can get eight or nine," Lowe remembered Harvey saying.[4]

At the Executive Leadership Summit, Lowe mentioned, "Dr. Harvey preached to me the importance of the work ethic. You go after perfection and arrive at excellence." He believes that no matter what position one holds, it is important to work hard and succeed at the job. For Lowe, the Harvey Model "sets the framework for your thinking as a leader, where you must excel to be successful. It also creates space for you within this Model to do your own thing. The work ethic is the engine that drives the model. You cannot be successful without it. That is so important to any person who has the tough job of leading any kind of organization. The part that makes all others work is the work ethic. If you don't work at things the right way, the right time, the rest of the Model will not save you."

Lowe also recognizes that as president, your role shifts from first mate to captain. "You have to go from rowing the boat to steering the boat. You need to put your best effort into steering the boat." After holding the presidency for eighteen months, Lowe stated that for him, "Harvey is becoming smarter and smarter every day. It has to do with things he has said in the past and the things he has made me do."

Dianne Suber, who trained for her role as CEO under Harvey, would no doubt agree. Apparently, she convinced Harvey that she was willing to go the extra mile, so Harvey gave the alumna of Hampton University additional responsibilities and experiences in preparation for assuming her presidency at St. Augustine's. Prior to her appointment as vice president for administrative services in January 1998, she managed the offices of admissions, financial aid and scholarship, the registrar, institutional research, and human resources. Suber also served as the assistant provost for academic affairs, dean of administrative services and as an adjunct professor in the Graduate College of Education. She chaired numerous University committees and directed the second phase of the five-year strategic planning initiative. She said of her preparation under Harvey, "I have had the privilege to be a student of Dr. William Harvey, who has provided me with the experience and the model to prepare me for the leadership of Saint Augustine's College."

At Harvey's first Executive Leadership Summit, Suber reminded the future leaders of the merit of being mentored. "It is important that you understand that you do not get to this point by yourself, no matter how good you are, no matter how competent you are, no matter how much you think of yourself. This level of administration is dependent on somebody with a level of influence, with an understanding of mentorship, who decides that you are the person in whom they want to invest. Dr. Harvey exposed me to the kind of responsibility that required me to discover, identify, and understand, and employ the principles of the Model." Suber described her mentor as "One of the most visionary persons I have met." Vision and innovation come in lock step, she said. "The visionary person is also the person who is willing to take risks. The person who is innovative must also understand those risks and share in them. Vision, innovation, fiscal solvency are the underlying variables in the strong leadership model." Suber said, "Innovation requires one to move far away from the comfort zone." She cited herself as an example. Though she did not have a background in higher education when was hired as the dean of administrative services at Hampton University, she believed, "Dr. Harvey saw something in me that encouraged him to invest in me."

During a personal interview, she said, "To whatever degree you agree with the implementation of principles in the Harvey Model, those [ten] key areas really do make a good model. You take those key areas and maybe you put your own spin on it. Maybe you use your own personality. Maybe you change a meeting date. But fiscal solvency is an underpinning of a successful higher education facility. It is important that your institution be creditably viable in order to be fiscally solvent." She also thinks academic excellence is a crucial component of the Model. "You can't argue with it. You can talk about whether or not to emphasize a liberal arts curriculum, or whether to emphasize a technical curriculum, or a 'college without walls' model, but you can't argue with the fact that you must have academic excellence in the model." She maintains," Vision is a given. Unfortunately, I don't think all administrators or presidents have vision. I think there are presidents who manage well. But I think one piece that has made a difference for Hampton is that Dr. Harvey is probably the most visionary person I have ever worked with in terms of thinking outside of the box and in terms of thinking ten years down the road."

For Suber, "The whole issue of fiscally running the institution like a business" was learned at the master's feet. She, too, has learned that "you can wed nurturing and fiscal responsibility. I have learned from him that you must be a master of managing and massaging people, that you cannot always call a spade a spade even though you think it and even though you are right, you must play to your constituents." When the CEO encounters resistance from constituents, she has gleaned from Harvey and his Model to "develop strategies to get people to come on board," and strategically develop team building. She also learned that it is important to have a "reporting network that prevents your being blindsided by situations. You must have a process at your institution that allows people to willingly share with you information about what's happening on the campus."

"If there is an issue that you expect is going to be problematic, then you disengage it or defuse it by going at it head on. . . ." These lessons are from the text of Harvey and his Model.

Harvey's mentoring does not end when his mentees assume their positions as CEOs. Suber acknowledged, "He helped me access his network. He has made sure that some of the key players in funding agencies all know my name, so that when I call or they call me, we have a direct link. So by association, there is some perception that Saint Augustine's College is worth investing in because I'm a product of the success of Hampton."

She said, "There is something about the tentacles of mentorship. No matter how far away you get, they are still right there. Harvey has been a good sounding board and actually, he has phenomenal ability to know when I need for him to call me. I have some days when I am saying this is not worth it, and he'll be on the phone. He'll call for whatever reason. Sometimes he calls just to check up and other times there are reasons. But it seems that the timing is always absolutely perfect. And then whenever I get a 'sick-of-it day,' and pick up the phone, he is readily available."

"More and more, as I travel, I am beginning to see a very, very broad-based community articulate respect for him—the President of the Bush Foundation, the Mellon people, the federal agencies—there is virtually nowhere I have been in higher education where people don't say to me, 'Oh, you worked with Bill Harvey.' 'Oh, you're one of Bill Harvey's protégés.' And then after that, there is a series of accolades,"said Suber.

Rodney Smith, who assumed a presidential post in 2001 at Ramapo College, has picked up the phone numerous times to speak with his mentor and Harvey was always readily available. "I have spent nine years as a student of leadership under one of the most admired and talented twentieth- and twenty-first century leaders in the higher education enterprise. I have spent nine years in service and leadership under William R. Harvey. The lessons have been invaluable. Both the Hampton Model and Harvey Model in combination spell success. He is a teaching president, a proactive leader, a humanitarian, and a man who cares about the future, a man who is totally committed to making society a better place for all mankind."

At the Executive Leadership Summit, Smith shared his thoughts on team building as a key component of the Harvey

Model. "William R. Harvey is known for quoting Langston Hughes in goalsetting," he said. "The dream becomes not one man's dream alone, but our dream, belonging to all the hands to build. Dr. Harvey has used this quote throughout Hampton to help build a sense of ownership toward developing goals of common interest. In addition to establishing and maintaining a focus on common interest, it is important in the Harvey Model to maintain a system of assessment. The key ingredient of effective team building and team maintenance, particularly at higher levels within the organization, is the fostering of the development of institutional interest to supersede personal or group interest," Smith exhorted. "The Harvey Model gives training, exposure, and experience to expand horizons. If you sat in Harvey's class, whatever you have done that is value added for the institution, Dr. Harvey has never forgotten to say 'Thank you.' He puts it in writing. Harvey always says 'Thank you' to let people know their work is being recognized and appreciated." For Smith, this quality contributes to team building.

Warren Buck, chancellor at the University of Washington, Bothell, knows that saying a simple "Thank you" or a simple "No" sometimes takes courage. It is the grit gleaned from Harvey and the Harvey Model. He said, "The lesson learned from Harvey's Model is to think on my own two feet and work with existing structures to further the goals for students. I learned that at Hampton University. That is a very strong and powerful weapon. Many of us may feel we are dependent on each other, and we are, but each of us has the power to effect change." To illustrate his point, Buck, who was influential in establishing the Ph.D. program in physics, told this story: "When I first arrived at Hampton and went in to see Dr. Harvey, I told him I would bring Hampton international acclaim and students would be able to get into high-level world-class physics programs. Dr. Harvey said, 'That's good, Dr. Buck, but I am not paying for that.' And that was a shock to me. I said, 'Doesn't everyone pay for things like this? It is a wonderful thing to pay for.' What that did was to give me strength to go out and work with my friends, my colleagues, and find ways to pay for it. His comments were quite appropriate and the results speak for themselves. That I learned at HU and other things have sustained me during my two years at Bothell."

Another one of Harvey's mentees, Leon Scott, President of Consolidated Bank and Trust, echoed what all the other presidents underscored—the necessity for fiscal solvency. "I think I learned from my tutelage by Dr. Harvey that fiscal management is as simple as common sense. You have to raise revenues and then you need to spend wisely. You need to make sure you keep a reserve. You need to not spend revenue you only anticipate. If one has only a dollar, one cannot spend a dollar and a quarter. You need to invest and not merely spend. Invest in people; invest in programs; invest in facilities, and of course, invest in endowment and the future."

For administrators who move on, Harvey believes this "constructive ambition is good." Thus, he takes great pride in what he does with the development of administrators, since it is his altruistic desire to place good leadership throughout the ranks of other higher education institutions, as well as other venues. Still, for Harvey, it is more than positioning leaders, he stated, "I am interested in their doing well." When Dianne Suber was named president of Saint Augustine's College, for example, he gave her names for fund-raising and, as the keynote speaker for a UNCF fundraising event, he invited Suber and her assistant to attend in order "to give them exposure." At one of her latter administrative council meetings, Harvey, who expected her to do well in the position of president, told her, "I can give you advice, but you are now the 'man.'"

In making presidents, Harvey, the leadership developer, offers the Harvey Leadership Model for Academic Administrative Success, a ten-step model that he has employed during the twenty-five years of his presidency. He said that some critics didn't like his model when he first took over Hampton University twenty-five years ago, especially when it came to tight money management. Now, many of his top administrators can recite the Harvey Model verbatim. "We try to pick very good people who can understand the model, who fit into the model, and who support the concept," Harvey stated.[5]

He said, "Since one of my most important jobs is to assist in the growth and development of my administrative colleagues, I have encouraged them to adopt the components to their use."[6] "They may not make it their model," Harvey said of his administrators who go on to take top jobs at higher education institutions, "but I believe they will incorporate a lot of it into their daily work schedules and lives."

"When colleges and universities are looking for leadership, they come to me," said Harvey, "and that's the ultimate flattery. That validates the model we have here. It validates the way we are doing things—how we do it and what we do. Others across the country are noticing that what we have here works. Our Model has been validated and emulated."[7] Judging by the success of his first Executive Leadership Summit in 2001, it is clear that leaders want to emulate his Model.

Harvey, in his opening remarks at the Executive Leadership Summit, said, "I believe so strongly in leadership, I believe so strongly in mentorship, that I wanted to start a series of conferences and institutes where we can deal with a number of issues. I want to pass the torch on, not just to my colleagues at Hampton, but to those of you as well. We have had excellent moments and we have had pitfalls, and I want to share them with you. If we can pass that on, and we can interact, I feel that is truly a worthwhile venture."

Harvey, building on the tradition of its founder, Samuel Chapman Armstrong, has rekindled the spirit of Hampton as a venue where servant leaders are "gathered to scatter."

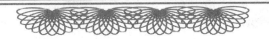

The Legacy of a Living Legend

*"Be not afraid of greatness: some are born great,
some achieve greatness and some have greatness
thrust upon them."*
—William Shakespeare

"An institution is the lengthened shadow of one man."
—Ralph Waldo Emerson

Whether one believes President William R. Harvey was born great, achieved greatness, or had it thrust upon him, whatever the circumstance, he was ready to receive his place in life and act on it. Like the Earl of Chesterfield, he thinks, "Whatever is worth doing at all is worth doing well." And what he does well is to build from the material and nonmaterial world. Unquestionably, the builder, "loves bricks, mortar, and steel or anything metallic and a mixture to hold those together." said Charles Wilson, the longtime Board of Trustees member. The majestic buildings that rise along the campus seashore, since his presidency, bear testament to his penchant. But his legacy is more than that of a material man of brick and mortar etched on the lifeless cornerstones of edifices. More importantly, it is a living legacy of a spiritual raiser, engraved, like the foundation stones, in the hearts and minds of all those who, since 1978, have walked through the hallowed halls of Hampton University. Like David, a stalwart warrior who made the City of Jerusalem the fortress of faith, Harvey, the stouthearted change agent and builder

361

of a world-class university, has sealed Hampton as a citadel for excellence and has made, in the words of Aurelia D. Parker, a friend and supporter of the university, "the sun shine upon Hampton" by raising the bar and by pushing the limits of possibilities toward a quality education, particularly for African American youths. As stated in Proverbs 24:3–4, Harvey, too, knows that "Any enterprise is built by wise planning, becomes strong through common sense, and profits wonderfully by keeping abreast of the facts."

So when the time comes for Harvey's departure, the lasting legacy of the perennial builder and "Renaissance Man"—educator, entrepreneur, art collector, sports enthusiast, innovator, and bridge builder—will be his passion for education and for creating a culture of excellence in education and in all things. He will bequeath to the landscape of higher education, and in turn, the world: a spirit of educational entrepreneurship; a policy of sound management; a model for moving an institution to the cutting edge of higher education; a model for black leadership in higher education; an amalgamable paradigm of education as an academic, business, and moral enterprise; a legacy of innovation and change in the quantity and quality of academic offerings and of increasing opportunities for African American youth; a gift of producing servant leaders; a legacy of gender equity, diversity, and civility in the workplace; a legacy of standing firm on principles; a strong work ethic; a legacy of incalculable tangible and intangible results. Without question, the builder will leave a situation better than he found it.

So when asked, how would you like to be remembered, Harvey rejoined with, "As one who made a difference—a positive difference."

> It is no doubt that we have made a difference. I am very proud that we have enhanced the quality and the quantity of our academic offerings. Fiscally we have operated in the black for all twenty-five years. Fiscally, we have been able to do some things that many did not think we would be able to

do. We have built eighteen new structures; we have built a shopping center; we have built apartments; we have increased the endowment from $29 million to $180 million. And if you look at our academic enhancements, we have now provided four doctoral programs, some sixty-four new degree-granting programs. All of this is designed to provide mainly African Americans an opportunity for higher education. So I think that there is absolutely no doubt that my leadership has made a difference. But I didn't do it alone. The theme that I always operated under is that it may very well be my vision, but it takes people to take ownership in that vision to make it a reality, and that's what has happened at Hampton. You have faculty, students, alumni, the board, parents, corporate people, political people, friends, donors and others that have taken ownership in the vision that we have for Hampton.

In making a difference, he expressed gratitude for his chance to serve. "I am very pleased that I was given the opportunity to provide leadership for Hampton and the wider community, and to do a number of things that I have been able to do as it relates to a leadership role. I am very thankful. I am blessed. I thank God for that, and I thank the trustees for their confidence and support.

For future generations, Harvey wants to pass on this legacy of service. As he so often has said, "The life that counts is the life that serves." In addition, he offers the gift of these life lessons:

I think that it is important for people to have a spirituality. I think it is important for people to have a love of family. I think it is important for people to have a good work ethic. I think it is important for people to be able to work together to achieve common goals. And as you look at the Harvey Model of Administration, it includes high academic achievement, high academic expectations, fiscal conservatism, and it includes work ethic and being results-oriented. And I think that's a pretty good model. What I hope that we can do here at Hampton, as an educational institution, is to make useful, responsible citizens. That's very important to be a good person and that's what we ought to be here. We ought to be about high expectations; we ought to be about citizenship; we ought to be about values, morals, and ethics. All those things are incorporated into a good citizen, a good person. If one is successful financially, does not have these ingredients that I am talking about, then I don't consider him/her successful. So to be a good person, to serve others, to do the kinds of things that help someone who is perhaps more downtrodden than you, that's what we ought to be about.

When we see Harvey through the "looking glass," we can ask, "What manner of man is he? What is he about?" If a person is known by the consistent nature of his creed and deed, we can rejoin with a thunderous praise and say, in the words of Parker, "You made the sun shine upon Hampton." Though it matters what we think of him, more importantly, however, like the poem, it is what "The Man in the Glass" sees.

> When you get what you want in your struggle for wealth
> And the world makes you king for a day,
> Then go to a mirror and look at yourself
> And see what that man has to say.
> For it isn't your father, your mother, or your wife
> Whose judgment upon you must pass
> The fellow whose verdict counts most in your life
> Is the man looking back from the glass.
> He's the fellow to please, never mind all the rest
> For he's with you clear up to the end,
> And you have passed your most dangerous difficult test
> When the guy in the glass is your friend.
> You may be like Jack Horner and chisel a plum
> And think you're a wonderful guy
> But the guy in the glass says, "You're only a bum"
> If you can't look him straight in the eye.
> You can fool the whole world down the pathway of years,
> And get pats on the back as you pass,
> But the final reward will be heartaches and tears
> If you cheated the guy in the glass.

For Harvey, an image of a perennial builder looks back from the mirror. At his feet lies a cornucopia of fruits, produced by the sweat of his brow, that glows in the looking glass, and on his head is a diadem of excellence that crowns the living legend—the "old country boy from Brewton, Alabama." When the sun sets on Harvey's time at Hampton, the "man in the glass" can proudly step aside and say, like Paul in 2 Timothy 4:7, "I have fought a good fight, I have finished my course, I have kept the faith." He will then let his life's work at Hampton, in the covenant of its *Alma Mater*, do the singing. For the master builder and master dreamer understands, like Richard Bach that "You are never given a dream without being given the power to make the dream come true."

Epilogue

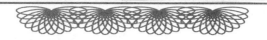

Taylor's Song
by
Papa Harvey

Down by the river
every day
Looking at the boats,
hey, hey, hey.

The sky is heavenly
blue, blue, blue
It makes me feel wonderful
When I'm with you.

We sing our song
Papa and me
Love is in the air
As I sit on his knee.

We feed the ducks
with old toast
I jump back
When they get too close.

We sit on the bench
to feed the ducks some lunch,
All of a sudden
they start coming in a bunch

I go to the playground,
So I can ride,
We get on the seesaw,
swings, and slide

We run behind the birds,
as they walk by,
Some get scared and begin to fly.

We continue our walk
in and out of trees,
Papa picked me up
when we saw a bunch of bees

I'm a little tired
But will not cry
'Cause the birds make me laugh
as they fly by.

Freedom in great
and it's no joke
Papa explained this to me
at the Emancipation Oak

Past the chapel and Papa's work
we continue to roam
Feeling a little drowsy,
I fall asleep going home.

During our walk,
we see lots of animals and even a mouse
O what great fun I have
At Papa's and Nana's house.

Notes

Introduction

1. "HI Prexy in High Gear," *Journal and Guide* (Norfolk, VA) October 8, 1980, 6.

2. Abraham Chapman, ed., *Black Voices: An Anthology of Afro-American Literature* (New York: Penguin Books USA Inc., 1968), 99.

3. William R. Harvey,"The Legacy of African-American Leadership for the Present and Future," keynote address delivered for African-American History Month Observance, Veterans Affairs Medical Center, Hampton, Virginia, February 4, 1999, 4.

Chapter 1

1. William R. Harvey, speech delivered to the 100 Black Men of the Virginia Peninsula, Inc., in accepting award as "Role Model of the Year," Saturday, April 17, 1999, Radisson Hotel, Hampton, Virginia, 7.

2. Harvey, "The Legacy of African-American Leadership."

3. Donald O. Bolander, ed., *The New Webster Quotation Dictionary* (New York: Lexicon Publications, Inc., 1987), 248.

4. Kirk Saville, "Confident Leader Drives HU to Top, *The Daily Press* (Newport News, VA), March 28, 1993, A. 11.

5. Bolander, *The New Webster Quotation Dictionary,* 35.

6. William H. Harvey, *President's Annual Report, 1982–1983: A Five Year Review,* Hampton Institute, Hampton Institute, Hampton, Virginia.

7. Sandra Tan, "Harvey Model Molds Leaders," *The Daily Press* (Newport News, VA), October 5, 1999, A 10.

8. Bolander, *The New Webster Quotation Dictionary*, 48.

9. Robert Francis Engs, *Samuel Chapman Armstrong and Hampton Institute, 1839–1893* (Knoxville: The University of Tennessee, 1999), 70. This work is a good source for a discussion of Armstong's life and work at Hampton University.

10. Times-Dispatch State Staff, "Hampton is One Man's Vision," *Richmond (Virginia) Times Dispatch*, September 20, 1981.

11. William R. Harvey, "Unity and Preservation for the Future," speech delivered at the Hampton University Alumni Association's Eighth

Annual Southwest Regional Conference, Dallas, Texas, November 12, 1983, 4.

12. William R. Harvey, speech delivered at the North Capital Annual Dinner, New York, May 27, 1987.

13. William R. Harvey, speech delivered at the Hampton University Faculty Institute, August 27, 1979.

14. William R. Harvey, Remarks on Planning made at Saint Augustine's College, January 6, 1981.

15. Ibid.

Chapter 2

1. See Derek T. Dingle, "Terms of Endowment: Keeping Our Colleges in the Black," *Black Enterprise* September, 1985. In the cover story, Dingle called Harvey a "money magnet."

2. William R. Harvey, "God and His Steadfast Love is the Answer to Crises," speech delivered at the Thirty-third Quarterly Leadership Prayer Luncheon, First Presbyterian Church of Norfolk, Norfolk, Virginia, February 13, 1989.

3. William R. Harvey, "The Christian Man in These Times," speech delivered at the 119th Session of the Middle Eastern Original Free Will Baptist Annual Conference, Inc., Wilson, North Carolina, October 29, 1987.

4. Ibid.

5. Ibid.

6. Ibid.

7. Stacey Burling, "Hampton's Best Seller," *Virginia Magazine*, July 10, 1983. Reprinted in *Hampton Institute 1982–1983, President's Annual Report—A Five Year Review,* Hampton, Institute, Hampton, Virginia.

8. William R. Harvey, Introduction of John Warner," at the John Warner-Mark Warner Debate, Virginia Beach, Virginia, November 1, 1996.

9. Marvin Leon Lake, "Hampton Institute's President Dedicated to Excellence," in *Hampton Institute's 12th President presents "The Year in Review" 1978–1979.*

10. Scott Walsh "Money, Power and Education," *Port Folio*, February, 18, 1986.

11. Stacey Burling, "Hampton's Best Seller," 17.

Chapter 3

1. Bolander, *The New Webster Quotation Dictionary*, 119.

2. La Verne M. Gill and Paris Davis, "Hampton's Dr. William Harvey Offers Prototype for Black College Solvency," *The Metro Chronicle* II:13, Virginia, Washington, D.C., Maryland, April 9, 1987.

3. Susan Friend, "HU President Builds on Prestigious Legacy He Has Formed," *The Daily Press* (Newport News, VA), Monday, October 5, 1998, A 2.

4. Nancy Felgenbaum, "HU's Greatest Endeavor," *The Daily Press* (Newport News, VA), October 4, 1998, A 1.

5. Friend, "HU President Builds on Prestigious Legacy."

6. Walsh, "Money, Power and Education."

7. Minutes of the Annual Meeting of the Hampton University Board of Trustees, October 25, 1996 and February 21, 1997.

8. Ron Sauder, "School's 'Mystique' Draws Top Students," *Richmond (Virginia) Times-Dispatch*, September 20, 1981, 3.

9. John Templeton,"Hampton's Harvey: Quality the Key to Survival of Black Schools" *Richmond (Virginia) Afro-American*, November 6, 1982, A 1.

10. Sandra Tan, "HU President Knows How to Raise Funds," *The Daily Press* (Newport News, VA), October 25, 1999, C 1.

11. Burling, "Hampton's Best Seller," 18.

12. Walsh, "Money, Power and Education."

13. Ibid.

14. William R. Harvey, opening remarks given at the Fall Faculty Institute, Hampton Institute, August 27, 1979.

15. Felgenbaum, "HU's Greatest Endeavor," A 6.

16. *The Daily Press*, Newport News, Virginia, September 17, 1981.

17. Sean Sommerville, *The Daily Press/Times-Herald*, (Newport News, VA), February 11, 1989, B 1.

18. William R. Harvey, Testimony Before The Committee on Education and Labor, U. S. House of Representatives, Washington, D.C. December 10, 1990.

19. Felgenbaum, "HU's Greatest Endeavor."

20. Friend, "HU President Builds on Prestigious Legacy," A 1.

Chapter 4

1. Paul R. Baker, *Richard Morris Hunt* (Cambridge. Massachusetts: MIT Press, 1980), 193.

Chapter 5

1. William R. Harvey, *President's Annual Report, 1980—1981*, Hampton Institute, Hampton, Virginia.

2. Victoria L. Jones, "HU Tops in *U. S. News* and *Black Issues* Magazine," *Hampton Life*, XIX:2 (September, 1999): 1–3.

3. William R. Harvey, *The President's Annual Report, 1978–1979.*

4. Martha E. Dawson, *Hampton University: A National Treasure* (Silver Spring, MD: Beckham House Publisher, 1994), 119.

5. Ibid., 120.

6. Harvey, *The President's Annual Report, 1978–1979*, 4.

7. Office of University Relations, Hampton University, *Hampton Highlights* XI:24 (1991): 1.

Chapter 6

1. Richard J. Powell, "Seeing and Thinking About the Unexpected in American Art," *American Visions*, March 15, 1999, Washington, D.C., 24–25.

2. Ibid., 25.

3. William R. Harvey, "Afro-American Art," lecture presented to University 101 class, Hampton University, Hampton, Virginia, September 25, 1989.

Chapter 7

1. William R. Harvey, *The President's Annual Report, 1989–1990*, 15.

2. Tom Foster, "HI President Joins 700 Club: Sports 'More Than an Entertainment," *The Daily Press*, (Newport News, VA), January 23, 1983.

Chapter 8

1. William R. Harvey, speech at the Governor's Prayer Breakfast, John Marshall Hotel, Richmond, Virginia, January 26, 1984.

2. Victoria L. Jones, "Scholarship Fund for Graduate's Children Established." *Hampton Life*, Hampton, Virginia XIX:1, 1.

Chapter 9

1. William R. Harvey, "Economic Empowerment: The Avenue to African American Liberation," speech delivered at the Economic Trade Fair and Exposition, Hyatt Regency Hotel, New Brunswick, New Jersey, April 9, 1992.

2. William R. Harvey, "Toward the 1990s: Uplifting Through Education and Economic Development," speech delivered to the Alpha Alpha Chapter, Omega Psi Phi Fraternity, Achievement Week Awards Program, Fort Monroe Officer's Club, Hampton, Virginia November 24, 1985.

3. William R. Harvey, *President's Annual Report, 1991–1992*, Hampton University, Hampton, Virginia, 21.

4. Ibid.

5. Ibid.

6. Ibid.

7. William R. Harvey, speech delivered to the 85th Ministers' Conference and 65th Choir Directors'/Organists' Guild Workshop, Hampton University Convocation Center, Hampton, Virginia, June 7, 1999.

8. William R. Harvey, "The Christian Man in These Times," speech delivered at the 119th Session of the Middle Eastern Original Free Will Baptist Annual Conference, Inc., Thursday, October 29, 1987, Wilson, North Carolina.

9. William R. Harvey, "Economic Empowerment: The Avenue to African American Liberation," speech delivered to the Economic Empowerment Trade Fair and Exposition, Hyatt Regency Hotel, New Brunswick, New Jersey, April 9, 1992.

10. William R. Harvey, "Toward the 1990s."

11. Dave Schleck, "HU Proposes Charter School, *The Daily Press* (Newport News, VA), March 16, 2000, C 1, 2.

12. William R. Harvey, "Mandatory National Service," reprinted in *The Daily Press*, (Newport News, VA), November 21, 1999, H 1–4.

Chapter 10

1. William R. Harvey, remarks delivered at High School Day Welcome Program, Hampton University Convocation Center, April 2, 1999.

2. William R. Harvey, "Promoting and Insuring Teaching Excellence," speech delivered at the 1995 Administrative Retreat, Hilton Head, South Carolina, August 13, 1995.

3. William R. Harvey, in speech delivered at the 115th Founders Day Program, Virginia State University, Anderson-Turner Auditorium of Virginia Hall, Petersburg, Virginia March 2, 1997.

Chapter 11

1.   Bruce C. Ebert, *The Times-Herald* (Newport News, VA), November 19, 1986, A1.

2.   Harvey, *President's Annual Report 1990–1991*.

3.   Harvey, "The Legacy of African-American Leadership for the Present and the Future."

Chapter 12

1.   Victoria L. Jones, "College Presidents Created Under Harvey's Leadership," XVIII:1, July 20, 1999:1.

2.   Sandra Tan, "Harvey Model Molds Leaders," *Daily Press* (Newport News), October 5, 1999, A1.

Chapter 13

1.   Joy Jefferson, *Hampton Life* XVI:7 (March 20, 1997):1.

2.   Victoria L. Jones, "College Presidents Created Under Harvey's Leadership," *Hampton Life XVIII:1 (July 20, 1998): 2*.

3.   Victoria L. Jones, "Hampton Celebrates Rich History and Legacy," *Hampton Life*, February 20, 2000, 1.

4.   Stephanie Barrett, "Another Administrator at HU Named to Head College Elsewhere, *The Daily Press* (Newport News), March 30, 2000, C3.

5.   Sandra Tan, "Harvey Model Molds Leaders," *The Daily Press* (Newport News), Tuesday, October 5, 1999.

6.   William R. Harvey, "Leadership: Promoting Excellence, Equity, Diversity, and Civility in Higher Education," a speech given at the 13th Annual Black Faculty and Staff Association Conference, University of Maryland, College Park, Maryland, June 15, 2000.

7.   Victoria L. Jones, *Hampton Life* XVIII:1 (July 20, 1998): 1.

Index